M000101815

The Brothers of Bragg Jam

What happens when a happy, prosperous family experiences a tragedy beyond their wildest imaginings? In her memoir, *The Brothers of Bragg Jam*, Julie Bragg makes a journey on which none would voluntarily embark; one which embodies a parent's worst nightmares. When she loses her two beloved sons in an instant, Bragg begins a spiritual journey that will call forth every ounce of her considerable resilience, and an openness to new experiences— even supernatural ones—as she seeks to keep her dead boys close to her. Invoking maternal love at its deepest and most tender, Bragg's beautifully told story is one that will inspire every reader and which none will put down without tears of appreciation and empathy. Indeed, *The Brothers of Bragg Jam* is destined to become a classic among inspirational books, and one her readers will turn to again and again.

—Rosemary Daniell, author of *Fatal Flowers: On Sin, Sex, and Suicide in the Deep South*, and seven other books of poetry

They loved them most who knew them best. Poignant, sad, and uplifting—a must read.

—Larry Walker, writer, lawyer, and politician

MERCER UNIVERSITY PRESS

Endowed by

TOM WATSON BROWN
and
THE WATSON-BROWN FOUNDATION, INC.

The Brothers of Bragg Jam

A Mother's Memoir

❧

JULIE WALLACE BRAGG

For Renee
Believe It!
Hang in there!
Julie Bragg

MERCER UNIVERSITY PRESS | MACON, GEORGIA | 2018

MUP/ P566

© 2018 by Mercer University Press
Published by Mercer University Press
1501 Mercer University Drive
Macon, Georgia 31207
All rights reserved

9 8 7 6 5 4 3 2 1

Books published by Mercer University Press are printed on acid-free paper that meets the requirements of the American National Standard for Information Sciences—Permanence of Paper for Printed Library Materials.

ISBN   978-0-88146-658-4
Cataloging-in-Publication Data is available from the Library of Congress

Contents

For Jim, Susie, and Annie~
my love for you will never die.

And for our boys, Brax and Tate,
whose love we feel today,
as ever.

The Brothers of Bragg Jam

Prologue

July 3, 1999

That innocent Saturday brings cotton clouds
to the bluest sky of the Georgia summer.
We are missing you both
hoping you see the same sky
still three days west of home.
They're under it somewhere I think
picturing you spin along, listening to CDs,
brother content with brother
to join New Orleans friends for the Fourth.
Music will float around our Macon driveway on Tuesday.
The car will arrive, loaded with dirty clothes, guitars, water bottles,
postcards, happy travel stories.
I am innocent, so are you, so are we all.
Cheery goodbyes set it in motion ten days earlier
scarcely weighing how much we can lose.

—Julie Bragg 11/99

Macon Telegraph—Sunday, July 11, 1999
Small Texas Town Shares in Sorrow

Editors: I am from a small town in west Texas called Ozona where everyone helps out another when in need. It is a town where people grieve when a loved one of a friend has passed away. It is one of the most touching towns in Texas. Recently, you printed an article about Jim and Julie Bragg's only sons being fatally injured in a car accident in Texas. The accident occurred right outside of Ozona.

There is not enough words to say for the sorrow we all felt, not only the fire department or the EMS, but the whole town. Tears filled our eyes as the people here who had access to a computer found the Macon newspaper to see if there was any write-up, and what we all saw was overwhelming. We all learned about the boys' lives from your cover story online.

God bless the parents for the two boys who were killed on I-10. For they were no strangers or passersby; they were indeed friends to the small town of Ozona. Our hearts go out to Jim and Julie, for we all are grieving with you as well here in west Texas. Our thoughts and prayers are with you all.

Lacey Romanelie, Ozona, Texas

I.

୧

Saturday July 3, 1999

I had been home less than an hour when the Bibb County, Georgia, sheriff and a chaplain came that afternoon. I had met Susie, our grown daughter, at Sam's Wholesale Club to visit over lunch and do some shopping. My long list consisted mainly of supplies needed for my home-based swim school, but we had fun trying out the long-handled back massager I purchased for her seventeen-year-old brother, Taylor, whose scoliosis still flared into a lingering dull ache from time to time. I also bought a pair of earrings—tiny gold hoops, each holding a single gold bead—rationalizing to the clerk, as I inspected them in a mirror, that I didn't usually buy jewelry for myself but could think of them as a traveler's gift from my sons, Taylor and his ten-year-older brother, Brax. They were on the home stretch of a cross-country road trip, and in case they'd been too busy to shop for a gift, these would do just fine as a back up.

I renewed my Sam's membership card that day, requiring an up-to-date instant photo—a last image of myself, grinning, suntanned, reflecting my innocent, unbroken life. It was also the first that showed a noticeable blend of silvery and brown hair. I'd begun coloring premature gray strands when I was 38, weeks before Taylor, our fourth child, was born, so that should he ever compare younger mothers of his friends with his own, his might appear less shopworn. All four children encouraged me to discontinue the brown, though, and I had in April. Taylor, mostly called Tate, had snapped a Mother's Day picture of me, head tilted back to hide my new yarmulke-like white crown.

As we rolled heavy buggies across the glaring parking lot to our hot cars, I mentioned to Susie that her dad, Jim, wanted to stir up some interest for launching the family's green pontoon boat that night, to watch Fourth of July fireworks on Lake Tobesofkee, west of Macon, the middle-Georgia city where we'd spent most of our lives. I switched the ignition to cool my car while I loaded frozen stuff into a large insulated bag on the back seat.

"What do you think about fireworks?" I asked, as I slammed the lid on the trunk, crammed with junk food for the snack bar, a venture which Tate oversaw in our poolhouse during summer swim school.

"Well, it's Jewt's Saturday night with the kids," she said. "Could we just go tomorrow? We'd miss the fireworks, but Anna and Rob love the pontoon any time." Jewt was her ex and their children were 14 and 11.

"That'll probably work," I said. "Your daddy mostly just needs a distraction from missing the boys—sure seems longer than ten days. I'll let you know what he says."

We hugged, drove our cars toward exit lanes, waved goodbye, and headed east onto busy Eisenhower Parkway. Susie tooted her horn as she passed me at the intersection, where I waited for a left turn signal onto the I-475 bypass, toward the north end of Macon.

On the way home I called her younger sister, Annie. She was moping alone, she said. Her husband, Bert, was fishing somewhere with his preteen son, Boone, and would be home late, so she was thinking she might meet a programmer at one of her two beauty spas while all was quiet there. She'd left a voicemail for the computer guy, but even if that didn't develop, she said she wasn't in the mood for much else. "Let's just hold off till the guys get back from California on Tuesday," she said. "I can't wait to hear about their trip."

Because I was on the phone while driving, I missed the Zebulon Road exit that would've taken me home and had to drive on to the next little town, Bolingbroke, north of Macon. Lured by big Fourth of July banners stretched between porch columns of an old white house, I impulsively veered off the town's main drag to check out my friend's antique store. As soon as I'd walked over the scorching gravel parking lot and past an array of collectibles by the front door, I felt agitated and wished I hadn't stopped. I hurried through a long center hall, resisting odors of linseed oil and old fabrics, and rushed down wide wooden steps of the back porch. My friend Elaine waved from the door of a barn-like storage building in the backyard.

"This was just an impromptu stop," I shouted, "I was headed home but missed my Zebulon Road exit—I'm hoping to make up time by getting on I-75."

"We've got some good bargains," she declared.

"I'm sure—and I *could* use a mirror for above our piano, but I feel like I better get on home." I trotted around to the other side of the house where I'd left my car, its interior still cool, and buckled my seatbelt. "I'll be back," I called, pulling the door toward me, scattering gravel in my haste to return to my search for I-75.

I made another mistake by turning left onto a winding country road going under the interstate instead of connecting to it. When I dialed our house to tell Jim I was on the way, he didn't answer. The memory of having seen him on his mower earlier stirred my anxiety, but I reminded myself to slow down around these curves—how ridiculous it would be if I were in the hospital when our boys got back.

Thirty minutes later, when I finally turned onto our rural street, the home scene was as peaceful as ever. The sunny afternoon, now around 3:45, seemed a little less humid than usual, with cotton clouds dotting an indigo sky. Our property, nearly 20 acres, is nestled within a forest of gorgeous, majestic trees, which border terraces of lush grass, now freshly mowed, near the house. I inhaled delicious air as I reached into the mailbox at the top panhandle to our circular asphalt drive. Jim and I had talked that morning of not waiting three more days for the boys to return to get the lawn in shape. It had grown at least two inches since Taylor, who still lived at home, mowed it the day before he left with Brax; but things were fine now for my swim classes on Monday.

As I rounded the right side of the house, I saw a familiar dark blue, battered van in the back swell of our parking area. Willie, our burglar alarm man, had come, hopefully to finish installing a new system. Since the place was overrun with children and parents all week, he hadn't been able to tie the poolhouse into our main system, and I guessed that's why he was here again.

I parked my ten-year-old gray Acura Legend beside his van, popped the trunk, and gathered the first armload of stuff, which included a scanner for our computer. I also had two boxes of Kodak photo paper so we could finally start putting together photo albums for the four kids. I went through the kitchen and spotted the back of Jim's dark head resting on his jade leather recliner. The television was on, things looked normal. Thinking he might be dozing, I walked around to the front of his chair with the new scanner, hoping he'd offer to hook it up. He seemed tired from the huge mowing job, but satisfied, and as I went back out I heard sounds of the box being opened. I took the insulated bag of frozen food into the garage, where we kept a large chest freezer.

Willie met me on the connective breezeway there and asked if I'd come down to the poolhouse and tell him when I heard the burglar alarm sound off in our kitchen. In a few minutes I heard it, encoded the control panel to silence it, and headed down the steps to our stucco poolhouse, lugging a forty-pound bucket of chlorine tablets with me.

While Willie and I were standing in the air-conditioned building, I looked through the back wall of windows up toward the street, where two cars were coming into our driveway. As they crept closer, I could see *Bibb County Sheriff* on the side of a white car, which was trailed by an unmarked beige one.

"Gosh, Willie! I'm going to like this new system—it's fast. There's the sheriff already." He looked out, but both cars had disappeared around the front of the house.

"Impossible for the sheriff to hear it," he said, climbing back up the ladder in the far corner of the room. "It's on test mode—that don't even send a signal to their office."

"Well, maybe they're not busy downtown on the day before July 4th and have time to send somebody out to verify our address for when the alarm might actually go off," I mused, oblivious to the lack of logic.

"They ain't ever done that before," he mumbled, as he fiddled with the motion detector near the crown molding of the vaulted pine ceiling.

"Well, I'll just go up and tell them it's a false alarm," I said. I opened the glass door onto the pool deck, stepped into a wave of heat, and bounded up the flagstone steps. I jogged past my yawning car trunk, around the far end of the garage, to the right side of the front yard, where both cars had parked. Two men were on our porch, about to ring the doorbell.

"Halloo!" I yelled from the far corner of the garage at the edge of the clipped, fragrant grass. "Don't worry. That was just a test of our new burglar alarm system."

"Oh, hello, ma'am," said an enormous black man in a starched tan uniform, a black gun holstered at his waist. He stepped back off the porch, sunglasses in his hand, his back to the afternoon sun. "Are you Mrs. Bragg?" he asked gently. The other man, in silhouette against the glare, followed.

"Yes, I am, and our man set off our alarm on purpose, to be sure it's tied into our poolhouse." I had passed both garage windows and stopped on the lawn at the corner of the garage, about fifteen feet from them. My right hand formed an awning above my squinting eyes. "He can't figure out how you knew about it, though."

"Mrs. Bragg, we're not here about your burglar alarm."

"Lord," I exclaimed, triggering the recent agitation of feeling lost. "You look so serious—am I in trouble?"

"No, ma'am," the sheriff said kindly, as they continued walking toward me. "You're not in trouble." The other man was smaller, in white shirtsleeves, and reminded me of an insurance salesman, with the same look of empathy that my father, who'd been an insurance salesman, had had. They introduced themselves then as Sheriff Somebody and Chaplain Somebody for Bibb County.

"Well," I said with a nervous half-giggle, "I never know. I mean, the sheriff has been here before—once it was to deliver a lawsuit from that old lady on the hill, claiming we'd cut down two of her trees..."

"We haven't come for anything like that," one of them interrupted. "Is your husband at home with you?"

I scanned their solemn, steady gazes—my own needled by the sun—and I nodded. One of them, I don't remember which, said he had tried to call us a while ago, but got no answer. My hand flew to my heart and I knew they'd been humoring me about not being in trouble.

"What is it, then?" I asked, feeling the pulse of real alarm, like an alert on the keypad, warning you that the main siren is about to scream, shattering peace. They balked, like they weren't able to tell me. My last bit of innocence flew in the split second that sped panic to my brain. "Oh, no!" I gasped. "Is this something about our sons?"

"Let's go get your husband," said the sheriff, his hand reaching for my arm.

"Wait!" I cried, flinging my hand in the direction of the road, "Our boys are on a car trip..." My sandals were Velcro on the soft grass. "You can't be telling me there's been a wreck." The image of a dark green SUV, two brothers cruising happily toward home on some distant highway, under cotton-ball clouds, on this beautiful summer day, offered balm to nerves, now petrified by such a horrible possibility. The men with their pained expressions blurred into my view of tall dark woods behind them.

"Has one of them been hurt?" I could barely breathe as the significance of the chaplain hit me. "But *you* wouldn't need to be here if one of my boys was only hurt, would you?" When he placed his hand on my left shoulder, I gripped the back of his neck with my left hand to keep from dropping to the ground on buckling knees. "You're telling me there *has* been wreck. A bad one."

The dejected chaplain nodded.

"Where?"

"In Texas."

"Which son?" The horror of such a question and their obvious reluctance to give up its unbearable answer made me take off running in panic for Jim. When I reached our front door and found it locked I ran around the left end of the house to the back of the screened porch, up its stack of wooden steps, and across the porch to the glass door of the front room, our office. I lunged for the knob, throwing the door hard against the inside wall. My sudden appearance, as I burst wildly into the den, brought Jim to his feet, still holding the new scanner, which he tossed to the sofa. "Jim! These men have something terrible to tell us about Brax and Tate!"

The two sad men followed close behind as I fell against my husband. His arms around me, I faced them, "Now you have to tell us."

I recall little of what muted voices said after that. I was in an airless haze, like a brittle, putrid field, amid trees scorched black by a fire. A gray film of sadness washed over Jim when I asked him if we would make it through this. "I guess we'll have to," he said flatly, his handsome face now haggard. I heard him ask the sheriff where we could go, to be with the boys, and felt his lungs deflate when the sheriff replied, "They will be brought home to you." Our heads hung as we held each other, too stunned to move, or weep.

I asked the chaplain to pray with us. What I remember of his prayer was his plea for God to send His peace and helpers into our lives. I made the sign of the cross on my head and heart and followed Jim's gaze to our mantle clock—it was 4:45.

The answer to the chaplain's plea for helpers began to come as soon as we muttered *amen*. We hadn't noticed a dark green SUV pass around the two cars in our front driveway until it parked by the breezeway at our kitchen door, and for one delirious second I thought it was our family car. We watched through kitchen windows as a young woman, whom I recognized as Jalaine Ward, mother of two of my little swim students, got out and rang our doorbell. I looked at the sheriff in bewilderment. His kind expression encouraged me, and I moved woodenly toward the door, feeling a different kind of panic—to tell anybody about this would substantiate our nightmare.

"Oh, Julie!" Jalaine exclaimed, "What's wrong?"

A stranger's voice, guttural and distant, spoke through my tight lips, "You're going to be the first person I tell this terrible thing to."

Jalaine was more than qualified to be first in an unending parade of helpers who would come to us—she was an FBI agent. Her composure returned in an instant, transforming her from stunned friend to poised investigator. She focused on getting details we would need, such as Texas phone contacts and case numbers, and she began to guide us through the thick fog of how to begin notifying our families. She also insisted on taking on the job of contacting eighty-plus swim students who would be showing up here in two days for their second week of class. We later learned that her reason for dropping by had been to search our poolhouse for a missing swimsuit, which eventually turned up in her little boy's bedroom.

I knew Susie would have gotten home by now, and I also knew we couldn't call her with this. Jalaine said she would go for her. Annie would have to be brought here, too, only we weren't sure where she would be. We felt that her husband, Bert, would be best to break this news to her, so I called his mother, Sarah, to locate and prepare him. Hopefully, he would have his phone wherever he was fishing. We would call the rest of our family as soon as we were sure our girls were with us.

The next few hours passed in a slow, thick-liquid-like medium. It was like that unforgettable scene in *Contact*, the sci-fi movie with Jody Foster, when she is walking on a beach and sees the approaching figure of her father, who had died in her childhood. When she reaches out to him, her fingers cause a ripple in a shimmering liquid space separating him from her real world.

I would have expected such a supremely hideous tragedy as this to throw the world into darkness, but it truly was not like that for me. Instead, my eyes felt inflated, making everything seem brighter and liquefied, as though I were swimming with a wide face mask or being carried inside a giant teardrop. Shock, and the need to stay strong for what would follow, kept tears suspended.

As soon as the sheriff and chaplain left and Jalaine had gone with her little boys, who had remained unseen in her car, to retrieve Susie for us, Willie, the alarm guy, and his grown daughter, who was his assistant, eased up to us. I don't know for sure, but he must have spoken to the sheriff as the cars pulled around the pool side of our circular drive. Misery was etched into deep creases on his face and his daughter stood beside him, pale and expressionless.

Ironically, none of his state-of-the-art technology could warn or protect a family from such demoralizing destruction. I was sorry they'd been here for this. It was the second tragedy they witnessed during the time they worked on our alarm system. Earlier in June, six days before our boys left, Willie had come during my midday break from swimming lessons to begin his work in the poolhouse. That was the day Jim had come home early to carry our sick, aging Rottweiler, Katerina, to the vet to be put to sleep. We'd all known that day was coming and had agonized over it. After Jim drove away with Kat riding innocently in the back of the pickup, Taylor and I walked around our yard, separately, each of us crying. Willie said that had been one of the saddest things he'd ever seen—until today. That had been sixteen days ago.

I don't know when Willie's blue van left because Jim and I, like mute zombies in our separate cells of numbing shock, afraid to collapse, unsure if we could rise again, had begun gravitating toward the small comfort of familiar motions, like straightening the house. I remembered snack-bar supplies melting in my hot car and went outside to unload them.

10

Initially, my FBI friend, Jalaine, had said I should call *the sisters*. I resisted, thinking she meant *my* sister, because I wanted our daughters told before anyone else, but after she left for Susie, I dialed my younger sister Margaret's number, as though I were Jalaine's robot, replaying an embedded command. I tried to convince Margaret to come to our house without having to be given a reason, but naturally she insisted on knowing what was wrong, so I blurted that the boys had been in a terrible accident. She wanted to know more, and I told her the worst possible thing had happened—to both of them—and that we needed her to hurry and come be with us. I also asked her not to tell anybody yet.

Not telling anybody wasn't realistic and she knew it. She immediately tried to reach our older brother, Bobby, who lives with his wife, Harriet, about fifteen minutes from us. When that failed, she called Hazle, their grown daughter, who knew they were riding with their neighbors to a pre-Fourth party in Monticello, forty miles north of Macon. When Hazle reached her dad on the neighbor's cell phone, he told her he had only minutes earlier pointed out our house to his friends, and they were now passing the rock quarry less than four miles north of us. They turned around at once.

After my call to Margaret, I went back to my hot car to carry candy and drinks down to the poolhouse. Humidity that typifies Georgia's July afternoons had descended. Kat's son, Sculley, a huge black Rottweiler-Lab mix, his panting tongue nearly dragging the ground, tailed my every step. The two quiet cars in the front drive hadn't disturbed his nap, but the familiar-looking green SUV surely would have roused him from his shady place under the back wooden deck.

On one trip to my car, I watched Jim walk slowly to the garbage can with what looked like a stack of neatly folded khaki shorts. When he dropped them into the can, I thought, *poor man, in shock, knows they won't be needed anymore.* When I mentioned it days later, he was hurt, thinking I assumed he would trash our boys' clothes when, in fact, he had been dumping a pile of bronzed-over newspapers from the screened porch.

After more labored trips to the pool area, I called my little sister again, this time from the phone down there. She answered on the first ring. "Why are you taking so long?" I complained.

"I had to take a shower, Julie; I was making a little stone wall in my backyard—my arms were a mess with cement." She reminded me that she'd be here for the rest of the day and into the night. "It's only been twelve minutes," she said. When she confessed to having called both Hazle and our mother I felt a sense of relief. "I'm going to bring Mama," she said, "we wouldn't want her to drive alone after this, and Hazle's called back. She said Bobby's on his way."

Crushing sadness, not only for the boys, but for their sisters, made it hard to keep walking. I couldn't let myself imagine what would be happening at Susie's house as this stranger with an FBI card and two little boys in a green SUV told her there was bad news from her mother. I learned later that Susie had been sitting barefoot on her sofa, working on her laptop; her first thought was that something awful was wrong with her daddy. She couldn't find her shoes or purse after she got the news—Jalaine had to search the house for them so they could leave. They drove by Annie and Bert's on the way to take Jalaine's stunned little boys home to stay with their dad, but Annie's front doorbell went unanswered and windowless garage doors were locked tight, so they left. It turned out that Annie's plan to work with the shop's computer never materialized. She had been home, sitting peacefully out of earshot on her canopied back porch with her dachshund and a glass of wine, reading a magazine, when her husband rushed home with the news.

I thought of Jim's mother, Richie. How could we tell her this? She, nearly 80, was a widow, like Mother, but with the added burden of having already lost one precious grandson. It had crushed her when Jim's sister's 16-year-old son Eric had a fatal asthma attack ten years ago. Now, to hear that she had lost her remaining two devoted grandsons...maybe we could wait. When I thought of Carolyn, her daughter and Eric's mother, a reflexive sigh, like a gust of despair, blew through my mind, scattering worries that were too much to absorb yet.

I returned to the den where the scanner was repacked in its box. Jim mumbled that he would never touch the thing again. He kept going in and out of our back door while I rearranged clutter, loaded the dishwasher, and wandered through downstairs rooms. Whenever our sad eyes met, just long enough to see that we were still standing, there was a clear sense of futility of speaking. This bombshell had blown us into a nightmare, where memories or disbelief or grace gave us some buffer, and we waited for the others to come. When I got to our front room, our office, I stopped at a window facing the street to watch for Bobby and Harriet.

There was a slim, pale young man, dressed in a dazzling white shirt and pants, moving at the right side of the driveway by our mailbox. Cropped pure-white hair, despite a youthful image, was like a shimmering Afro. I watched him jump across the roadside ditch onto our lawn. He was alone, but he seemed to be reaching for someone's hand as he turned back, arm outstretched, toward the street. He turned again to our yard and walked slowly, head lowered, around the azaleas and cement bench that stand under an ivy-covered oak tree. He seemed to be searching for something in the grass, back and forth, nodding his head and talking to himself, or possibly into a cell phone. I couldn't make out his features.

I thought he might be a daddy from one of last evening's infant swim classes and maybe he had come this Saturday afternoon for a lost pacifier. I watched, hoping he'd find whatever it was and come no closer. There was an open view of the street and entrance to our drive and I wondered where his car was.

Bobby and Harriet startled me as they came through the den door behind me. He, wearing a bright red shirt, printed with white tropical flowers, had his arm around Jim, whom they'd found in our garage. Through tearful embraces, we could only repeat how unbelievable all this was and how horrible. When I asked how they'd gotten here, Harriet said neighbors dropped them off at the street. Though I hadn't seen them or a car, I associated the young man with them. "Oh, that's who that was," I said. Bobby nodded with a vague "Yeah." But I knew their friends—the connection didn't fit.

Within an hour Susie, barely able to speak through sob-swollen lips, and Annie, with Bert supporting her limp frame, had been brought to us. His parents were waiting for them here. Mother and Margaret had arrived, and we knew that word of the tragedy would spread quickly. Jalaine, our FBI friend, offered to put a call through to Texas for us. She began talking to a gentle-voiced trooper who had worked the scene on I-10 at 1:30 that hot day of a holiday weekend. When he needed to speak to a parent, Jim motioned for me to take the portable phone from him because his hearing aid made phone conversations so difficult.

I was in too-deep shock to agonize over shattering details of the wreck and simply parroted, as the trooper's report dutifully droned on: "Younger one was driving...wearing seat belts...may have fallen asleep...hot in Texas today...papers, postcards, belongings all over the highway...flipped four times...no signs of alcohol or tobacco..." Jalaine took notes. I was listening, but in my dreamlike state, I had become mesmerized by a strange white vase that had not been on our piano before. Speckled coral-pink daylilies were crammed down over its lip and the thing actually seemed to be glowing. Susie followed my stare and noticed a warm white light inside the milk-bottle-shaped vase, too. *Who had brought it?*

When a distraught friend, the mother of Tate's friend, arrived and wailed loudly during our embrace, I thanked the trooper for everything he'd done and passed the phone back to Jalaine. The few people in the room had listened to details as I repeated them and we stood around not knowing how to absorb the shock.

Family and friends began filling our house, and sounds of activity came from the kitchen as space was created to accommodate a steady arrival of food. Someone answered the ringing phone and necessary calls were made, but I wasn't aware of them. I heard a vacuum cleaner and noticed that someone had brought whirring white pedestal fans to assist the over-taxed air conditioning. Weeping came to all of us in waves, but so did smiles over recalled memories. I think shock had cinched an increasingly tight life jacket around my chest which would probably stay forever.

Father John Cuddy, our pastor, was called, and he came to pray with us and to set up funeral plans. Both boys had been altar boys for him at St. Joseph Catholic Church, so he shared our loss on several levels. The funeral would be next Tuesday morning, in time for him to leave for Europe that afternoon. Milton Heard, Hart's young funeral director, was there and made arrangements for someone in Texas to send our sons' precious bodies home.

Sometime after midnight, when everyone had gone and our house was quiet, Jim and I went upstairs to bed. Too exhausted to speak or weep, we fell asleep in the familiar shelter of each other's arms.

The next day, Sunday, was the Fourth of July. There was an instant of normalcy when I awoke at daybreak, before my heart recoiled, remember-ing. I went downstairs in a daze, set the coffee maker, and wandered outside in my pajamas. To my disbelief, nature was running her usual routine. Misty rays of sunlight sliced through leafy branches, which rang of birdsong. A triangle of honkers flew over on their way to a lake on Bass Road, and squadrons of honeybees droned over tiny white nandina blooms by our back deck. *How was this possible?* But when a freight train clattered toward its crossing beside the Ocmulgee River a mile away, there was clearly an echo of mourning as its whistle trailed through our trees. I had no energy for releasing screams of rage building inside the cinched life jacket. With coffee in hand, I went upstairs to dress. When I returned, friends were already in the kitchen with Jim, making breakfast.

After breakfast, people moved quietly through our house, acting as hosts, shielding us, while the family sat at our dining room table, layered now with photographs of our boys, as we struggled to fill out the obituary forms that Milton left the day before. An appointment was made for us to go to Macon Memorial Park Cemetery, so in mid-afternoon Bert, Annie's husband, drove us—Annie, Jim and me—there. Kind staff members, called in on their holiday and still wearing vivid summer clothes and sandals, guided us through the ordeal of selecting a burial plot. We decided on a shady hill under a tall long-leaf Georgia pine—a perfect spot for a family picnic.

On our way home, Bert, an anesthesiologist, reacting to his instinct to relieve pain, pulled into a CVS drive-through, scribbled on a pad, and passed a vial of Valium to Jim and me in the back seat. He made us promise to take at least a half pill at bedtime.

At 7:30 that evening, Milton, Hart's Mortuary's owner, used a two-way radio to converse with drivers of two black hearse-vans bearing our beloved sons' bodies from Atlanta airport, where they had been flown from Dallas, over 300 miles east from an obscure little west Texas town, Ozona, where the accident happened. He had arranged for a stop at St. Joseph's rectory, where Father Cuddy blessed their transport coffins and softened their crude appearance with large white liturgical palls. Milton relayed the progress of their approach while our brave group of twenty or so family and friends stood in his parking lot, bracing ourselves for first sight of the convoy. Milton said Taylor would be in the first vehicle, its license plate reading Harts 1, and Brax in Harts 2.

It took my breath away as Tate's vehicle slid around the corner on Cherry Street, into the driveway toward us, before parking under a portico. When its back door was opened, and before someone gently held me back, I was able to crawl in to touch the edge of his coffin. Then, when Brax's van parked beside it, our group rushed to his open door, too. Our hearts breaking, we followed their draped coffins into a long, cool interior hall where we prayed, reminisced, and began our tearful goodbyes—our only consolation being that they were now united forever. We instinctively knew our sons wanted us to remember them as we last saw them, unhurt and beautiful, so their caskets remained closed, but I heard Milton promise to give Jim locks from each son's hair.

At 9 P.M., as we were about to load into cars in the parking lot, two dark gray pigeons flew past the huge clockface on the sunset-reddened dome of the Bibb County Court House. All of us watched them soar across Cherry Street, and then, like expert air-show pilots, they underlined two tall pink-tinged cloud formations hanging above the huge, circular verdigris-copper roof of Macon's City Auditorium. Like giant, lumpy snowballs, clouds had been gathered into dramatic, indisputable numerals: 1 and 2.

I drifted in slumber that night, dreaming of holy smoke, the effect of my sons' burial in the clouds, rising through Macon skies, curling above streets and rooftops, some of it lighting on tree branches, or on a passing train, some floating along with the river, leisurely making its way toward heaven.

Finally, early Monday morning, July 5th, while I sat on the wooden back steps of our screened porch, clutching the newspaper, tears—like a rush of amniotic waters making real the pain of birth—flooded in racking sobs. Nothing, not even the dawning of a lovely sunrise, could soften the hopelessness of black print proclaiming the deaths of brothers Braxton and Taylor Bragg.

A continuous wave of people, flowers, and gifts of food increased. I eventually changed the outgoing message on our phones to express thanks for thoughtful comments and prayers, relieving anyone from having to answer the nonstop ringing. That night we moved through hundreds of mourners at a memorial which overwhelmed the air conditioning and crowd capacity of the funeral home. Young friends had arranged readings, collages of photographs—which I dared not look at—and music. It was our first time to ever hear a recording of Brax's singing voice, when "Just a Minute of Your Time," one of his new songs, came through the sound system. I still recall the shock of that. A handkerchief, handed to me by Tate's classical guitar teacher, to replace my wad of drenched Kleenex, is one of my keepsakes from that Monday night.

A touching newspaper article, sensitively written by a journalist after her Monday evening phone interview with me, appeared in Tuesday morning's *Macon Telegraph*, inspiring even more public response, overflowing St. Joseph Church before the ten o'clock requiem Mass began.

Our extended families, dozens of them, had interrupted their holiday and had come from everywhere. As we processed with Father Cuddy toward the altar, where two more priests were waiting, the church resounded with "How Great Thou Art." I was a member of the choir, and my fellow members had assembled above us, wearing white robes in the already sweltering, non-air-conditioned choir loft, to bring their cherished gift of music.

I felt carried through most of the long requiem and burial of our sons' combined ashes in a bubble, where my spirit, at least, felt protected, but I expected the spells of crying, a new experience for us all, to last forever.

I had lost my two wonderful children instantly, on a lovely, normal day. Whatever remained of my future had been robbed of dreams that disappeared with them. I tried to believe that God had a purpose for this cruel rewrite of my life's script—it had been all my nature desired: a good husband, two daughters, two sons, and a future brood of grandchildren—and I prayed that He would care enough to pull me through it. I clung to hope that spirits are alive and still love each other after death, but I had no real expectations of experiencing proof of it on this side of heaven, wherever that existed.

Three years later, on the morning of August 11, 2002, I sit in our poolhouse with my first laptop, still shuddering at the shock, but no longer hesitant to share what I learned from the other side.

2.

❧

Thank-You Notes

Thirty-nine days after the funeral, Mother and my friend Cile Messer came to help me begin the bittersweet job of writing thank-you notes. Stationery, envelopes, sympathy cards, lists of food and memorial gifts, and pages from the mortuary's visitation book were in organized piles, covering the round maple table in our breakfast room. Both women were committed to helping me with this note project, and whenever it began to overwhelm me their relentless dedication would steer me back.

Two days before, Monday, the 9th, had been my widowed mother Peggie's eighty-sixth birthday. Always a power source for our Wallace family energy, she planned to see me, her middle child, through this crisis as she had any of the others in her long life. She had begun her day by driving her classic celery-green Olds Cutlass to eight o'clock Mass, dressed in a bright yellow and black linen suit from one of her well-kept closets. Her cheerful outlook keeps Mom from getting emotionally bogged down, so, when the epicenter of a crisis calms, she promptly begins to put the past behind and look toward the next promising thing, saying "...and that's that." She had alphabetized, by sender's last name, all the sympathy cards and filed them away in a lidded Georgia peach crate.

I still clung to the hope that God would offer solutions for grappling with this demoralizing watershed in my life, but aside from grace, healing tears, and a sense of relief from completing this note project, offerings seemed to lack divine luster. My mother would never have accepted the offering that was coming that day as being an item on her prayer list for me, but our outlooks were about to be altered.

Jim and our girls, Susie and Annie, had gone back to their jobs the week after the funeral, despite heartbreaking grief. I don't know how they did it. The strain showed on each of them, but especially on Susie, the big sister. Divorced years before, she'd recently decided to put her house up for sale and had finally accepted our offer of the poolhouse as an interim place. She planned to move her waterbed in and stay through the sale, after which she would find another house, hopefully on our side of town. But I seriously doubted if I would ever be able to teach children to swim again, so it was fine with me if she stayed forever. That day, though, she was home on medical leave, granted primarily to revive her exhausted energy and provide much-needed solitude.

Susie's children, Anna, nearly 14, and Rob, 11, had already been spending the summer here, hanging out with Taylor during weekdays while Susie worked, spending weekends at home with her or with their dad, Jewt. We welcomed their presence even more now and were relieved they'd be here through the next months, at least. Susie would still have the massive task of getting their three-bedroom house emptied, painted, and on the market. Though we always seemed to know how to help each other, neither of us could face tackling all that work.

Wednesday, August 11th, was another of mid-Georgia's steamy "dog days." Piercing rays of late afternoon sun ricocheted off the corner of the screened porch on the west side of our house, bathing a white orchid and other plants on the pine bay window seat beside Mother, Cile, and me in creamy light.

School had resumed, following the summer break. The house was peacefully quiet after such a chaotic period, and clean. Earlene, our long-standing housekeeper, had come through, and worked her magic everywhere, leaving signature scents of Pine-Sol, starched ironing, and lemon Pledge behind.

Annie, 32, two years younger than Susie, was settling into her third year of marriage, with its inherent stress of a ready-made family with two young teenagers. Her ramped-up creative energy split between redecorating their big two-story house, a few miles from us, and running two bustling beauty spas in town. She now spoke openly of longing for a child of her own.

We had returned home on Sunday for Mom's birthday after spending a week at Amelia Island Plantation in Florida. The nine of us—Susie, Anna, Rob, Annie, Bert, his children, Marilyn and Boone, and Jim and I—had traveled in a procession of two cars and our old green pickup, loaded with bikes and towing Jim's Carolina Skiff on a boat trailer.

We'd needed to be alone to start dealing with this new sad way of life. Bert suggested the trip as a step toward shifting away from pain, and had made all rental arrangements. The four-hour trip was hard. When we met at rest stops, the girls and I cried as we compared I-16's blistered concrete, with its watery mirages, to that long, flat stretch of I-10 in west Texas. Sadness for Tate—thinking how he must have struggled with the same dulling drowsiness as he drove into the midday sun beside his dozing brother, only one month before—was unbearable.

Lethargy clung like a wet towel most of that week, our first ever at the beach without them. We forced ourselves through familiar pastimes— lolling in the surf, fishing, tossing bread to gulls, biking—tenderly protective of each other. Nobody wanted to be the one to spring the first leak, though we seldom fell into the same depth of misery or disbelief at the same time anyway, so we'd felt supported. We spoke of waves of gloomy despair that washed over us like the restless tide of truth, rolling with the gray Atlantic, but also had surprising spells of silliness, recalling old beach memories, until the dark rhythm repeated. I watched a gleeful young family of five pose for a photograph beside the lifeguard stand and said a prayer for their future.

One night had been the distinct, bright highlight. We were gathered in the small, second-floor condo, where Susie, Jim, and I were staying, overlooking beige sand out beyond tall, spindly loblolly pines. Annie and Bert housed the four children in a larger place within walking distance; however, a plumbing problem there made our place the logical one for dinner that night.

My girls and I braved a trip into the village that afternoon for our first grocery shopping trip together, praying for strength to withstand being ambushed by vacation memories. Oblivious of other shoppers, all three of us broke down; we were exhausted when we got back to the condo. But by sunset, the men were enjoying cold drinks on our covered balcony while everyone else was occupied in some stage of dinner prep. Corn was shucked, salad tossed, garlic bread sliced, and rich smells of Annie's famous seafood stew wafted above a huge pot bubbling on the stove. A long glass-top table was set with white ironstone. Sarah McLachlan's "I Will Remember You" played loudly on a boom box, her words speaking so utterly to our collective need, and we were even singing along.

During dinner we began swapping stories and laughing over our unforgettable experiences with our two boys. Sweet memories flowed with the chardonnay and cold beer around that table that night, and for a while their absence felt less permanent.

We hardly noticed that an electrical storm had dropped down over Amelia Island with heavy rain and gale-like winds. Lightening, with roaring thunder, flashed over the dark ocean, finally hitting something nearby and our lights went out. Cousins Boone and Rob ran out to our balcony and yelled back to us that ours was the only dark condo on the whole beach. But dinner and happy storytelling were more important; we looked around for candles so the spell wouldn't be broken.

Our condo owner had outdone herself with elaborate decorating. When we first settled in, to make it more homelike, I had moved three silk floral arrangements and a pair of ornate burnished brass candle holders, stuffed with fat, fluted pink candles, to thick off-white carpet under the front windows. I walked across the dark living room and brought them, in their tacky two-foot splendor, to the table. Jim lit them with his lighter and sparkling light reflected on the mirrored wall above chair rail molding.

We all relaxed, responding to the magical aura around us that night. We were convinced that the boys must have loved watching us have this kind of family get-together that had been so natural before. At some point, after the rain stopped, the glare of returning lights startled us. Reluctant to bring the night to a close, we eventually extinguished the pink candles and began cleaning up. After goodnight hugs, Annie's crowd trooped off to their place, and we all went to bed.

Early next morning, the guys left for an offshore fishing trip. Before we girls left the condo to cruise Fernandina shops and have lunch, my sister, Margaret, called to say there was an article about our family in the *Macon Telegraph*. Journalist Ed Grisamore, whose gift for writing stories of the heart is widely known, had come by our house for an interview with Jim and me on Sunday afternoon, the day before we'd left town. We suspected his article might be published while we were away.

On that Sunday, he'd driven to our back parking area where we stood talking to Skipper and Belinda Zimmerman. Ed joined us beside a white station wagon, parked off the paved area, in a dogleg under three tall oaks. The Z's, family friends for two generations, were there to buy back an old Volvo wagon they had sold to Brax a few months earlier once their teenaged twins had advanced to newer wheels. Skipper had asked to retrieve it so they could hand pick its next owner instead of selling it publicly.

Skipper runs a popular seafood restaurant, Jim Shaw's, named after his own son, and both of ours had worked there together all summer. Brax had worked the bar off and on for years, since graduating from Mercer University, and Tate was doing back-bar work for him before his upcoming senior year at Mount de Sales Academy. The busy restaurant, across from Annie's Vineville salon, was in public mourning, with a black wreath still on the door. Business was off, Skipper said, as folks seemed reluctant to face depressing changes, especially in the bar and grill section.

Skipper told Ed how he and Brax had developed their mutually accommodating routine, satisfying Brax's wanderlust, which most bosses probably wouldn't have put up with. He said Brax would work a spell, living on tips, rarely cashing paychecks, and then give a two-week notice. After he traveled a few months, he was back, reapplying for his old job. It was uncanny, Skipper said, chuckling, but an opening always appeared and he rehired the vagabond.

There was a lot of stuff in the longish car. Brax had left his keys with us on the night of June 23rd, when they left, but no one had touched it since. We began loading a cardboard box with spiral notebooks full of his tiny scribbling, pens, CDs, tapes, and books, plus black shoes and a bar-apron. An amplifier for his new red guitar was in the far back. I found a charcoal-gray velour slipover that I'd given him for Christmas back there, too. I folded it as a pillow and held it, redolent with memories of his bear hugs, against my cheek. I knew I'd keep it.

Everybody who knew him had Brax stories, and Skipper lightened the mood with one of his. He said he'd gone to the restaurant early one morning, soon after the car sale, and there it was—across busy Vineville Avenue, in the parking lot in front of Annie's salon—keys dangling from the driver's door. According to a waitress, Brax had done a quick, futile search for keys at closing the night before, then hitched a ride with one of the cooks. He either walked the mile to work the next afternoon, as in his between-cars days, or called his kid brother to give him a lift. Luckily, the car had still been there.

Belinda and Skipper had obvious affection for the old car and for its recent owner. She deferred to her husband when Jim held out the keys, and Skipper got behind the wheel. The motor cranked right up. He backed into sunlight and drove out of sight around our wooden deck. Belinda followed in their white truck, leaving us, hands raised in halfhearted waves, in our driveway. Ed, our journalist friend, cleared his throat, reached through his open window for a pad and a tiny recorder, and we walked toward the house to begin his interview.

Brax and Tate had left for their summer road trip on June 23rd, heading first to New Orleans, on to Los Angeles, and then back to New Orleans by Sunday, the Fourth of July. We expected them home, in Macon, on Tuesday the 6th. There had been plenty of discussions about this cross-country trip. I can't forget the look of surprise on Brax's face as they sat on the sofa across from Jim and me when we finally agreed to let him take his little brother with him; I find it hard to admit now, but there had been a split second of relief when I first heard that the big brother wasn't at the wheel that day in Texas.

They happily accepted our offer of the family car, a newer model dark-green SUV, rather than adding mileage to the old Ford pickup, which had passed down to Brax and on to Tate after their dad had finished with it. They spent weeks mapping their trip, packing enough CDs to occupy long hours on the road, making connections with friends along the way, and Tate had seen to all the SUV's travel readiness. I knew they didn't need money because he turned down my offer of any, and I felt sure Jim offered as well.

The previous summer of '98, they drove the truck to New York and Montreal. The summer before that, Tate and I met Brax in Amsterdam to travel for two weeks in his low-key style in the Netherlands and France. He had been in Europe for several months and stayed on after we left, finally getting home as a surprise for his little brother's sixteenth birthday in late October.

Their encased guitars were loaded, along with a large black rolling duffel bag they would share. Taylor spent the afternoon tying up loose ends, and they worked together at the grill that night. They came into our bedroom around midnight that Wednesday, June 23rd, to say goodbye. Both had showered to banish the smell of smoke and frying fish. They promised to take lots of breaks. As they pulled out of our driveway and up the hill past our house, Brax honked the horn twice in cheery farewell. Taylor made the first entry in their journal: *Brax at the wheel.* Although family trips were great, they clearly preferred a road trip with each other, especially now that Taylor was experienced enough to be a relief driver. When I went into the kitchen the next morning, I saw that Brax had left a small, well-worn used book on the counter—*The Loved One*, by Evelyn Waugh—with his inscription: "Dear Mom, I hope this cracks you up. Dear B—," scrawled on the title page. It was a few weeks before I thought of it again, and by then it really did crack me up. The book, written in 1948, is a dark and brutally funny satire of America's funeral business: the timing of its gifting would've exactly suited the brothers' sense of humor. I hear the movie, an oldie, is hilarious.

The boys got into New Orleans next morning, slept at their friend Bart Stephens's apartment most of the day, and continued west. They had no cell phones, but called us several times on their way across the country, including once from a restaurant near the Grand Canyon, while they waited for the nearly full moon to rise so they could play their guitars at some perfect spot on the South Rim. From the next call we learned that they'd locked their keys in the car at the canyon and had to accept a lift from a park ranger and a night in the canyon lodge. I was relieved to know they had slept so well. We laughed at this accidental family tradition—we'd locked our keys in a rental car at the canyon during a family trip seven years earlier.

The boys made a quickly ended call from a booth on San Francisco Bay while waiting to ferry over to Alcatraz. They were staying in a nice hotel and the weather was perfect.

Their last call was from Nepenthe, a famous cliffside restaurant on Big Sur, in California, with Taylor reporting on the great time they'd had in San Francisco. They were taking pictures, but he said the prison tour was bleak. It was around 9 P.M. here, and I wasn't in the house with Jim, but down in our poolhouse running a vacuum, setting things up for my swim school the next morning. I have a busy summer program of teaching babies and children to swim, and my base of operations is in our backyard—over six hours a day, five days a week.

By sheer luck I was able to speak to both of them that night. After Taylor's call, Brax placed a call to his friend James Morris in Los Angeles to say they'd be arriving around midnight. As agreed, long distance calls were charged to our home phone, requiring an operator to call us for approval. I was able to slip in "Hello, Brax" before a click cut us off. The phone rang again, with a different operator, for the same purpose. The first number had called James's office, which was closed, so they were calling his home. This time, when the operator cued Brax for his name, he said, "Brr-ax, my-Mama," and when she gave me space to accept charges, I rushed in, "Have fun in LA!" They were back on the road, and I was back to my regular life.

After several fun-filled days with their friend, a writer for an NBC series, which I think was called *The Dead Zone*, they began the long trek back across country. We learned later, when James wrote us, that they had slept late into that day, Friday, July 2nd. He spoke of their noticeable love for each other, even as they snored, crowded together in his only guest bed. We read and reread his long letter as he shared his memories of the fun times they had. He sent several copies of a photo he took of them leaving his apartment that afternoon, freshly showered and obviously happy.

Later, Jim studied their credit card bills, tracking gas fill-ups through California and Arizona until, at some point on Saturday, Taylor must have begun his shift at the wheel. Driving into blazing sun, it's possible he got distracted or began dozing. The car careened off Interstate 10, twelve miles west of Ozona, Texas, flipping several times. Brax, despite a seat belt, was ejected from his reclined front seat, and Taylor was pinned behind the wheel. Both boys were killed instantly, at 1:30 P.M. CST.

* * * *

At Amelia Island, the morning that my sister called about the newspaper article, we decided to include a stop at the Fernandina library before lunch, to get online and read Ed's article—we'd bring copies back for our fishermen.

We aimed for the library's big white-topped circular table filled with busily clicking keyboards. As soon as a chair was vacant, we moved as one toward it, five of us—Susie, Annie, Anna, Marilyn, and me. Susie logged on to the *Telegraph*'s site, and the rest of us crowded around to read over her shoulder.

I had felt anxious about our interview with Ed, not wanting to cry or preempt its purpose with our sadness. He sensitively described our relationship with our sons and the admiration others held for them, but his real focus had been to publicize exciting plans for a future heritage greenway along the winding, brown Ocmulgee River. Since the boys' obituaries had suggested that, in lieu of flowers, donations could be sent to a community trust earmarked for the proposed greenway, we felt a real interest in the future project. Such a lasting alternative seemed like a perfect way to remind us of the boys and their love of nature. Ed wrote about a memorial concert that was given by a group of Brax's musician friends, twenty days after the tragedy, at the Rookery, a popular downtown pub. It tied in perfectly as a fundraiser for the river project.

Brax and his newly formed band of four college friends, the Buckleys, had set July 23rd as the date for their premiere concert, mainly to showcase his songwriting. Shortly before he and Tate left town, the group made a recording of their last rehearsal and left it for the others to practice by. After the tragedy, the group, freshly grieving, was determined to carry on with the concert and went about promoting it locally, renaming it Bragg Jam. Eleven additional entertainers, including friends from New Orleans, came to perform for the bittersweet event. John Wood donated memorial t-shirts from Imagewear, his downtown store, to be sold as fundraisers for the greenway. They became touching keepsakes.

The Rookery owner, Jim Kee, hosed the old building's roof that afternoon to dispel 100-degree heat, and by nine o'clock there was no standing room inside. Taylor's underaged friends manned outside tables, stacked with t-shirts and brochures about the greenway, alongside a tripod stand with a topographical display of the project.

In Ed's article, he also wrote of the struggle it had been for us to compose a two-line epitaph for our sons' grave marker, which we wanted to order before we left for the beach. Words, not to define our loss, but to affirm their lives, had failed to come. I told Ed about having asked the boys for inspiration as I stretched out for a nap on the afternoon of the concert, and of how, as I awoke, two perfect lines had been given:

James Braxton Bragg
March 10, 1971–July 3, 1999
Taylor Wallace Bragg
October 29, 1981–July 3, 1999
We had music, we had love, we had life
The best gift is my brother

* * * *

At the Fernandina library, huddled toward Susie's monitor, tears ran down our cheeks as we read, and then we giggled, embarrassed over our failed attempts to whisper. Library regulars cast polite glances our way as we rushed to the desk for copies and were gone.

Another night at the beach, after having sampled several local restaurants, we decided to duplicate the night that had felt so magical. Annie concocted her stew, we set out the landlady's big pink candles, played the music and...just had supper. Nothing tasted or felt like before.

We were grateful for our week of privacy, a luxury unavailable to many grief-stricken families. Nonstop coverage of the Kennedy/Bessette plane crash, exactly two weeks after the boys', was a clamoring reminder of public intrusion into a family's world of shock and pain.

Being away from home's sad reminders of loss required us to rely solely on memories. I figured we could survive absence of places, maybe even of people we love, as long as memories stayed intact. My growing fear was that they would begin to fade. Inspired by the family's resilience and my need to protect beloved images in a journal, or even a memoir—anything to keep them alive—heartened me to go home, try to reconstruct a peaceful life from heartbroken shambles, and find a way to save memories.

3.

❧

Wunnerful, Wunnerful

Before any thought could be given to ways of saving memories, the project of thanking heart-weary friends and family who had abruptly stopped Fourth of July vacations was the first priority. As our trio progressed steadily in my kitchen, there was barely any small talk among Mother, Cile, and me. Even the phone was unusually quiet. Many notes required personal touches, referencing a relationship someone had with our sons. For example, the note to the church's folk music group, honoring their part in Taylor's life, as he played guitar and sang with them. Notes to their friends, to their friends' parents, to teachers, to musicians who accompanied the Requiem Mass.

Although our adult choir disbanded in summer, over twenty-five fellow members returned that sweltering Tuesday morning to sing for us, requiring many to leave work in time for early morning practice, opting to wear long white robes in the church's un-air-conditioned attic-like choir loft. Our soprano, Laura, fought tears during her role as Mass cantor, and I don't know how she made it through the gorgeous "Ave Maria." Tate's classical-guitar teacher, Terry Cantwell, played Bach's "Jesu, Joy of Man's Desiring," filling the cathedral-like church with heart-wrenchingly exquisite sound. Tate, at 14, had accompanied our choir with that beautiful piece, which Terry had taught him to play.

Mother had a knack for writing colorful remembrances of food gifts, while Cile mainly addressed envelopes, stuffed with stationery provided by the funeral home. I loved the stationery's printed verse, which we'd borrowed from a plaque which hangs on the trunk of a poolside oak:

28

There is always music amongst the trees in the garden,
But our hearts must be very quiet to hear it.

I had bought the black cement plaque at an antique sale two years earlier but left it in a flowerbed without much thought, not even noticing that
two boy angels flanked the white lettering, until Saturday morning, a week
after the funeral, when our assistant pastor came to pray Mass with us, al
fresco by the pool. Before breakfast we had helped Father Tim McKeown
set up an altar in the shady curve of the pool deck. We placed candles and
two wooden crosses, which had belonged to the boys, on antique lace covering a tall mahogany end table, under an oak tree. The diving board and two
white benches were pews. After breakfast, I marked the spot by rescuing the
black plaque and hanging it on the oak tree, above scarlet and white peri-
winkle. Cile's husband Jim later made a photo of it, which John Wood used
as the t-shirt centerpiece for the Bragg Jam memorial concert two weeks
later.

To continuously write each son's name, such a simple thing, was
draining. To keep from falling apart in front of the others, there were times
when I would go outside, sit on the steps under drooping fuchsia crepe
myrtle blooms and let the tears flow.

Around 4:30 that afternoon, our kitchen phone rang. Annie, en route
to her downtown spa, was starting to get her business life back on track.
Her busy, upscale salon staff had scheduled their regular monthly after-
hours pamper party for a group of doctors, and even though a drug rep
would handle food and expenses, Annie usually made it her job to coordi-
nate staff services—makeover, massage, manicure, and hair styling—and to
see that necessary ambiance was supplied. Because of the tragedy, there had
been no July gathering, but Tate had played his unforgettable classical guitar music for the event in mid-June. Annie had loved watching women
gather around her handsome little brother, charmed by his music, the last
time she ever saw him. Since she feared walking into an emotional mine-
field, she had only, at the last minute, decided to go. She was calling me to
help her brace up for it.

We talked of arranging plants in the sad hole where Tate's stool had
been and of allowing time for crying. Once the salon's heavy glass doors

opened, I heard happy chatter as her staff gathered around her, welcoming her back from the beach trip.

"I'm okay now, Mama," she said. "The girls are surprised to see me. They want me to meet a lady who's here donating her long hair to a child having chemotherapy. I'll talk to you tomorrow."

She later told me what followed: they led her back to where the lady was sitting, inspecting her radically new hairdo in a hand mirror, which reflected the back of her hair from a tall, gilt-framed wall mirror.

"Well, I'm not surprised it's *you* donating your hair," Annie remarked, recognizing the pleasant lady she'd met once before in her suburban salon on Vineville. "It's *Olivia*, right?" Olivia put down the mirror and reached for Annie's hand.

"Yes, it's been a while," she said. "I've had you and your family in my prayers—my heart breaks for all of you. I especially can't get your mother out of my mind."

Annie acknowledged her sympathy, admired the new hairstyle, and was drawn away to speak to other clients. Then she went into the product area in the front of the shop, gathered a bag of hair-care goodies, and took them back to Olivia. The stylist had removed the black salon cape from her shoulders, and as she rose to leave, she asked Annie for a quick word in private. Annie led her to a break room in the rear of the shop.

"First, I've got to give you a hug," Olivia said. "May I speak about your brothers?"

"Of course—I didn't realize you knew them."

"I didn't, but I have to say that I believe, in my own way, that one of them has been with me since before their funeral."

"Really?! *With* you?" Annie's jaw dropped. "How exactly do you mean that?" Annie told me that it was then that she recalled how impressed she'd been with the lady's intuitive sense the first time they were together—nearly a year ago.

"He just appeared in my car one Sunday. It was on July 4th. At first I had no idea who he was; but that's often the way it happens."

Annie recalled how this lady had seemed to read her mind before, when Annie was harboring so much stress, adjusting to her new role as stepmother to her husband's teenagers. Their conversation had helped her that day. She nodded for Olivia to go on.

"But then," Olivia said, "once I read the newspaper article two days later, I realized he was one of those brothers from that tragic accident—one of *your* brothers. Since then he's been riding with me *everywhere* I go." Her tone was quietly confident. "He keeps saying, 'Talk to my mama, talk to my mama.'"

Annie was speechless.

"I couldn't allow thoughts of contacting their mother, because I would never do anything to add to her pain, but I've been beside myself for over a month, trying to placate him. Do you understand?"

"I think I do," Annie said. "Tell me, though—are you saying you've had a vision of one of my brothers?" Her brothers' faces floated through her mind's eye, causing tears to gather. "How do you know who he is? How do you see him?"

"There's only one of them," Olivia said. "I see the young man with the exotic eyes. Didn't one of them have both a blue eye and a brown one?"

"Gosh," Annie said, "neither of them had eyes like that. Brax's were blue and Tate's were brown." Disappointed, but not surprised that something like this would be too bizarre to be true, she was struck with inspiration. "But what if you could be seeing a sort of combination of them?"

The brothers, though ten years apart, had formed such a bond that at times we felt the loss of one huge entity with two lively, connected spirits. To merge physical characteristics—Brax's sky blue eyes and curly dark hair with Tate's big brown eyes and walnut prep-cut—would have made a striking composite.

"That could be it," the lady said, glancing at something in her peripheral vision. She nodded, as though admiring the fit of a puzzle piece. "That's right, a merged image, so we can know they're together."

"Can you tell if they're with you now?" Annie asked.

Olivia smiled, implying guests waiting off-wing. "Yes," she said assuredly, "they're here."

"Are you hearing anything?"

"They want you to know they are with an older man, an 'R,' who loves your mother very much," Olivia said. "They show him as a smallish man with white hair. He is just getting to know the younger boy, but he's with them all the time now—making music with them. Do you know who this man would be? They say to tell you he signs his name with a flourish."

31

"Yes! That has to be my granddaddy—Mama's father! His name was Robert. He died from cancer right after Tate was born."

Our three children, Susie at 16, Annie, 14, and Brax, 10, were so excited about the pending birth of a baby brother that they had already dubbed him Sweet'Tater. Annie, too, took every chance she got to bend close to my bulging middle to talk to him in there, shouting, like Charlie Brown characters, "Bawonk, bawonk, bonk." When Jim wheeled Taylor and me from the delivery room to greet his joyous siblings, after their long night of waiting there, she began the gibberish that he had heard faintly for weeks. When he rolled his big eyes toward her voice, it was love at first sight.

"Mama needs to hear this!" Annie said.

Olivia may not have planned to reveal this incredible news now, but the opportunity had appeared, with Annie so receptive—maybe it seemed like an affirmation that timing was right. "I have no idea if I could ever contact her, though."

"Well, I can!" Annie said, dialing our number on the wall phone in the break room. Olivia signaled she'd be right back and left for the restroom.

This all took place in the few minutes since we'd hung up before. I was back to writing notes with Mother and Cile—*Your thoughtfulness in making a donation to the library in Brax and Taylor's names is such an appropriate way*—when the kitchen phone rang again.

"Mama! You're not going to believe who's here!" Annie exclaimed. "Remember when I told you about the lady buying Aveda cologne at the Vineville shop last year? The one who explained chakras to me?"

"I do," I said, remembering that Aveda, the shop's major product line, had launched a new promotion, linking aromas to the seven chakra centers. I assumed Annie hadn't read their marketing material yet. "Didn't you call me after she left?"

"Right, that's the one! I thought she might be a psychic, remember?"

I hadn't forgotten Annie's excitement about a lady whose violet blue eyes seemed to *look right through* her. I was surprised that she'd asked the lady if she had ESP, but when the lady admitted to being able to see things at times, Annie had asked her if she could see anything about *her*. The lady answered that she saw two children behind Annie and sensed stress connected with adjustment to married life. I think Annie gifted her with some cologne, a harmless exchange.

"I don't recall the word *psychic*," I said, uncertainty rising like before, "but yes."

"She was kind," Annie reminded me, "and it helped me."

"Right," I agreed. "Basically, I thought you needed to shift perspective from trying so hard to be the perfect stepmother. Maybe you could talk to her again."

"Well, she's in here now, having her hair cut for Locks of Love. And, Mama, she says she *has the boys with her!*"

I could tell from the quizzical look on Cile's face that my look of surprise was going to require an explanation. "Annie," I said in a lowered voice, as I began walking the portable phone out to the front room, our home office, "What could she mean, *she has the boys with her?*"

"She says she *sees* them—in her car!"

"What does she really do?" I asked. I wished I were beside Annie to keep her from grasping something like this so quickly and to have a look at this lady myself. "Who else knows her?"

"I'm not sure," she said. "But listen to this! She said she's only been seeing one boy—he has a blue eye and a brown eye—that confused us at first—but then we realized it was their way of showing that they're together. Isn't that amazing?! And they've told her they're with Granddaddy!"

"Well, how does she know *that?*" Caution bordering on protection for my child, this grieving sister, was what I felt. "I mean, we already believe they're with Granddaddy—that's one of the comforting things."

"Yes, and she said they're making music with him. He's told her he loves you very much and to remind you he signs his name with a *flourish*, whatever that means. And the boys want us to know that they're so happy—they're saying 'We are wonderful, wonderful!'"

I stopped in the front hall a few steps from the office door. A silken cocoon of memories had slipped around me. My daddy's musical talent was one of the best gifts to pass along to our four children. He played saxophone and clarinet, sang bass in his Baptist church choir, and had perfected a beautiful warbling way of whistling, which became his trademark. I could see his signature, his way of swirling three rolling loops in the "W," when he signed Robert Wallace—definitely a *flourish*.

It had irked that sweet man, when I was a third-grader in Sister Madeline's cursive writing class, when I argued with him about that "W"; Sister said all those loops weren't allowed. Though my brother was permitted to walk with our neighbors to nearby Joseph Clisby, a popular public school, Dad had conceded to his Irish Catholic wife's wishes by driving my sister and me downtown to the parochial school. He never liked how the nun also taught me to drop his mother Anne's name from my signature, making it appear that I was named only for his mother-in-law, *Miss Julie*.

"So, what do you think, Mom?" Annie asked. "She'd like to talk to you if she knew it wouldn't hurt you in any way. She said she keeps hearing, 'Talk to my mama, talk to my mama!' Can you talk to her?"

"Of course I'll talk to her. But, let's just be careful here, too, about letting anything upset our balance. We're working so hard these days just to survive." My heart thumped as if I were about to jump off a high dive—a fearsome thrill all my life. I walked the few steps into our office and closed the folding doors.

"Hold on," Annie announced. "Here she is!"

"Hello, Julie," Olivia said. She expressed sympathy first and then an apology for the unplanned intrusion. "Are you and your husband doing all right?"

"Amazingly, I think we are," I answered, "but only because of prayers and love from others, breathing life into our flattened spirits."

"Your family has been on so many prayer lists," she said. "You have wonderful children. These sons of yours are incredible."

"Annie tells me you think you've gotten messages from them," I said, surprised by a wave of possessiveness. "That sounds fascinating. I want to hear about it; when has it happened?"

"First," she said, "I have to say they are fully aware of the unimaginable pain you are in from this. They've been saying *talk to my mama* for weeks. I agreed to try, when *you* felt the time was right," she said tentatively. "I had no idea how it would ever happen—this may not be a good time for you, we can wait."

"No, no, this is fine. They're really all I want to talk about anyway; I've become obsessed with them. I've always believed there's a life after this one and that we'll recognize each other when we get there, but life until then is almost unendurable. Maybe Annie told you we're Catholic."

"I knew that," she said.

"I really believe souls are connected forever. Ever since I was a child I've loved the promise of a communion of saints."

"Souls are connected forever," she said.

"But I've never met anybody who says she actually hears what they say," I said. "It probably worries some people when you say that."

"I try to be considerate," she said, "but some are afraid, yes."

"Well, don't let me give you the wrong idea," I said, "no doctrine exists that could stop me from hearing whatever you have to tell me. Has there been something today?"

"Oh-h, yes," she said, in what I thought was a casual way of dealing with messages from beyond the grave.

"You told Anne a boy has been in your car. How do you see that?" Life-sized luminous faces floating in a car came to mind when I first heard that part.

"In little images, like on a screen—like a little TV on my dashboard."

"I can picture that," I said.

"Your sons want you to know they're wonderful, wonderful," she said. She repeated what she told Annie about my dad. "Does any of that resonate?"

"It all does." I answered, enthralled.

"And they seem be using a special accent when they pronounce 'wunnerful, wunnerful,'" she added, chuckling. "I feel like I need to say it their way—maybe to let you know they're with your father?"

"Absolutely! That confirms it all right." I said, chuckling. "Lawrence Welk! Daddy loved the Lawrence Welk Show. We had to watch it every Saturday night when I was a teenager. For our thirtieth birthdays, he and Mother even took my husband, Jim, and me to the Atlanta Civic Center to see the Welk orchestra in person. In his distinct accent, he'd say *wunnerful*—so we said it that corny way, too." I chuckled again.

"They've mentioned an important birthday—did one just pass?"

"Yes, my mother's was Monday, two days ago," I said, relaxing my grip on the phone.

"They know," she said, "and want you to let her know they're sending love to her. Will you tell her that?"

"Oh, I will," I answered. "She's with me today; she'll love it." *Would she*, I thought. Thinking of telling somebody else about this, especially my mother, instantly throttled the flow of excitement.

Olivia went on to say the boys were with me all the time. "They say they haven't left you since the big three," she said. "Does that make sense?"

"The third of July," I said with a sigh. "The day they died."

"They especially want you to know they were with you when you lit pink candles," she said. She waited a second for a reply, but if that was a clue for something, it missed its mark. She went on. "Did one of the boys love wood?"

"We're in a much wooded area," I said, looking beyond the window at the thick stand of hardwoods and pines all around our house. "They both loved woods."

"No, this is lumber that I can smell—not trees. Did one of them build something out of wood? With his dad, maybe? Recently? There is the smell of fresh-cut lumber."

"Yes, Taylor! He and Jim just finished a deck on the back of the house in May. They stained it on Mother's Day." Tate enjoyed that project with his dad. They shared a love of structure and design. "Brax came by and joined in, too," I said. "We all did."

"Well, I think this is Taylor talking. He wants you to know he's here. There's an October birthday or anniversary."

"His birthday..." I felt tears, *I wasn't going to cry now.*

"That's just his way of confirming which son is speaking," she continued. "He wants you to know that when you are standing on that deck he is there with you. And he says he was there with the pink candles, too, with all of you."

That was her second mention of candles. *On a birthday cake maybe? Not pink for the boys.* I remembered some pink ones in a dining room drawer but doubted the boys had seen them. We'd never used them as a family, certainly never on the new deck, but I'd find them.

"Did one of the boys wear a special blue tie?" she asked, speaking faster now. "I see a photograph with a big smile; looks like he's wearing a blue tie."

"They hardly ever wore ties. I'm trying to think," I said, wanting to check every reference but feeling like I taking too long.

"Well, you may come across a picture like this," she continued. "Watch for it—he's raising his glass high."

Maybe then she changed the channel, but I got the feeling that Olivia's visions were gone. She began talking more as a friend. She said she had learned of the boys' deaths from her daughter, who heard Father Cuddy announce it at Sunday Mass on July 4th, the day after the accident. "She told me he was so sad," she said, "people gasped when they heard."

"Someone from here called him," I said, recalling how we'd needed his prayers and comfort, "and he came right out that Saturday evening. That's when we planned the funeral for Tuesday morning—he was leaving for Europe Tuesday afternoon."

Olivia said that when she heard about Anne's brothers she decided right away to attend their funeral out of respect for the lovely young woman who ran the spas. It was soon afterward that she sensed the presence of an unfamiliar young male spirit.

Obituaries, compiled amidst mounds of photographs on our dining room table on Sunday morning, appeared in Monday's paper, and on Tuesday, the morning of the funeral, there was a touching article, written by a female journalist, after a Sunday night phone interview with me.

"I was getting ready to attend the funeral," Olivia said, "when I read the *Telegraph* article describing your sons as traveling romantics who played their guitars at the Grand Canyon. I was pretty sure then that my visitor was one of those boys—one of Anne's brothers. The whole thing broke my heart."

She said she removed the dress she would wear to the funeral and just went to bed. The boy's pleading for her to talk to his mother convinced her not to be around his family. "I had to trust him to show me when there was a better time," she said. "I guess this has been it."

"I'll never forget this, Olivia. It's all I really needed—just to know they're happy and still love us. I can't describe how much I miss them. Do you think you'll ever hear from them again? Could you call me sometime if there's more?"

"Oh, there'll be more," she said with cheerful assurance. "If you ever wanted me to meet with all of you at your home sometime, I'd be happy to do it. Why don't you talk it over with your husband and girls?"

It crossed my mind then that she might make her living this way. I wrote her phone number on a clear spot on the large, doodled-on graph paper desk blotter. As elated as I felt, a sense of vulnerability surfaced, too, reminding me again of our progress. We had relied on faith and time, never dreaming someone could speed up our progress or dull the reality of our pain with a promise of supernatural contact.

"You know," I said, "a lot of satisfaction comes from seeing how this has validated my faith in life after death. I can't wait to talk to Jim and our other daughter about it."

Annie was back on the line. "What do you think?" she asked, as excited as before.

"I'm thrilled, of course." I assured her. "But we're so fragile, Annie. Maybe we shouldn't be too impulsive. She does seem purely sincere, but with the newspaper articles, some of those clues wouldn't be too hard to come up with—no matter how welcomed they are from the *other side*." I heard someone join them in the break room. "And let's be cautious about telling this."

"I agree, but are your arms completely covered with chill bumps?"

"I wondered the same about yours," I said.

I walked back into the kitchen, nearly giddy over what had just taken place and a little naive about the impact it would have. "Y'all aren't going to believe this," I said, holding the receiver like a diploma against my chest. "That was Annie again—this time there was a *psychic* with her!"

"Oh, my Lord," said Cile, her tone more of an *uh-oh* than excitement. Her hand held a note midair, in route to its envelope, her blue eyes huge behind bifocals, waiting for more.

"What are you saying?" Mother asked. "What's going on with Annie?"

I was nearly breathless as I ran through all that transpired during the phone call, disregarding the advice I gave Annie and deflecting Mother's effort to interrupt me.

"Well, I sure hope you're not planning to talk to that woman again," she said finally. "I know all about those gypsies." She wagged her pen for emphasis. "We had them in Pennsylvania. They come around telling fortunes and end up trying to take your house away."

"Well, she definitely has a Southern accent," I said, replacing the phone on its wall charger. "But I probably won't do much more about it."

Cile, head down, failing to suppress a grin, was back in motion. As friends in a tight group since first grade, there had been long discussions about spiritual matters, which, as parochial school children, we learned about so early in life. Talk of angels was as regular as roll call. I knew we'd get back to this when Mother wasn't around.

"Of course you won't," Mother was saying, her voice softened. "You're doing all you *can* do." She stuffed a folded note into an envelope, inadvertently licked a new-style self-stick postage stamp with a lily on it, and slapped it to the corner of the envelope. "Annie should watch what she's doing, letting people like that in her shop," she groused, troubled blue eyes peering over sparkly blue-rimmed glasses. "We'll get through this like we get through everything else."

"She does sound like a sincere person, though, Mom, and she's lived in Macon for years. Besides—isn't it comforting to hear that Daddy's with the boys? And that they even mentioned your birthday!" She harrumphed at this. "But, no question," I said, "we'll give it plenty of thought. Like I told her, I'll just wait and think about it. There's probably nothing more, anyway." I sat, picked up the list and tried to focus on it.

I was thinking how unlike *everything else* this agony was—why would a person want to get through it at all. What would be left if you did? My hardest experiences had mainly been time-related challenges, such as pregnancies, children's illnesses, and breast cancer. Yet there had been lights at the ends of those tunnels and looking ahead was always fortifying. This torture was unfixable, unbearable, and no outcome would bring resolution. Wanting to live longer, to be involved in the lives of a growing family, no longer carried the same optimism.

I needed a break and headed down to the pool area to get Diet Cokes from the fridge in the poolhouse, with the primary aim to call Jim at his office. He was a supervising engineer at Blue Bird, a major school bus manufacturing plant in Fort Valley, forty-five miles away. I thought of him all during the day, wondering how he managed waves of grief as he tried to push through his long hours.

I tried not to look at the chartreuse water in our neglected pool. The prelude to fall always drops the driest yellow leaves in August, and our pool floor was littered with them. My sudden entry into the wooded area set off a shrill shirr-eez, shirr-eez alarm from the cicada world in tall trees overhead.

I expected Jim's resistance to talking to a psychic. I knew he would be skeptical. His left-brained, logical mind would trigger his ever-vigilant security system, and he would warn me of the risks involved. But maybe, I thought, when I've told him all I just heard, he'll find comfort in it, too, and want to hear more.

Just during the past week in Florida, he'd spent hours on our condo balcony reading a compelling true story by an attorney in Johannesburg, South Africa. The man's son, Michael, and his fiancée had been killed in a wreck during a summer holiday trip. The man wrote about being able to speak to Michael through a psychic medium whenever he took a hundred-mile drive for an appointment with her. Susie and I read most of it, too, and we'd talked about it together. Another first-grade friend, Beth McKinnon, had mailed the photocopied manuscript from upstate New York, where she was living in a Siddha Yoga ashram. She said she'd found it in her closet the day of the funeral and, though she hadn't thoroughly read it, hoped it could somehow help us. After glancing through a few riveting pages, albeit a little far-out and sad, I had tossed the big brown, padded envelope into my reading bag. Our minds opened to the idea of extrasensory connection as we shared the loose, dog-eared pages of that story.

I felt that Jim's main concern was that my talking to Olivia could upset me and be a possible way for someone to exploit us financially. As usual, our conversation was brief. His saying, "Go ahead, but be careful, don't spend a bunch of money," was enough acquiescence for me. I remember he also added, "*And count me out.*"

It was approaching dinnertime, so we decided to call it a day with note writing. Mother made a final check on a meal she'd put together—we were still taking food gifts from the freezer—and gave me a searching glance and a hug, then followed Cile to their cars. My cheerful role-model mother must have wondered, from day to day, when the real crack-up would take place out here. It often loomed these days, but for now the fuse seemed longer, the moment lighter. I called Susie as soon as their cars drove away and asked her to come for supper. After hearing about the call she was eager for more. We wished there was more, and we wanted to see what Jim and her kids thought about it.

I was anxious for Jim's blessing. His reaction, while clearly impressed with specific details about the boys and my father, was tempered by his characteristically cautious approach to most uncharted courses. I could sense his relief that my mood was lighter, but also his unease with my promise to leave him out of this adventure.

My interpretation of "pink candles" was simply that I could feel Tate's presence if I took a pink candle out to our wooden deck. I had some in a dining room drawer; I had used them years ago in a children's etiquette class. After dark, while Jim read the paper in his recliner and the others cleared the kitchen, I went to the mahogany buffet for a pink candle, carefully avoiding piles of heart-wrenching photographs still on the table.

I took it outside to the deck and lit it and waited for a possible sign. I whispered to Tate to make himself known in some way. I wanted to call aloud to both boys, as I did so often when I was by myself in the yard, and then I began to cry, as I had done when I felt only cheated and alone. I asked God why I should believe that deaths of precious children were part of some divine plan. I needed to trust today's unconventional gift as a healing part of the plan, and I resented the pang of guilt I felt from wanting to accept it. Why had He chosen to give such an amazing gift, the ability to receive present thoughts from spirits of my loved ones, to this ordinary, plainspoken stranger? I recognized my true emotions then: more envy and skepticism than pious guilt. It was bewildering.

Susie heard me and came out. Through tears we accepted that neither of us could feel Taylor's presence. We admitted how pathetic a situation could get if we began setting up little stages, not unlike a séance, to call the boys back. The pink candle had no significance for either of us—we couldn't think of a single time the boys had seen one.

There were instances, though, when we had spontaneously felt their presence. Maybe that was all we should expect—from them or from God. But we reminded ourselves that since placing our broken hearts into His hands, every healing gift that came to us had come freely. We had not sought out this lady. Nor should we be expected to turn away from an offer of a focused connection with the spirit world, if it really did exist. Susie and I were convinced the idea was not some new-age thinking, but has existed since the beginning of time. We would not overthink this. The preview had been too thrilling to ignore. We were thankful for grace, which strengthened us, as the feeling of abandonment slipped away once again, and we wanted more.

4.

❧

Q and A

I called Olivia the next morning, Thursday, August 12, to say we would all be very excited to talk to her if, like she had said, there was more to tell us; we settled on Monday. Both girls definitely wanted to be here, so it would be late afternoon, giving Jim a chance to be in on it. Our conversation was fairly businesslike, except that I forgot to mention the matter of a fee.

During that weekend the family talked again about July 3rd, less than six weeks before, when our world was shattered. We were still filling in the scenario of where everybody was and what they were doing when the news came to them and sharing reactions. Stories were gradually fitting together so that each person was accounted for. Most gatherings on those summer weekends included various generations of family and friends, few of whom had any idea what the girls and I were planning for Monday.

We began an outline of topics for Olivia, as though she might monitor a Q and A between us and the spirit world. Three unsolvable mysteries topped our list: first was the lingering question of the accident itself. Maybe she could help us understand why such a terrible tragedy had been allowed to happen.

Second would be what we now considered my *apparition*, which many of our visitors had heard me talk about. We'd definitely have to ask her about the man I saw at the end of our driveway that afternoon while I stood at the window waiting for my brother and his wife. Though Bobby and Harriet's friends dropped them off near that same spot at the end of the drive, none of them saw him. And I didn't see *them* as they passed in front of the house. If I had, I would have run to them, preventing their continuing around to the garage, where they found Jim. I was still watching the man when they all walked through the door behind me. Such a mystery, easily excused as a figment of my shock, will always be real to me, and I'd given up expecting to get an explanation in this lifetime. To me, he was an angel, sent to calm me as I stood alone. Apparitions would be less fantastical to someone like Olivia.

But the third mystery, the most bizarre, was that white vase which had begun to gently glow while I was talking with the Texas trooper that horrible afternoon, before even a dozen people had arrived. My sister, Margaret, said she knew instantly it wasn't one of mine and was impressed that somebody had gotten flowers here so fast. Bobby said I pointed to it at some point, saying, "Look what a sweet neighbor brought us; I don't know who, though." Such a trivial thing didn't really interest him; he thought it had must have been there before.

The vase is in the shape of a foot-tall opaque milk bottle, and on that day held four pinkish coral-striped lilies, whose ragged stems were too short to reach the scant water in the base. My first reaction was that it seemed to have been thrown together on the run, snatched from someone's daylily bed. Had there been any like them in our yard, I might have thought they'd been grabbed on the way to our door. By Tuesday the lilies had died and Mother refilled the vase with zinnias after washing away a tiny gold sticker that read, "Hand-formed, Mouth-blown in Poland." The vase had been the center of many discussions over the next few weeks. Jim even checked our phone bill to confirm the time of the call to Texas, fixing its appearance before 6:16 P.M. We made a list of everyone who was here by then and questioned each one. No one had brought it. I avoided asking if anyone, other than Susie and me, had noticed its soothing glow.

A choir friend, Ellen Harvey, gave me a book by George Anderson, a medium she followed on TV, because she had heard him describe an *apport* as a physical object that is transported by energy from the spirit world. We began to wonder if our vase could be an apport. We believed in our hearts that it was connected to the boys somehow. The girls and I agreed to use the vase, without its backstory, as a touchstone for Olivia's credibility. If she could shed light on any of these mysteries we would be grateful. Despite how imbedded these two bizarre things were in our memories, it felt awkward to mention them to friends; most were too kind for open skepticism, but even subtly raised brows could erode our confidence.

Regarding questions about the wreck, we weren't sure we would ever need to hear more about it. We were certain, if we were to continue moving through our difficult recovery, we weren't meant to dwell on its horrific details. Maybe such details, recounting conditions of departing this life for the next, should fall in the same category as those of departing womb life for this world. Both are natural. Both cause fear and pain, and if we have a memory of it, it surely pales in contrast with the outcome. But it is tempting to become obsessed with fear about each milestone, to get stuck in a quagmire of details, instead of accepting each passage as divine solutions for Birth and Life and Rebirth. At each passage, as our frail bodies face the end of a world, God allows loved ones to greet us. My lifelong challenge will be to accept this terrible role reversal—I had planned to be the greeter for all my precious children at both passages.

Olivia and I had several phone conversations on Monday concerning her time of arrival. As a person tuned to the spirit world, she seemed understandably challenged in dealing with life's practical side. Following directions to our house seemed to confuse her, so her daughter agreed to drive her out on a test run first. That would move the time from 5:00 to 7:30. These quick chats served to break the ice, and we discovered that we each have a good sense of humor. It would be better now, anyway—we wouldn't be pressed to stop for dinner.

I got into the shower about 3:30 that afternoon. As often happens, the steady beat of hot water shut out the rest of the world, allowing my imagination and memory to relax and stretch, along with my body. A favorite memory from six years earlier, when Tate and I visited Brax on a weekend trip to Charleston, began to run like a comical video.

Brax and his friend Russell Walker were apartment- and cat-sitting for a young English woman named Colleen Kelsall, whose cats had been left behind in Charleston while she worked in Los Angeles, her recent home. She was a movie wardrobe designer working on *The Rich Man's Wife*, a film starring Halle Berry. Brax and Russell had graduated from Mercer University in Macon more than a year earlier, but neither had found jobs doing anything remotely equal to their intelligence yet.

Colleen and Brax had met a few months earlier at a rental-car counter in Savannah's airport after he had flown from Macon to visit Luke, a college friend in nearby Charleston; but the friend had not, at the last minute, been able to meet his plane. Colleen walked up as Brax had lost hope of being able to rent a car to drive the next hundred miles because, at 22, he was under-aged for car rental. He had called me several times during the past aggravating hour to see if I could help somehow, but the tone of his last call was joyous.

"There's a very nice lady here who's driving to Charleston, and she's offered me a ride!" he exclaimed. I could tell she was standing there. Colleen had just finished working on a film in Savannah and was driving over to Charleston to see about moving there from LA. After her move to Charleston, she would have to go back to the west coast for her next movie job, leaving her apartment and two cats behind for several months. As it turned out, their meeting was more than accommodating all around.

Brax and Russell gladly accepted her suggestion that they house-sit for her. It would give them a chance to gather speed before heading out to pursue more suitable occupations, and, besides, as novice cat fanciers, they saw no problem with sharing the two-bedroom apartment with her cats. Brax got a job tending bar around the corner, and I think Russell worked a few leads for a while, but they loved Charleston, and I think, though Brax wouldn't have told me directly, there was a romantic relationship developing between Colleen and him by then, too.

Brax affectionately referred to her sleek black felines, whose tender feet had never touched real dirt, as Colleen's Malibu kitties, but mutual affection quickly deteriorated since neither fellow commiserated with the homesick cats' need for regularly cleaned litter boxes. Colleen had left clear protocol for feeding and hygiene in exchange for rent of her second-story apartment. The eclectic, feminine décor included white linen slipcovers, polished floors, and antiques, which, except for a state-of-the-art stereo and extensive CD collection, these two younger guys hardly noticed.

Our car trip, Taylor's and mine, had been prompted by a frantic call from Brax saying the two cats must have turned feral—they were having a *pissing war* all over everything. When he complained to Colleen, on the far side of the country, about her temperamental cats and the malodorous condition of her precious worldly goods, she ordered a case of expensive disinfectant and had it shipped to Charleston with instructions to scrub everything.

When Tate and I arrived, duvets, pillows, and covers hung all over the railing and wicker furniture on the once-elegant second story porch above a busy travel agency in the historic district. Piles of laundry blocked double doors to the laundry closet. A dainty eyelet lace curtain, meant to conceal a pair of well-tended litter boxes under the bathroom sink, hid shameful neglect.

I laughed out loud in my shower remembering that time with them, wishing there was some way to start to protect all the precious and hilarious family memories, when the words *short stories* came through the streaming water. Short stories? I wouldn't have to begin at their births and go chronologically through their lives, and there were plenty of family stories to write about.

"That's my answer!" I said aloud, turning off the shower, "I'll write short stories."

For years I'd regretted not keeping a journal, not recording our mostly happy lives and escapades. Now, driven by fear of cherished memories slipping away, writing was becoming an obsession. I just couldn't formulate a beginning. Even if it focused mainly on the children's lives, wouldn't it have to go back through my own youth? And then further back to my parents'? Considering so vast a project always overwhelmed me.

I wrapped in a towel, turbaned my wet hair, and, delighted by this inspiration, picked up the white portable phone by our bed. I needed to tell Jim about it. While the switchboard buzzed him, I toweled my short hair, now blondish silver all over, having been spared any bottled brown since April.

"Jim, I've solved my writing problem," I said when he picked up. "I can just start with short stories about the boys, not get so involved in long histories."

"You have?" he said, failing to hide his lack of enthusiasm. "Please tell me you won't start anything else until all those funeral notes are in the mail."

"Oh, I won't. This just lets me stop worrying about how I *will do* the writing one day. I'm not even thinking of starting now; but what a relief to know it can be short stories." Despite the brakes that he was able to push on most of my impulsive schemes, he was right—there were more pressing things to think about for a while. But, as fog vanished from the mirror, I smiled at the resolve in the brown eyes looking back at me.

"When is your *guest* coming?" I could tell that he had cupped a hand over his phone's mouthpiece, hoping no one was near his office door. Jim's the quiet type of man who, to say the least, guards his personal details. He would have structured a safe range of conversational topics at work, and explaining his relationship to a psychic would come nowhere close to it.

"She's postponed her visit until after dinner," I said. "Now you'll have a chance to meet her if you change your mind."

"I'd like to maybe say hello, but I'll leave readings, or whatever you call them, to you girls."

With no clue what Olivia looked like, nor having ever known anyone like her, I realized my imagining a woman with deep skin tone, possibly wearing a long skirt and bangle earrings, was the result of overlay from my mother's perspective about gypsies. I was getting excited. Maybe there was specific protocol—candlelight, soft music, incense? And what about the fee? I hoped she'd take a check.

After dinner the girls and I were ready. We would use our office or maybe the screened porch if the night cooled off some. Candles, incense, and matches were on hand. Anna and Rob hardly knew what to make of our merry moods and conspired to escape to their rooms as soon as the lady arrived. I think Jim had probably decided the same thing, although he stayed downstairs watching television until nearly eight o'clock, when the kids ran into the den announcing, "She's here!"

"Can I light candles now, Mimi?" Anna asked.

"I guess it's time," I said, "be careful."

5.

❧

Shattered

By the time Olivia parked her dark green Jeep Cherokee by the lamppost at the flagstone walk and was on our front porch, we had all gathered at the door. My first impression was of a gentle, young-looking matron with an engaging smile and indigo eyes. She was wearing knit slacks and shirt with watch and wedding band as jewelry.

We each exchanged hugs with her, as if welcoming a long-lost relative. Even Jim hung around the bottom of the stairs for a quick hug. In that moment she noticed his pensive aqua-blue eyes; later she would mention the deep sorrow they held. Susie's children said goodnight as they flew up to their room, rolling their eyes in my direction, as if to explain, "Mimi, we wish we could stay, but this is all too *we-ird* for us!"

Olivia said she and I had met some years back at Kroger's. It must have been when I wore a little hat to warm bald spots, because she guessed I was having chemotherapy. She said I was humming along with the piped-in music and that we'd spoken, but I didn't remember.

"I'm enjoying my short hair, Anne," she said, fluffing her thick, shiny brown hair. "It's so much easier and definitely cooler." The bob, because she had insisted on giving extra length, barely covered her ears, emphasizing her eyes. She followed us through the short entry hall toward the office.

"Oh, I see a big Rottweiler here." We looked around to be sure Sculley hadn't sneaked through the front door. "Do you have a Rottweiler?"

"Yes," I said, "I mean, we did have. We just lost a wonderful dog, Katarina, about eight weeks ago. That part-Lab who nearly knocked you over on the porch is her son."

"Well, she's here, too," she said.

"Here?" I said. "Oh, you mean *here,* as in there," pointing to the ceiling.

"A mother dog," she continued. "She was there to meet your sons."

"Really?" I said, "Gosh, I had hoped that could be true—you're saying animals *do* go to heaven." I visualized Kat's sweet, wide face, hoping she knew how we loved Sculley, whose first birthday was one day before Tate's.

Susie said, "Maybe we should apologize to her."

"No need," Olivia said, and smiled. "She's happy, taking care of your sons, with you taking care of her son—that's what she's saying."

"Amazing!" I said, finding this easy to believe. "I feel the same way."

Susie led us through the folding doors into the office. Without a pause, Olivia said, "There's a man here." She had turned back to face the fascia above the doors, just inside the room. "He wears a brown leather glove, but only on one hand," she said, "I wonder why—maybe that hand is hurt?"

Before I could respond, she said, "Yes, they say an accident...to himself...a gunshot wound?" Then she looked at me. "Whoever he is," she said, "he loves you very much and hates to see you go through this."

Though unprepared for old family history, I knew immediately whom she referred to. Susie knew, too. "Your grandfather!" she exclaimed. "Uncle Vernon told us how his father's shotgun went off, shooting himself in his hand while they dozed by a log on a duck-hunt in Charleston. We heard that story a hundred times!"

"Vernon was my daddy's big brother," I explained. "He was 9 when that happened, a year before my dad was born. He said he rode behind his father's saddle that morning, carrying their guns, sobbing, until they reached the other hunters. It was the only time his father ever told him to shut up. Grandfather Wallace covered the ugly scar in a leather glove for the rest of his life. He died when Daddy was only 5; I believe it was 1917. He never even knew any of us!" Chills flew over my arms. I hadn't imagined that someone other than my father and boys would be aware of this meeting.

Olivia then asked if she and Anne could be alone for a few minutes. Our family uses "Annie," my grandmother's name, as a term of endearment, but most people call her Anne. "I have a few things to tell her," she said.

"Sure," I said. "Susie and I'll go to the den."

Annie suggested they go out to the screened porch. I set a candle on the coffee table there and closed the glass door, leaving them alone. We knew she was overloaded with stress, from several directions. Her husband's ex-wife had recently been hospitalized due to an overdose, for one thing. Work proved to be her greatest solace and she was burying herself in staying busy. I hoped Olivia could help in some way.

Susie and I hung out in the office checking email. After twenty minutes I tapped on the glass. They were relaxed, chatting like old girlfriends. The sinking sun painted a blazing backdrop for the dense woods behind them. "Annie," I teased, "you'll have to consult with Olivia on your own time."

"Come on out," Olivia said, patting floral cushions on the wrought iron sofa beside her. "We've been waiting for you."

But humidity sent us back to the cool office. Olivia decided to talk to me then. The girls, taking the hint, backed into the den, closing the door, leaving us to stand facing each other.

"I want you to let me hold your hands now," she said, "and allow me to take away some of your pain."

"Take it away?" I said. "There's no way I could ever want another mother to take this kind of pain."

"I know what to do with your pain," she said, lifting my hands in hers. Her eyes, like marbles behind tortoiseshell glasses, searched mine, and her hands, though soft, conveyed surprising strength. "It can't hurt me; it won't stay with me."

For weeks I'd been offered relief from other willing, sympathetic eyes, which mostly held personal pain as well; but hers held a detached gaze, which allowed me to dissolve a need to be strong.

"Can you tell me the worst thing you feel, at this moment?" she asked.

"It's that I can't visualize Taylor's face," I said, my voice cracking. "I'm thankful I can see his brother's, but I don't think I can stand to live if I can never hold Tate's face in my mind."

Tears, which unless in private had usually been shielded by my hands, began to pour openly. For the moment there seemed to be more room around my heart. I don't know how long we stood like that.

"How can you endure that?" I finally asked, wiping my spattered glasses and face with a Kleenex. "What did you mean when you said you know what to do with pain?"

She smiled. "I gave it to God for you—as He's asked us to do. He can handle it."

"Oh," I said, feeling a little foolish with relief. "I need to remember that; like offering it in a prayer." I admit I also liked being reminded that a gift like hers could only come from God.

"That's all," she said. "Losing your younger son, the baby, must be so unbearable that pain blocks your ability to call up the memory of his face."

The hall clock reported the half hour in Westminster Abbey chime, but I had lost track of which hour it might be.

"Did he still live at home?" she asked.

I nodded. "He would've been a senior in high school. He was to be a millennium graduate at Mount de Sales Academy, where I graduated from forty years ago, when it was a small convent school for girls."

"Well, in time you will be able to see his face," she said, "he'll help you."

"He was a good student," I said. "He played classical guitar like an angel. His guitar teacher was helping him prepare for a recital in December."

She touched my shoulder, a big smile on her face. "Do you know how much those sons love you?"

"I think so," I said. "I did feel great love from each of them, all their lives."

"They never left you from the minute you heard about the accident," she said. "They say they floated you around on their arms, like a queen on a throne—let me show you." She clasped my forearms at the elbows. "They clasped arms and held the soles of their feet together, like this..." She lifted her foot straight out in the front. "They didn't put you down for three whole weeks."

I chuckled, getting the picture exactly. "It amazed me that I was able to walk at all," I said, "I really did have the feeling of floating."

Her face lit up and she tapped my shoulder again. "By the way," she said confidentially, "they want me to say they *love* the short stories idea."

"That idea just came to me this afternoon—they never knew about that."

"They know."

"How could they? I was taking a shower when I had that idea!" That gave us both a laugh. I turned to see what she was looking at behind me; it seemed to delight her.

"The two of them are sitting on that shelf over your computer," she said, and pointed to the top of the bookcase Taylor helped me assemble from a kit last winter, "ready to inspire you with one funny story after another. They really are—right there!"

I pictured two elfin boys and wondered how they looked to her. "But we can even be followed into a shower?" I said.

"Makes no difference to them where you are," she shrugged with a smile.

"I'll have to remember that," I said and laughed again.

We sat, then, in chairs by our big walnut desk. She seemed lost in thought, as though enjoying a memory from a movie we were discussing. Since I figured her reading for me was finished, I was about to stand and tell the girls to come hear all about it.

"Who is this older lady with us?" she asked, undistracted by my confusion at her rapid gearshifts. "I'm surrounded with a feeling of luxury here—satin pillows, lovely, lacy bedclothes. This lady says 'beautiful in bed.'"

Something familiar stirred in my memory.

"There is a strange bell on a bedside table." Olivia laughed. "She says, 'I ring it loud and often.' She can be funny, can't she?"

"My gosh! It sounds like you're describing an aunt of mine, Annie Moore Wallace. She kept a copper cowbell by her bed—I still have that bell!" Olivia had nailed the description of my bedridden, arthritic aunt who had died in 1980. "She would actually tell us she hoped to look beautiful in bed," I said, "like her mother had done. And that cowbell—she rang it from her upstairs bedroom to summon their housekeeper, Ernestine, for at least twenty-five years. She was married to my dad's brother, Vernon, the one on that duck hunt with my grandfather."

I pictured the white painted brick house, which she had built in the thirties, on a shady, azalea-covered slope in Shirley Hills, an exclusive older neighborhood across the river, before she married Vernon. He and my daddy, ten years apart, were close brothers and looked so alike that people often mistook them. Vernon suffered greatly when his little brother died in '82.

"I loved spending time with them, like their little princess," I said, "more like the child they never had than as a niece. Before her housebound days, she took me shopping for frilly party dresses to wear at tea parties she had for her socialite friends." It had seemed like luxury.

"Your aunt's saying, 'I am loving being with your boys, and especially meeting the little one,'" Olivia said. "They've heard many stories about your childhood now. She says they're *swapping* stories about you."

"This is incredible," I muttered. "She died a year before Taylor was born."

"She wants to say that you and your Jim should be very proud of these two. Both beautiful, smart young men."

Tears of joy filled my eyes as I relaxed, recalling those happier times. "Can you tell if Uncle Vernon is here, too?" I asked. "He was always like the grandfather my siblings and I never had, and after Daddy died, Uncle Vernon took up the grandfather role for our four."

"We can wait and see," she said, as she folded her arms across her chest, chuckling, "because she says she has others with her, so we're going to sit right here and have our party while they play their lovely music."

"That sounds just like her," I said. "She ran the show from those pillows." Then, realizing she might hear me, "And planned loads of nice parties."

Again, I thought Olivia's pausing indicated the end of our time together. I was anxious to get Annie and Susie.

"So-o," she said, "You got flowers you didn't like, huh?" Her voice sounded mildly sarcastic and distant, then amused. "Goodness, Julie, have you ever gotten flowers you *didn't* like?"

"That I didn't like? No, why do you ask that?" It wasn't easy to shift from an idea of my sons making music in another world and having loving conversations about me.

"That was a strange question," she replied. "Maybe for the funeral? Some pink ones possibly? But who ever heard of not liking flowers? Especially gifts."

"No, we loved all of them," I said. "Wait! Before you say anything else about flowers—see that vase? Would you say there's anything special about it?" I followed her to our piano. The vase, full of colorful zinnias from our neighbors, the Browns', garden, was now shrine-like to us.

She touched it. "Hmm, odd," she mused, moving both hands along the vase's smooth sides. "Is this a new vase, Julie? Maybe a replacement for a broken one?"

"New, but not replaced."

"Shattered," she said. "I'm hearing *shattered*. But then it wouldn't be here if it were, and you haven't gotten a duplicate of it?"

"No, but we've been so interested in what you would say about this. Wait a second; you've got to tell the girls what you told me." I opened the door and they popped to their feet. "Listen to what Olivia just said about this vase," I said excitedly.

She smiled like someone missing a punch line. "Well, I felt like Julie's vase was shattered at some point, but since it's obviously whole, I had to guess this one is a replacement." She went on before we could say anything. "Maybe it was a gift—was it a gift from your sons?"

The girls and I began speaking over each other, wanting her to know that we felt the same way—which was that it was somehow connected with them. "Your describing it as shattered wouldn't really surprise us, though," said Susie.

"Remind me how they crossed," Olivia said. "A car crash, wasn't it?"

We nodded.

"Maybe they were bringing it to you; did you get their things back?" We nodded.

"It would've been shattered in a car crash," Olivia said, touching the vase once more. "But, then, how would it get *here*?"

"That's what we hoped you'd tell us," we chorused.

"Does she know about the man in white?" Susie asked. I shook my head.

"The man in white?" Olivia repeated.

"We think Mama had an apparition," Annie said.

"Tell me about that." Olivia lifted her glasses' nosepiece with her index finger.

"It was while I was waiting for everybody to get here, after the sheriff left that afternoon. I'll never forget it; but it's hard to expect anybody to believe it."

"There's a white aura around a person's face when they're telling the truth," she said. "See your mother's face, girls—how it seems so white?"

"Tell her, Mama," Susie urged.

I described the pale, slim man, his white hair and clothes, how he'd leapt the ditch, and I demonstrated his turning back, hand outstretched, as if to encourage someone following him.

"I didn't see a car or anyone else, though," I said. "He walked in slow circles by our bench, nodding and talking to himself." I pointed toward the dark street where the curved concrete bench from Uncle Vernon's yard stood by a white oak tree.

"You don't think you knew him?" Olivia asked. I shook my head.

"But they say he's a good friend," she said.

"Who says?" I asked. "The boys?"

"His name," as if she just received a text, "is Matthew. Can you think of a Matthew who fits that description?"

"They each had a friend named Matthew," Annie offered.

"Yeah, but this man didn't look anything like Matthew Gray," I said, referring to Tate's teenaged brunette friend who lived a few miles away. Then we all thought of Brax's lifelong, blond friend in Seattle. "Matthew Davis?" we asked in unison.

"You couldn't mean *that* Matthew—he's over 2,000 miles from here," I said. "Plus you mean somebody who's not living, right?"

"Oh, but he's your angel," she said. "And I hear that 'he'll be ringing your bell.'"

"Angel?" I repeated. "No, no. We don't want any more boys to become angels. Are you implying that he's going to die, too?"

"Not at all," she said, "but God uses people who may live long lives here. He needs lots of them as messengers and helpers. I think your friend is like that—very human, but able to travel if necessary, understand?"

"That's a whole 'nuther way to think of angels," Annie said.

"I hear that he'll be here in three months," Olivia said. "That's when he'll be ringing your doorbell."

"But how was he visible," I asked, "and what would he be doing here?"

"God could have let him meet his friends as they were crossing over, to accompany them home—so they could see that their family would be okay and could begin to deal with their deaths."

I imagined two beautiful forms floating above wreckage, being swept up, as if by an eagle's wings, to go with a friend for a guided farewell to cherished places. "I wonder if they were excited, or as heartbroken as we were," I mused.

"Would you believe they couldn't even begin their work on the other side until they knew that you all were okay?" she said, probably assuming that we understood more than we actually did.

"But Bobby and Harriet didn't see him; and I didn't see their car—it all happened at the same time."

"They could see you looking through the window."

"They said they didn't see me, though," I said.

"The *boys* could see you," she said. "You weren't crying."

"They are saying that?" I asked raptly. "No, I wasn't crying then—I was in total shock. I actually felt peaceful, even as I watched that man. I just didn't want him to come nearer. I remember feeling that our boys were where they had to be, and that we had to accept the horror of it. When Bobby, Harriet, and Jim walked in behind me I looked away."

"How could she have seen that, Olivia?" asked Susie. "Could he have made himself visible just to her? Does a person like him remember that, if it happens?"

"I don't know that answer," she said. "But you can ask him when he comes."

"Yeah, right," I said. "I'll ask him how it all worked—when I had a vision of him as an angel in our yard. Can't quite see that happening."

"Well, they say he's coming in three months."

"Do you think that's got any connection to the vase?" Susie asked. "I was at my house when an FBI lady came to tell me about the accident. I think the vase was already here when we came into this room together.

"An FBI lady?"

"An FBI agent whose little boys had taken swimming," I explained. "She happened to drop by while the sheriff was still here. She left to bring Susie to us."

"Oh, how sad...well, it could be," she answered, "but I can't say for sure. I think that's something you'll find out later. How it got here is a mystery to me, too," she said and shrugged with a smile. "They don't always tell us everything, you know. Julie's aunt is the one who brought up the subject of flowers."

"Your aunt?" The girls looked at me.

"Y'all have to hear about that," I said. "Olivia said Annie Moore was going to sit here while we have a party. She teased about flowers I didn't like, and that reminded me of how disheveled I first thought those lilies looked—then I remembered the vase."

We chatted on, unaware that Olivia had begun to feel like a traffic controller, until she exclaimed, "Y'all have no idea how crowded this room is!"

6.

≈

Santa Claus

"Now," Olivia continued, "which boy had these damaged eyelashes? Maybe they're singed, or...no, this appears to be done by him...'no accident,' he says. Did one of your boys cut off his eyelashes?"

"No," I said.

"Well, this young man has damaged eyelashes, and he says y'all know who he is," she said matter-of-factly.

"Eric!" we exclaimed together.

"He was our cousin," Susie said. "He died when he was just 16."

"Jim's sister's son," I explained. "He passed away in an Atlanta hospital in '89 after an asthma attack. It was heartbreaking—our family's first sudden tragedy."

"Well, he's here," Olivia said, "and he's having great fun making music with his cousins. He says he loves you all very much, too."

It was as though Olivia had raised an antenna into some high-frequency energy field, which, though it seemed effortless on her part, had opened a clear channel for spiritual sound waves.

"What about his eyelashes," she asked. "Did he cut them off?"

"Well, he didn't cut them," I said, "but with chronic asthma he needed strong meds, which could cause more anxiety than his asthma. During one of those times he plucked out his lashes. Thank goodness they grew back, but the look was memorable."

"He had such dreamy blue eyes," Annie said.

"Do y'all remember that time we were in an elevator at the Medical Center?" I asked. The girls clearly didn't know where I was headed. "I don't know why I'm thinking of this now anyway," I said, feeling guilty at this memory. Olivia gestured to go on.

"I was taking all six cousins—our four, his sister, and him—to visit Papa, Jim's dad, who was in the hospital. I think it was near Father's Day. Eric was a young teenager with more than enough hospital experience, but his obvious lack of enthusiasm got to me that day. I shamed him in front of the others, warning him that he best adjust his attitude and have a happy face for Papa when we got off that elevator. And he did. I wish now I had just let it go."

Olivia's hand shot up like a school patrol boy's. "Eric says, 'Stop.' He doesn't want you to regret anything; you were saying the truth." She smiled a crooked smile, not unlike his. "He says he deserved it anyway."

"Really?" I asked. "Are you sure that's what you hear?" The girls talked of how Brax loved his two-year-younger cousin and how depressed he was when Eric died. Papa had passed away less than two years earlier, or it would've killed him. Everybody felt bad about having so little time with both of them.

"Eric says, 'Tell them to stop crying—tell them to laugh!' He wants you to remember flip-flops and *laugh*!"

"Flip-flops?" I repeated, as I clapped my hand over my mouth. The girls stared at me. "Oh, my gosh...I haven't thought about that since the day of his burial."

"Thought about what?" Susie asked.

"I hate to say." I shook my head in disbelief. "It's so silly. Think back to the day of Eric's funeral. You remember how you four kids and I stayed at the cemetery until his casket was covered?" The girls, hardly kids back then, at 24 and 22, nodded.

"By the time we got to Jim's mom's crowded house everybody had begun lunch; y'all joined them. The door to the bedroom that Grandma devoted to Eric was closed, but I went in, thinking of saving her and Carolyn the sadness of its straightening, and I closed the door behind me."

"That was a good thing, though, Mom," Annie said.

"Well, wait," I said. "Several things from his last visit were scattered around. I folded a couple t-shirts, then noticed this pair of flip-flops sticking out from under the bedspread. They were so cool, *so Eric*—thick black-tire soles, spikey chrome studs on black leather straps, but small, about my size.

I slipped off high heels, fit my stocking feet into those flip-flops, and walked over to the mirror on the back of the door. I looked ridiculous, of course, and even whispered out loud 'I don't think so, Eric.' After I put them back under the bed, out of sight, I never gave it another thought. And I sure wouldn't have ever mentioned it to anyone."

"Wow," the three of them said.

"He was really there, Mama," Annie said, her face beaming. "And he thought it was funny...incredible!"

"Ten years ago," I said. "I'm embarrassed to remember it even now."

We were off again, talking about him, enjoying memories of three boy cousins and the mischief they got into, unaware that Olivia was patiently trying to direct invisible traffic.

"Let's sit down," she said finally. "There are so many others in this room, we'll be here all night." She shoved her tortoise shell glasses up again and looked at me.

"Now, who is this woman pointing to your hair—like she's lifting it away from your ear?" she asked me. "Another aunt?" She fluffed her own hair, exposing her ear. "It looks like she may be trying to put an earring in your ear?"

"Earrings? I can't think," I said. "Annie Moore used to do my hair in French braids close to my ears when I was little, but I didn't like it."

"No, you're grown here. This lady says, 'The earrings—they *were* meant to be a gift.' She wants you to know that. It looks like she's trying to put a shiny pierced earring in your earlobe." I reflexively touched my ear, feeling the familiar gold ball on a wire loop—the ones I got with Susie at Sam's that awful Saturday.

"My aunt Anne loved jewelry," I said "mostly costume, but not pierced." I was conscious of my chatter, feeling hyper, trying to hang on to this fast-track of memories, wanting not to disappoint anyone. "This was hers," I said, patting the brocade arm of my antique round chair. "She was the oldest of Daddy's three sisters. The others, Shelley and Beverly, wore pierced earrings. Shelley's still alive, so I guess she's not the one."

Olivia smiled. "You'll connect it later," she said, "just remember the earrings *were* a gift, that's how I hear it, but it's not clear who from. But now, let's find out who this little man in the Santa Claus suit is."

It only took a second for the girls to exclaim, "Granddaddy!"

"Whose father—yours or Jim's?" she asked me.

"Mama's," answered Annie. "He was always the one who sat under the Christmas tree, doling out everybody's gifts,"

"Yeah," said Susie, "he made everybody stop and watch each person open a gift before he gave out the next one." I remembered how that had tested the children's endurance each year.

"And he wore a Santa costume?" Olivia asked.

"Not a costume," Susie said, "a hat sometimes."

"This little man is wearing a full costume. He's come through that door eight or nine times, stacking gifts there by your piano." She pointed to our front door, tracing a left-to-right air path across the office to the pine floor under the window by the piano. I could visualize the packages.

A lump of sadness pushed up a precious memory. "I remember his wearing that costume," I said. "He wore it twice during the years I did museum guild work—in the late seventies and then again in 1981. He was so sick that last time. During that fall, when I was pregnant with Tate, I helped assign volunteer Santas for the guild's Christmas shop. I registered Daddy for early December, knowing our baby would be here to include in a cousins' photo with Santa, like before. We still had no idea about Daddy's metastatic colon cancer at that point.

"By Thanksgiving new baby Tate and Daddy's dismal diagnosis were all that was on our minds. When the museum called to remind me of his date as Santa, I explained that it would be a big effort for him now, but I would check with my mother before cancelling. With her usual optimism, Mom reminded us how much he had enjoyed it that first time—it would do him good, she said. So Daddy feigned enthusiasm and agreed to go again. We made our plan: baby Tate and I would take him to the museum and help with the costume, which was much baggier than before—he'd lost so much weight. Margaret would bring the others, now teens and preteens, to wait in line to visit their Santa."

"I remember that now," said Annie.

"Me, too," said Susie.

"His face was jaundiced and he looked exhausted," I said. "I'm feeling bad now, remembering how suspiciously other children eyed our fake Santa that day. I don't think we even took a picture of that time."

"You know," said Olivia quietly, "he did that Santa gig because he loves you all. He's saying it was the last thing he was able to do for you." Then, eyes twinkling, she wagged her finger at me and said, "He's pointing to that stack of gifts—he's been bringing them in for *you*! He wants you to look at every one of them. You'll know when the time is right."

"He and Mother moved in with us not long after that," I said, "to stay through our last Christmas together. We put twin beds in this room since he couldn't climb stairs, and after his seventieth birthday on New Year's Eve in '81 they went home. He passed away in less than a month. Baby Tate was three months old."

My mind drifted, wondering what gifts were in my father's stash for me. Maybe one of them would be a clue on how to share tonight's experience, though I doubted I could ever convince anybody to believe it.

"Olivia," Susie asked diffidently, "do you have any messages especially for me?"

Olivia crossed the floral rug to sit beside Susie on the celery-colored loveseat. "I do, Susie," she said. "Somebody is telling me there is a man who wants to help you with moving and painting. Are you buying a new house?"

Susie explained her recent decision to put her house on the market. "I just wish I had enough energy to face the humongous mountain of work ahead," she said.

"It feels like a good thing—to be selling that one, though," Olivia said. "There'll be a perfect one in time. It seems that you more or less just *settled* on that house; but it hasn't turned out right for you or your children, has it?"

"I feel the same way," Susie said. Then she chuckled and said, "But I really need to hear more about that helper."

"Let's see...," Olivia reported. "He's a dark man, a friend, not tall, with a short, curly black beard. I hear you'll be able to count on this man to see it through to the end."

"Well, wherever he is," Susie said gaily, "somebody bring him on!"

"He's going to call," Olivia said, "and then you'll get started."

Our first guess of a bearded friend was my brother, Bobby, but hearing of a black, curly beard ruled him out—his was snow white—and besides, he was tall. But Olivia reminded us that answers would come later, so we added this to the things to wait for.

THE BROTHERS OF BRAGG JAM

Then she lifted Susie's hand and enfolded it in hers. "You know, Susie, Taylor has a special love for you."

Susie nodded, lips compressed in a straight line, tears pooling in her big hazel eyes. "I always felt like we wouldn't have him long. I couldn't say that to you, Mama, but I cried sometimes just holding him, rocking in the front porch swing."

The hall clock chimed some late hour. When the house was quiet again, she said, "We'd watch Daddy ride his mower around the front yard and wave at us when he passed the porch; Tate had learned to wave back. I could never shake that feeling, that this precious baby would be gone from us one day." Tears slid down her full cheeks; she reached for the Kleenex box I held. "It made my heart ache when I heard he'd gotten his driver's license. It was like karma, or some sad thing, had been set in motion."

Susie had been 16 when Tate was born, and my only acceptable replacement—able to rock and bottle-feed him, freeing me to leave the house. The news, during his seventh grade, that he had scoliosis hit her hard, too. She'd been through it and knew about living with that cumbersome Milwaukee brace. He mocked his brace by wearing it on the outside of his clothes. Her prayers were answered when it was clear that Tate wouldn't need the surgery or bulky plaster cast she'd endured during her seventh grade.

"I always thought he was an angel," she said dreamily. "I know it sounds crazy, but I felt like he was a part of my life from long ago." She looked at Olivia, adding unsurely, "If that makes any sense."

Olivia leaned in, their faces close, almost whispering, "Taylor *was* an angel, Susie, and there *are* past lives."

We gasped when she next said that Taylor was crying. We began crying, too. None of us could bear his tears—ever—or imagine him shedding them in heaven. "His are happy tears," she soothed, "he's affirming a greater mystery, which he now knows that Susie understood."

"I wonder if Brax could've known that...," Susie said more confidently, wiping a cheek with the back of her hand, "about Taylor."

"Maybe so," Olivia said. "Maybe Taylor's role as an angel was to come help his brother. Brax's spirit knew that his own life would be short—so he made it a full one, didn't he?"

"Ah-h," said Susie, her features softening, as though she had just received a key to a treasure box.

"Someday," Olivia said to her, "we can go further into that if you want."

Talk of earth angels and past lives...something in my own psyche relaxed, too. The idea of reincarnation, while it had always intrigued me, had seemed to be for those who expected to feel incomplete after one physical lifetime—it hadn't been a necessary belief system for me. I had been taught to be hopeful, trusting that our spirits will settle into one final, blissful eternity. But now, hearing ideas which I believed could be Tate's, from paradise, with more wisdom than I could ever hope to have, with God watching us all, I knew I would rethink this subject.

7.

❧

Gigolo Monkeys

Time had been flying—it was after 11:00. It would be an understatement to say this had been engrossing, and it was, honestly, also intense. We stood to stretch and I moved to a small computer chair on the other side of the desk where Olivia was sitting. Annie left to get glasses of water from the kitchen.

"What's the age difference between Brax and Anne?" asked Olivia.

"She's four years older," I said, as Annie returned.

"Anne," Olivia said, "Brax has a message for you."

"Moi?" She curtsied, balancing a tray in one hand, like the waitress she'd been at Natalia's Restaurant during college, and placed a glass on the desk by Olivia's revolving desk chair. She put the tray of other glasses on a little table by the loveseat.

"He likes that you're in charge of organizing thin papers," Olivia said, looking over the top of her glasses as she sipped. "I hope that means something to you."

Annie, her dark brows arching higher, sat in the barrel chair, which had been handed down from her namesake, my aunt Anne Brennan. "Thin papers?" she asked.

"I'm seeing a cemetery," Olivia went on. "Did he take thin papers to a cemetery? Maybe he did tracings of tombstones?"

"He loved Rose Hill, the old cemetery by the river," Annie said. "He went there a lot to write in his journals. Thin papers? Maybe notebook paper?"

"He loved reading epitaphs," I said. "Cemeteries were big attractions in his travels." I remembered a hot August afternoon in Paris, when he'd dragged Tate and me to see Jim Morrison's grave. "I've never seen any tracings, though."

"Annie's collecting his writings so three friends can go through them," Susie said. "Poems, songs, essays—we've never read any of it."

"Kirby, Russell, and Bart are talking about making a book from it," Annie said. "Kirby Griffin is a published writer; they'll collaborate. I've been collecting boxes of notebooks, hopefully all his journals, cards, napkins, matchbooks, loose sheets. Some of it is typed, but he hated computers, so most is handwritten."

"He always talked of a book," I said. "He loved creating catchy titles."

"So, he's happy I'm doing this," Annie said, smiling contentedly. "It'll be a huge job, but his friends and I are excited."

"Brax stayed busy," I said. "He'd asked about moving into the poolhouse this fall to save money, with more time for writing and music. Somebody gave him a sofa that he left down there before their trip. He was shopping for an old upright piano. We were looking forward to it."

"He says he saw you," Olivia said, swiveling her chair around to me, "when you were holding his gray sweater not long ago."

"His gray sweater? Recently?"

"He doesn't want you to be that sad," she said. "He wants you to use it—'Maybe when you're sleeping.'"

"Oh, I wonder if he means that gray velour slipover I found in his car," I said. "His boss had sold him an old car and agreed to buy it back a few weeks ago. What a sad time." I recalled folding the big, soft thing, redolent with his hugs, into a pillow against my cheek. "I gave it to him last Christmas—maybe he used it as a pillow sometimes."

I expected that Olivia was tired, but there was something I wanted to show her. "There's a magical thing I want to show you," I said, as I headed to the den door. To answer the girls' curious glances, I added, "Tate's metronome."

Hearing pleasant chatter behind me, I recalled my nervousness about this visit and how I had been braced for sadness. But it had been so uplifting. Whatever coordination had drawn these energies together was impressive, as though our lost loved ones, who obviously weren't lost at all, had been planning this loving event for us to show what a brilliant life is in store for all of us. I wondered who would believe it.

Most people recognize a tall, pyramidal-shaped metronome when they see it, usually set on a piano. But the tiny black plastic box, a product of the electronic age and small enough to fit in Tate's shirt pocket, was unfamiliar to Olivia as she turned it over in her hands.

"How does it work?" she asked.

"This little switch turns it on," I said, "but its AAA battery's dead now. There's a bright red blinker to silently set rhythm and an optional ticking, for when a guitarist practices with no audience."

"It was Taylor's?"

"Yes," I said. "It came back with their things over three weeks ago; he had left it *on* whenever he used it last." I was anxious to talk about its magical homecoming, but she was preoccupied.

"The boys want me to tell their mother to go home," she said. Her hands were in a prayerful pose, cradling Tate's little box in a steeple.

"I am at home," I said.

"Not this home. Where did you grow up? Around here?"

"Yes, I grew up about seven miles away, in the Ingleside area."

"Well, that's where your boys want you to go. They say you left a part of your childhood there."

"*My* childhood? What could that have to do with his metronome?"

"Maybe you should go see," she said, smiling at me.

"There's nothing of mine there after all these years," I said. "Mother sold the house shortly after Daddy died, and the next family had a fire. Our kids heard lots about my idyllic childhood; maybe I'm supposed to think more about those happy times."

"Nope," she said with a hint of boyish spunk. "They say you left something in the little house. Was there a tool shed in the back?"

"We had a playhouse. But I can think of nothing I left. Except for good memories—and I still have those."

She opened her hands to peer at the little device. "The time-box...go look for the one you left in that little house."

"A time-box? Oh, good lord—my time capsule."

"What time-box?" the girls asked together.

"In our playhouse. Daddy had it built in the fifties, after a tornado damaged our roof and garage. It's attached to the garage."

"Right, but what about a time-box?" Susie asked.

"I called it my time capsule," I said. "When I was in sixth grade the nuns placed one in the cornerstone of the new St. Joseph's School on High Street, letting each class add to it. I thought it would be a neat thing to do with our playhouse. Daddy gave me a little metal box and the workers waited while I put stuff in it; then they nailed floorboards over it. I told Brax about it when we explored the playhouse during a visit—it was the kind of thing he loved. He and I speculated about what an 11-year-old girl would include in a time-box back in 1953. I'd forgotten about all that. It may've been just a Band-Aid box. Mom moved while Tate was a baby. I doubt if he knew about it. I wonder if it's still there."

"Why don't you try to find it," said Annie.

"Maybe I could," I said, smiling at thoughts of my safe childhood, itself such a solid cornerstone for my life.

"Tell me about the metronome's magic," Olivia said.

"Oh, Lord, here comes a story," teased Susie.

"I'll give a condensed version, I promise," I said. "After their wreck, the boys' belongings, which we were desperate to have returned, went to a body shop in San Angelo, Texas; our car was hauled to a nearby scrap yard. Eventually the shop owners phoned to say they'd packed a full auto-parts box onto a national freight line, which would bring it here within ten days.

"On a sunny Friday afternoon a local dispatcher called to say their truck was on its way to our house, where about twenty of us braced for its arrival. Out of the blue, a huge storm erupted, just like the one on the evening of the funeral, when the house was packed and no one dared to leave. We had imagined that the boys were having fun experimenting with the soundboard of the universe that night. We imagined Brax saying, 'Tate, toggle *Lightning Bolt*' or 'hit that *Thunder* knob again.' *Rewind* would blow another gust of wind, which kept our giant trees dancing perilously above the parked cars.

"The trucker unloaded his precious cargo in a downpour that afternoon. Jim and Rob carried the soaked, grease-stained box to a blue tarp in the center of the den carpet. No one spoke, our eagerness to go through its contents wilted—we just stared at it.

"Taylor's guitar case, covered with FRAGILE stickers from various flights, was the first thing out. There was a collective sigh of relief when Jim lifted Tate's polished, untouched Spanish guitar from it. My sister stood the guitar on the sofa by the windows and Jim slid its closed case in that direction, too. Next was Brax's new red guitar, also unharmed. I put it back in its battered case and someone placed it in here, by the piano.

"We gingerly handled other things, all dusted with specks of glass. There was a gray t-shirt from Alcatraz, a coverless *Einstein's Secrets of the Universe* paperback, plastic-wrapped Elvis videos, CDs, papers, harmonicas, and two rolls of exposed film in their duffel bag, along with dirty clothes.

"No picture postcards, though. The Texas trooper had told Rick Owens, our insurance agent, about cards scattered at the scene, and because Brax wrote his travel journal on cards before mailing them to folks who knew to save them for him, we hoped to find postcards.

"Margaret slid Tate's guitar case back to me, so we could recheck it for cards. I unlatched the felt lid to a small tool compartment, where he kept nail clippers, tuning fork, picks, and this metronome. It was wedged-in diagonally, face-up, from his last practice session. Its tiny red light began pulsing and its ticking noise was suddenly loud enough for everyone to hear, even from the kitchen. It was breathtaking. After we took turns holding it, this real link to Tate, I couldn't put it away in the case. It stayed propped on the coffee table all during supper."

"Did its red light stay on?" Olivia asked.

"Yes, even during most of the funeral video, which we decided to watch, since my friend Gina Hersh was with us. She hadn't been able to leave Virginia for the funeral because of surgery, but was in town then, visiting her mother."

"A video? How was it, to watch that video?"

"Surprisingly okay," I said. "I had asked our neighbor Phil Brown if he would video the funeral for us—without considering if he had a camera or not. Early that morning, he borrowed a camcorder from Coke's Camera Shop, where they gave him a crash course in filming, and he filmed the whole thing for us. He even climbed up to the choir loft in the rear of the church for an aerial view. Whenever focus meandered around the church, it matched my feeling of floating through the funeral.

"My daughter was there—she said the church was overflowing," Olivia said.

"It was. And *white* everywhere—priests' vestments, choir robes, sunlight gleaming through stained glass windows onto marble. Oh, the music...Terry Cantwell, Tate's guitar teacher, played Bach's 'Jesu, Joy of Man's Desiring,' and our choir's soprano, Laura, sang Shubert's 'Ave Maria.' My choir sang 'My Shepherd Will Supply My Need,' by Isaac Watts, so we could hear its last line: *no more a stranger or a guest, but like a child at home.*"

"I don't know if I can ever listen to 'Ave Maria' again," Susie said. "Daddy said he'd never hear it again with dry eyes."

"Me, either," said Annie. "Brax's friends were so struck by the beauty of it all that they joked later about not knowing if they wanted to live like a Catholic, but it sure seemed okay to die like one."

"I wanted to be there," Olivia said. "So how long did the ticking go on?"

"About an hour," I said. "And the light pulsed like a tiny red heart even longer. At some point during the video we realized it had stopped, along with the storm."

"And you had survived," she said quietly. "You did have a miracle."

"It was proof they were here," said Susie.

"It gave us hope to keep our hearts open for more signs," I added.

"And that was Mom's condensed version!" Annie said, laughing as she put her arm around me.

"Well, it's a powerful story, Anne," Olivia said, "and your brothers are some of the most energetic spirits I've encountered. So soon after crossing over, too. I feel like they enjoy this freedom to express love to you all."

"No more than we do," I said. "I thought the metronome was as lovely a sign as God could allow."

"People go on pilgrimages, praying for any little sign," Susie said. "I wonder if they see anything as positive as that."

"Well, I sure hate to break this up," Annie said, "but I have to get home to my husband and work tomorrow. This has been like nothing I've ever imagined, Olivia. I'm so glad we ran into each other last week."

"I am too, Anne—it was bound to happen sometime," said Olivia.

"Mama, I'll call in the morning to hear anything I miss, okay? I hope you'll take notes." We all stood, as she gathered her purse and keys from the piano bench.

"Olivia," I said, "I feel like we've probably worn you out."

"Actually, there are some things I want to talk to Susie about, if she wants to," she replied. She stretched her arms out and over her head. "Can you stay up a little longer, Susie? I'm really a night owl, and I'm enjoying this so much, too."

Susie was telling Olivia that she would definitely stay a while as I walked with Annie to the kitchen. I needed to learn what arrangements she might have made with Olivia for being paid for this incredible work.

"Oh, I forgot to tell you," Annie said, "She said she made an agreement with the boys—about bartering. She said they promised that their mom would help her, too. She said it's settled."

I frowned, thinking she'd probably already paid Olivia, who'd surely extended her usual time by several hours. She rolled big brown eyes, like she didn't understand it either, but that it was okay.

"So, how do we settle it, then?" I asked. "I expect she charges for a reading or by the hour for this, and I want to know that she's satisfied." I turned on back porch lights, causing dazed Sculley to climb out of his pile of bedding on the breezeway.

"Oh, she does get paid that way—ordinarily. But this was to be different."

"I can't imagine how I could help her," I said, unconvinced.

"Maybe it'll come to you later, like she says." She gave me a hug, opened the door, and headed to her car. A recurring concern for her nagged at me as I stood watching the red taillights of her Mercedes disappear into the dark. At times I'd noticed her exuberance, or diminished melancholy, and wondered if she were numbing her feelings somehow. Her marriage to a compassionate doctor made relief very accessible, like the Valium he prescribed for all of us after cemetery shopping that day. But it wasn't for me. Even half a pill did nothing for my sleep, but left a residual dullness in the morning. My daughters were resilient women, capable of dealing with pain, but some pain can't be fixed with man's remedies.

I looked at my watch—it was after 1 A.M. A sliver of waxing moon was bright above the eastward trees. I headed to the poolhouse for commemorative concert t-shirts to offer Olivia. Stars are extraordinary in our area, away from the city lights of Macon, and I felt taller under my immense velvet sky that night, more visible in the wondrous scheme of it all.

When I got back, Susie and Olivia were standing in the office. Susie had been crying. Heartbreak from losing brothers was compounded by being a mother herself, and her hasty return to work had added unbearable strain. But her eyes now shone with relief. Olivia probably reminded her that God's hands are always there to lighten our load. We were lucky that this woman was willing to work this openly for Him. Many people helped us in so many ways, but most of us aren't prepared to absorb another's pain. Olivia was reminding us of things we'd forgotten and teaching us more than we'd ever known.

When I brought up the subject of payment, she verified what Annie said about her deal with the boys and appreciated the shirts as a token of our appreciation. "We'll have lots more to talk about," she said, collecting her things. "Even though energies have pulled back, there wasn't enough time to hear from them all."

"You mean more people had messages for us?" Susie asked.

"Sure," she said, "Lots more."

"I wish I'd listened more than talking so much," I said. Before Susie could ditto that, I admitted, "—the story of my life."

She had an idea to show the boys' pictures to Olivia. "Have you ever seen what they look like?" she asked.

"No, but I'm not ready to see pictures yet. It could break my heart— I'd be no help after that. I see them in my own way."

I was in the hall, turning on front yard lights, when Olivia's laughter drew me back.

"What?" Susie was saying. "What's so funny?"

"Oh, my goodness! This really is so funny—they are laughing and it makes me laugh." Olivia chuckled, hand on her jaw, obviously delighted.

"What?" we asked in unison.

"You don't have monkeys here, do you?" she asked.

"Monkeys?" I said, "No, what makes you ask?"

"Because they say, 'Tell Mama to go look at the monkeys!' Do you have a lot of stuffed animals—maybe some monkeys? They want us to go look at monkeys."

Susie and I stared at each other. We did know about some monkeys. She took Olivia's arm. "Come on, we'll show you monkeys."

Olivia carried her bag and the shirts and followed Susie through the den and into the kitchen, leaving our office for the first time in over five hours. The stove's hood lamp filled the room with soft shadows.

"There they are," said Susie, pointing to two black, hard rubber gorillas on the countertop over the dishwasher. One, about six inches tall, stood on all fours, and a smaller one sat beside him.

"We just got them from Brax's apartment on Saturday," I said. "His friend Mick brought them with a load of things from the place he rented to Brax. I had especially wanted them back."

"Where did they come from?"

"The Museum of Arts and Sciences. Taylor had been asked to play there for the opening of a Picasso pottery exhibit, as a community-service-hours gig, and needed to go one afternoon to line it up. He was 15, with no license yet, so I drove and waited in the gift shop. I got them as a little Christmas gift for Brax. Tate thought they were cool, too."

"A community-service-hours gig?" she repeated.

"He donated playing time for things like that, earning school credit for community-service work; otherwise he was paid," I explained.

She patted the head of the smaller, seated gorilla.

"Brax kept them on his coffee table and included them in conversations with his friends. He called them *the monkeys*, and when visitors came..." At that point Olivia sat the small gorilla on the back of the larger one. "He created little scenarios with them, like sitting the smaller one...*just like that.*"

"There," she said with an impish grin. "There are your monkeys—and there are your boys." She broke into a big smile then, jabbing me on the shoulder. "There are your *gigolo monkeys*!" She looked as surprised as we felt. The hum from the refrigerator suddenly seemed loud in the quiet. "They say, '*And how's that for a book title, Mom?!*'"

I'll never forget the startled look on Olivia's face.

"This feels so funny," she said. "Do you know what that means? They're laughing at their own cleverness now—it would make an unusual book title."

Susie shrugged. "Titles were Brax's specialty."

"I think I get it," I muttered. "But I cannot believe he remembers that."

"What...? Tell us," urged Susie.

"Brax just got revenge."

"Whatever for?" she asked.

"Something I said a couple years ago," I said, feeling heat in my cheeks. "I hardly ever had to reprimand these guys—Susie can tell you—but one morning Brax stood right here at this counter complaining about the stagnant state of his relationship with an older, lovely girl. You know who I mean, Susie. Well, I'd heard it all before. He'd moved from Charleston back to Macon by then, and I think she was visiting local friends. I reminded him that he was a grown man, and it seemed to me that they should just break it off. He'd grinned sheepishly, as though he agreed, but said he wasn't sure he wanted to—just yet. I think he found support in that prayer of St. Augustine, one of his heroes: 'God, help me become a holy man, but not *just yet.*'

"I remember looking out the window, where he'd parked her sporty Land Rover in our driveway. Rather than come right out and accuse him of being a user, I said, mostly teasing, 'Well, one good thing, Brax—as long as you stay young and good-looking, you can always earn a living as a gigolo.'"

"Whoa," said Susie.

"I guess that was awful—," I confessed, "coming from his mother. I remember he looked down, pretending to squeeze crocodile tears from those blue eyes. All he said was 'Gosh, thanks, Mom.' It was like a quick sermon—I didn't mean to hurt his feelings."

"Looks like he's letting you know that even gigolos can get to heaven, doesn't it, Mama?" Susie spoke like the true fan she was.

"And don't forget monkeys," Olivia added.

"I hope this means he's forgiven me," I said.

It was nearly two o'clock when Olivia and Susie left. They promised to call when they got home. I jotted notes while I waited so I wouldn't forget any details from that night. Then it hit me—a lot of people would never believe any of it.

I thanked Olivia again when she called. She said to phone any time I needed to talk, and I knew she meant it. She also said she would probably be up the rest of the night writing and processing.

Later, as I brushed my teeth, I noticed that my mirror did seem to reflect a brightness in my face, as Olivia had mentioned. I was more convinced than ever about that afternoon's decision to save my memories in short stories. Had that been only eleven hours ago? Since then I had been handed plenty of ideas, along with a possible title that could only be described as an original Braxism!

8.

❧

Covenant

I was cleaning up from breakfast, having promised Jim and the grandchildren, as they flew out the door, that they'd get a full scoop from last night at dinner. At 7:20 the phone rang.

"This is Tommy," said the familiar voice of our yardman and Jim's fishing buddy. "Mr. Bragg said something about your daughter wanting to get her house fixed up for sale. I'm calling to say I can help her out, if she still needs it, whenever she's ready—even today if you say so."

"Tommy!" I exclaimed. "You will never believe this, but a lady who visited us last night told Susie that a dark man, with a short, curly beard was going to call and offer to help her with that."

"What lady?" he asked. "Talking about me?"

"We didn't know *who* she was talking about—y'all don't know each other—but I bet you'd love to hear some of the stuff she told us." Since his efforts to grow a beard hadn't produced a memorable effect yet, it was hard to tell where Tommy's chin ended and little goatee began. "I forgot you had a beard, Tommy."

"Well, it ain't much of one, for sure. Listen, I'm in a phone booth at the store near our house. Linda took the car to work. If you could take me over to your daughter's place, I could get started washing down the walls. Mr. Bragg said they need paintin'."

"Have y'all talked about it—about what you'll charge and all?"

"Not yet—I've only met her in passing—but y'all know I'll treat her right, and I really do want to help her."

I knew this was true. Tommy was as much a friend as a worker and heartsick with all that happened. He didn't know our other children well but had spent a lot of time with Tate. By Brax's having been gone from home for several years, it had fallen to Tate to be the main helpmate for Jim, so they usually did bigger jobs as a trio. I'll never forget seeing him make his way to us from the end of a long line of mourners at the memorial the night before the funeral. His face crumpled at the sight of Jim's, and, as we hugged, I caught a whiff of whatever had fortified him to come.

"Susie was over here until late last night," I said. "It's too early to call her now. How about calling me back after 9. I'll have talked to her by then."

After we hung up I stood with a cup of coffee, gazing at the little gorillas. I placed a votive candle beside them and added the last picture taken of Brax and Tate, their shining faces smiling into James Morris's camera as they were leaving his Los Angeles apartment for home. I had obsessed over this picture since he sent it. Brax, hair damp from a shower, toothbrush sticking out of the pocket of a new plaid shirt, held a bulging yellow Towers bag in one hand, with a newspaper and another new plaid shirt folded under that arm. His right hand was in a fist. He leaned slightly forward, looking eager to get on the road.

Tate's face, tilted in his engaging, attentive way, looked rounder than when he'd left and older. His aqua t-shirt with an unidentifiable white logo was also new. Shopping, rather than wasting time in a Laundromat, was apparently their solution for clean clothes. He held an odd-looking pipe, which James identified as an antique Chinese pipe that had been his mother's.

On the wall behind them was a rare 1983 Stars Wars poster, *Revenge of the Jedi*, likely their choice as backdrop. On Brax's right was a poster which featured two angels superimposed over two dark-suited Blues Brothers-type men, wearing bowlers, facing a row of tall, identical trees, their backs to the viewer. We had dug for symbolism in this odd poster, for subtle coding, but Dot Brown, our art-teacher neighbor, had explained that instead of angels, the figures were cloned images of Flora, Mother of Flowers, from Botticelli's *La Primavera*. She was lifted from context and now faced both east and west, instead of eastward with the wind, as in the master's glorious 10-foot original, which Jim and I would later get to see in Florence, Italy. And instead of Blues Brothers, the men had also been reworked, by Rene Magritte, a Belgian surrealist known for his passion for shifting subjects out of context, so that a viewer cannot assume that an image is really what it appears to be.

Eventually, studying my boys' beautiful faces, close to the real thing but now so horribly out of context, caused deep sadness. Could that be a reason we were being offered these little black gorillas—these *monkeys*—instead?

I recalled a similar covenant from thirty years earlier, when we vowed to use green ivy as our family's symbol of connection. The children promised to transplant Boston ivy from our yard into theirs, wherever in the world they lived, as a reminder that we were bound forever. No matter which of us went first, the survivors had a reliable symbol of our promise—they weren't alone. Years later, in 1994, I framed small prints of a new family portrait in verdigris ivy frames for each of us. That was the year breast cancer came, with all its insecurities and possibilities. It had been reassuring to talk again of our pledge with mature children.

We would be seeing the monkeys every day, hopefully without forgetting our sons' cheerful suggestion that we use these comical little forms as reminders of their real, though invisible, presence. To me, it doesn't take a big leap to correlate that to the covenant made by God's greatest spirit, His Son, offering us bread and wine for the same loving purpose: as a way of communing with His spirit—as Remembrance.

I read my notes from last night as the sun's piercing light, rising higher through trees, laid a white path across the kitchen floor tiles.

The first person Olivia brought through, my grandfather Wallace, with his gloved hand, had been 52 when he died in 1917, leaving his 44-year-old widow, Annie, with five children. She sold their big house on Tradd Street, his piano store on King Street, along with a car she couldn't drive, and bid household help, friends, and her dreams goodbye when she moved from the beautiful city of Charleston back into her family home in Perry, Georgia. She told me of crying into a faint on his grave there; but I was young, incapable of imagining real grief. I wonder if she ever felt his efforts to contact her. I wanted her to know I was proud of her strength and courage and of her children, whose adult lives impressed mine in such positive ways. She'd been a devoted letter writer, on regularly mailed penny postcards, to all of her children and grandchildren. No one could squeeze more onto front, back, and around margins of a postcard than she and her three daughters, my aunts. I still have some from all of them.

My dad, her curly haired baby, was 5 when the trauma of his father's death hit, and I sensed, even when I was a little girl, that his casual whistling might have been his solution for disguising a core feeling of loss. Maybe it evolved as a way to cheer his mother and siblings in that stark old house in Perry, crowded with somber old relatives.

Then there was the aunt with the earring, and I even imagined a tingling in my right ear lobe. *Aunt Beverly*, I thought out loud, *you forgot to give me those earrings!* She was the middle of Dad's three sisters. I recalled a September day in 1980 when she caught me looking at her, sitting beside me at a luncheon table on a screened porch in Allentown, Georgia. The quintessential little Southern town was named for Aunt Annie Moore Daughtry Wallace's grandfather, J. W. Allen. We had gathered for her funeral.

"What are you looking at, honey?" Aunt Beverly had asked me.

"I'm just admiring your earrings," I said.

"Can you see all those facets?" she asked, removing the solitaire, in gold Tiffany setting, from her left ear, closest to me. "I had a jeweler use an antique, mine-cut stone; see that tiny table on top?"

"I do," I said, learning something new about diamond tables. I think she'd had these, or at least one of them, made to duplicate antiques of her mother, Annie's.

"Here, try it on," she said. "I can never see how it looks on myself."

I was happy to remove my own earring and slip hers into my right lobe for her inspection. "Oh, that really is lovely," she said, "one day I should give them to you."

Admittedly, that was no promise, but now I wondered if she'd at least considered leaving them to me. Next time I saw my cousin Jack maybe I'd ask what became of his mother's earrings. His sister, Bev, probably had them, or his wife, Sue. But I liked the forgotten memory and possible intent, nonetheless.

At 9:00 I called Susie, assuming I would probably wake her. "Susie, guess who your dark, curly bearded helper is!"

"Huh?" she said groggily, "Oh...who?"

"Tommy!"

"What makes you think that?"

"He called at the crack of dawn to say he wants to help you with washing the walls, then painting—right away."

"That was fast," she said, more awake then, chuckling.

"He said Jim mentioned it to him, and I guess he's ready to make a little money. He'll be fair and it sounds like he wants to get started right away. Is it okay with you if I bring him over this morning? That's what he wants."

"And *he'll see me through to the end*, I bet." She laughed, echoing Olivia's words. It was good to hear her energy come alive. "Sure, give me time to get dressed."

I couldn't wait to tell somebody about our visit from Olivia, and now Tommy would be my first, if captive, audience. I put a bucket, some rags, and a radio in the truck, as he'd asked on his second call, and added some Cokes.

The truck had been Tate's prized possession since his sixteenth birthday, when Brax had ceremoniously turned its keys over to him. It was always more presentable after that than when either his dad or brother had it. I had a lighter feeling riding in it that morning. A miniature Marilyn Monroe, her white skirt flying high, sat on the rear view mirror—Brax had left her—and R2D2 stood on the dashboard. I guessed others weren't so far away. Maybe Kat, our Rottweiler, ears and tongue flapping in the morning breeze, had resumed her spot in the back.

Tommy was on his porch when I drove up and hadn't forgotten that I mentioned talking about stuff from last night, so I ran through some of my little stories, explaining necessary references. He had no trouble believing that spirits can be anywhere they choose or that there are certain people who can see them. He cautioned about evil spirits, too, but I said I wasn't sure about that.

Susie was in her doorway, hand on heart, tears on her cheeks, when we stopped in her driveway. She said she first thought it was Taylor when the green Ford truck turned the corner. "He ran an errand for me last time I saw it," she said. After a minute she added, "But things seem better this morning, don't they? Y'all want some coffee?"

"None for me, thanks," I said, "but I'm leaving some Cokes. Oh, and I told Tommy all about last night. He may be too spooked now to get any work done."

He chuckled. "Not if you leave me a radio, some rags, and a bucket."

They were working together when I left a half hour later with a truck-load of discards for a Goodwill kiosk in the shopping center at the corner. There was no doubt that his willingness and staying power had already motivated her. I wondered who had been so sure of that last night. Probably Taylor, I figured. I turned up the radio and headed for home.

Susie came for dinner that night. We sat around the table telling Jim, Anna, and Rob everything we could remember from the night before. We referred to my notes, and Jim took a few of his own.

"You know," he said finally, "I'm kind of surprised Dad didn't show up." Jim's father, Ernest, well-known for his gregarious nature, had passed away in 1987.

"Me, too," said Susie. "Papa would really have wanted to be in on all that storytelling, wouldn't he, Daddy?"

"I wonder how so many of them knew about it," he said, apparently having disarmed his skepticism, at least for a while.

"Olivia said the room was full of spirits," I said, "and that they had a way of pulling their energy back. But don't you think he'd have spoken up if he was there? He's got to be hanging out with those three grandsons."

We turned to the subject of Susie's house and her long day with Tommy. She was tired, but invigorated. She had made the right decision to accept the offered medical leave from work. To return so quickly, before having time to begin processing the grief, had caused a health problem. Her job as an auto insurance agent meant long hours in a cubicle, wearing a headset, dealing with often-mindless questions from around the Southeast. She'd kept her high sales rank even after a week off, but finally one day the pressure of having to sandwich crying breaks between incessant calls was too much. Her heart was beating erratically, and she collapsed at her desk, hardly able to catch her breath. A painful rash had appeared on her arms and torso—she said she was falling apart. A coworker offered to take her to a med-stop, but she wanted to go alone.

The doctor ran tests, prescribed cream for her rash, and suspected it might reduce her blood pressure to just lie there a while. When a nurse took Susie's hand, saying her own child had been taking swimming lessons from me during the time of the tragedy, they both broke down. Only Susie couldn't stop crying. She wouldn't let anyone call us. They kept vigil on her, lying in the darkened room for hours, until her body accepted relief that only tears could bring.

But now, with the free weeks ahead, she looked forward to having Tommy, such a willing worker, help her through this hard, physical task. We talked about her moving into our poolhouse sooner, and she agreed that it made sense to go ahead, to escape the paint fumes and dust. The work, along with her move home, would be a relief all around.

Having Anna and Rob with us was a tonic, too. They clowned around that night after Susie left, as we did dishes, speculating about ghosts, with lots of laughing. Rob hadn't brought himself to move into Tate's bedroom yet, but seemed content to share Annie's twin beds with his sister. They'd been spending the summer with us, swimming with Taylor during my mid-day class breaks, listening to his guitar practice, and riding with him on errands while Susie worked. Their weekends were with her or their dad, Jewt, and his wife in Crawford County.

Because the kids were with him for the Fourth, news of the tragedy went by phone. Before Susie could ask Jewt to tell their children, knowing how crushing this was for him, too, she broke down and passed the phone to Bert, who assumed she didn't want the children to be told until they got here. Jewt closed himself in the bathroom for an hour, the children later told us, while he tried to compose himself enough to honor that request, despite their begging to know the big secret. When they drove up late that night to our fully lit house, surrounded by cars, they guessed his big secret was that Mimi and Pop were having an early Fourth of July party. I met them at the door, not knowing of their innocence, and with arms around all of them, burst into tears. The shock must still be registered on their hearts.

Their survival was surely helped by having each other to talk to long into the night and by knowing how much we needed their company for our own survival, especially as we faced abrupt changes in nighttime routines. Jim's early work schedule meant he was often asleep before Taylor and I went up to bed. By 10 P.M., with homework done, he would come downstairs to practice guitar while I emailed or chatted online with friends. After *Seinfeld*, we'd head upstairs, tiptoe past Jim, close the bathroom door, and engage in a silly tooth-brushing-swishing-spitting war, which had begun in his toddler days, with him on a stool beside his big brother, learning to brush. Spitting strategy was key; so was aggressive elbowing to gain control of the small oval sink, to avoid being hit by spitfire. Over the years Tate's height advantage forced me out of bounds, but the silliness of such carefree rituals before bedtime had always been a comfort for the children and for me. Bedtimes brought special agony.

Weeks afterward, in the yard searching through night skies, crying out to God and the boys to tell me where they were, I'd feel a strong hand on my arm, and Rob would be standing beside me. He would just say, "Mimi"—nothing else.

9.

~

As the World Turns

The next day, Wednesday, August 18, Earlene would arrive, as usual, at 7:45. An irreplaceable part of our weekly household since Tate was 3, she'd seen me through nearly fifteen years of ups and downs, and we shared spiritual convictions. I knew I'd tell her about Olivia.

While I stripped beds and loaded the washer upstairs before coming down to wait for her, I thought back to the Monday morning before the funeral, six weeks earlier, when Earlene called to say she and her church ladies were home from their Nassau cruise. Though she intended to tell me about her cruise when she came to work on Wednesday, something told her not to wait. She hadn't seen the paper. When I told her about the boys she gasped in horror, then said she'd get her daughter and come right over.

About twenty people were here when Earlene came through our door with her daughter, Dorothy, the pastor of a little church in Fort Valley. Through a round of introductions, Earlene's arms encircled my friends, people she'd heard of for years but never met. When she asked, with fitting maternal pride, if Dorothy could lead us in prayer, it reminded me of how I'd asked friends if they'd like for Taylor to play for us.

Reaching for hands, with heads bowed and eyes closed, we filled the den with our circle. Dorothy's deep, gentle voice, rolling in soothing waves, gathered our emotions along with our spirits, and our circle seemed to breathe in cadence to her praying. "Yes, Jesus" and "Amen, Lord" could be heard as various souls responded. Charismatic religions may have an edge over the more ritualized in times like these, when emotions are under so much pressure, leaving rote prayers to often fall flatly on broken hearts. I wished more could've been here for that moving experience.

Earlene always rings the doorbell, even if she sees me through a window, but I was waiting on the porch for her that day. I was in running clothes but planned to wait a while for my run. Sculley's huge tail flapped against her blue-checked dress as he escorted her from her black Cadillac.

"Earlene," I said into her gray curls as we hugged, "I've got so much to tell you!"

"It sure is good to see you looking more chipper," she said. "What you got to tell me?" She put her big purse in a chair, slipped off her shoes, and headed for the sink.

"Well, I don't know how you'll feel about this, but Annie called after you left last week, saying she had just met a lady who could see spirits and who knew about the boys and that they were with my daddy in heaven, making music."

Earlene straightened up slowly, clutching a bottle of Pine-Sol and a spray can of furniture polish from under the sink. "Anybody'd know that much, Mz Julie."

"Yes, but then I talked to her—it was amazing. At first I realized anybody could've known some of the things she knew, but I was convinced she was real when she told me how she heard them say 'wonderful'—like *wunnerful*. Do you remember Lawrence Welk, that TV bandleader from the fifties?"

"I remember that show."

"We watched it every week at home," I said, "and made fun of how he talked. Nobody would know that except my daddy. I really wanted to hear what else she had to say, so we set up a time for her to come here and she did—the night before last."

"Mr. Jim talk to her?"

"You know better than that, Earlene. But after the girls and I told him everything she said, he's no longer a skeptic."

"Well, that's really somethin'," she said. She smiled and began moving through her normal routine of gathering dishtowels, trash bag, a mop, and various things to carry upstairs. I stood in the upstairs hall as she padded from laundry room to bathrooms—I'd given up trying to convince her that support shoes might help her aching knees—and together we made beds while I talked on about my experience with Olivia.

"I've heard of people like her," she remarked. "I've never met anybody who could talk to the dead, but it does make you believe there's a heaven."

She seemed to have heard enough, as if it made her nervous, or perhaps because she felt protective of me, but she mentioned the temptation of being distracted from the real business of accepting the death of loved ones.

"I understand," I said, "but this has helped me do that by reinforcing everything I've been taught—in an astonishing way."

I left her to her ironing with a hyper Bob Barker yelling about *The Price Is Right* on our bedroom television, and headed downstairs, enveloped in the comforting scents of Clorox and heated spray starch wafting through the house. I felt a caveat in Earlene's reaction, though: I should be more cautious about bombarding folks with my enthusiasm over this experience. She was curious and didn't doubt my version of things, but seemed relieved to let it drop and get on with her work. Nevertheless, whenever she asks if I've heard anything from the lady, I know what she means.

Mother called soon after and we planned to get back to thank-you notes around lunchtime, something we hadn't worked on for a week,

"I'm going for my run," I yelled up to Earlene. I plugged in earphones and headed for my two-mile run through my neighborhood before the sun got too high. Some days it began with vim and on others my shoes trudged like ski boots. It's liberating to know that a runner's face, squinting with effort, doesn't usually impress passersby, even with tears sliding in horizontal streaks, so running provided a double outlet for my pent-up energy. Invariably, music from my pocket radio has a special message to get me moving. *It's All Right* (*to Have a Good Time*), by the Impressions, started that day's run.

Mother and I had talked little about Olivia. But she, like Earlene, was mainly concerned with my well-being and wouldn't be comfortable hearing much more. Regardless, though, while we ate ham sandwiches and pound cake, I risked telling her about Annie Moore, Daddy's Santa costume, and the time-box I left in the playhouse. She didn't ask for details, but listened, lowering her guard a bit, and could go far enough to agree that this woman had hit some nails squarely on the head. After more grumbling about gypsies, ingrained from her childhood in rural Pennsylvania, she said she was glad we seemed to get so much out of it, and *that was that.*

The television played quietly in the next room while I cleared away lunch dishes and we talked about note writing, intending to tackle only ones that evoked less emotion. Our black-and-white Boston terrier, Lucy, dozed on the mustard-colored armchair by our back door. Since turmoil had come to her household our little dog had seemed depressed and tears slipped from her soulful, bulging eyes whenever she snuggled near any of her humans.

The phone rang as soon as I picked up my pen. "Hello, there, how are you doing?" I said, when I realized it was Olivia, ignoring Mother's mouthed, "Who is it?"

"I'll be right back, Mom," I said, and headed to the office, turning up the volume on a soap opera as I passed through the den. Lucy, her collar tags jingling, trotted after me.

"Are you busy?" Olivia asked.

"Just writing notes with Mom," I said. "I should write you one. Monday night meant so much to all of us."

"Me, too, but I'll get right to the point," she said. "I think you're the one who can tell me who this big well-dressed man is, sitting here in a huge reclining chair."

For a second, before clicking into her context of *here,* I thought of suggesting she call the police, then chuckled. "Tell me more about him."

"He's dressed in business clothes with a beautiful striped tie, and the odd thing is that he's snapping strange-looking, long purple beans; but he's no farmer, Julie. Even his shoes are stylish—brown-and-white wingtips."

"Good Heavens!" I exclaimed. "That sounds like Ernest, Jim's dad."

"Well," she said, and laughed, "I had to call you because he insisted."

"He died in 1987," I said. "And he wouldn't be snapping beans—he'd be shelling purple hull peas."

"I never saw peas like these in Tennessee, but they're in piles all over the room, spread out on newspapers."

That made me laugh. "They were his favorites and that's exactly how he did it. He'd buy bushels of them every year at the farmers' market and spread them on newspapers to prevent mildew. Then there was a big rush to get them shelled and into one of his three freezers."

"Well, he is in a hurry. I guess that's why I had to call you right now, so you would make the connection?"

"That's it—he always went home for lunch. Since everybody else was at work or school, I was the one available to go help him with shelling. We'd watch *As the World Turns*—more watch than listen, because we were usually talking. Sometimes he'd doze off, but the soap opera's sign-off music was our signal for him to go back to work and for me to get Brax from nearby Tinsley Elementary; so we stashed the shelled peas in the fridge, turned off TV, and left. We still lived in town, closer to them in those days. I enjoyed those times."

"That explains the dapper clothes—he was on his lunch break."

"Yeah. Clothes were a big part of his self-image. He liked shopping—for himself and Richie, Jim's mom." I thought of all the outfits he'd bought her, many of which she secretly returned to the store.

"Well, he's been sitting here saying *call Julie*. He wants me to say he was at your house the other night, too, but nobody let him get a word in edgewise."

"That's hilarious," I said. I glanced at the TV in our den as the commercial ended, and there were familiar faces from eons ago, still dealing with the same crises, with offspring aging to adults within a season, to no one's notice. "His soap is on right now."

"Here, too," she said.

Lucy danced on hind legs, scratching my knee, wanting to go out. "I can't wait to tell Jim about this," I said, closing the front door on nearly 100-degree August heat.

"Did Ernest fuss about your getting too involved in stuff?" she continued. "Like working too hard?" Before I could answer, she chuckled. "He says *somebody* had to."

"Well, after he retired, he did. His emphysema worsened, threatening congestive heart failure, and he made it clear that he wished we'd all slow down so he could spend time with us and his grandchildren. We probably should have listened to him."

"He's nodding," she said, "but he's smiling."

"I remember a day that really stands out," I said, "when he couldn't hold his disappointment back. He drove an old mint-green GMC truck, which Jim had ceded over to him, to Baconsfield Shopping Center, where I was setting up to open our third frozen yogurt store. His breathing was labored and he was clearly exasperated. He said he had to come ask me something. He wanted to know why I needed to stay so busy. Why were we opening another store? Didn't his son provide well enough? He reminded me that he had seen Jim though Georgia Tech and his sister through Auburn so they would have easier lives than his generation had."

"I remember those yogurt stores," Olivia said, "especially that one on Tom Hill with the drive-thru. How did you get into all that?"

"In a real roundabout way," I said. "One morning, when I was 40, I was half-watching *Good Morning America* while I fed baby Tate. I was still in pajamas, there was cereal in my hair, plus I was feeling isolated from my friends who had outgrown this routine; all our older kids were in upper grades by then. Anyway, the show's guest grabbed my attention. Marjabelle Young Stewart was about to franchise her etiquette school for children: "White Gloves and Party Manners." Right away I could see what a perfect fit that was for me, with my years of Girl Scout work and teaching swimming. Within a few weeks I'd bought franchise rights for Macon, Savannah, and Atlanta. By February of '83, after professional make-up lessons and haircut, and a spree of clothes shopping, I was actually teaching Saturday classes at Belk's at Macon Mall."

"Well, it didn't take you long—once you set your mind to it," she said. "So where did the yogurt shop come in?"

"The next fall I expanded to Belk's at Oglethorpe Mall in Savannah, which is where I first tasted frozen yogurt. I came home raving about it and about how busy the shop was. So the next Saturday, while I taught etiquette classes, Jim hung out in the mall's yogurt shop, counting customers and researching franchise possibilities. By spring of '85 we were in Dallas, becoming proud franchisees of "I Can't Believe It's Yogurt!" That August we launched our first shop in Warner Robins, our next-door city, and it did so well that we contracted to open three future shops in Macon."

"Life sure changed for y'all then, didn't it?" commented Olivia.

"You can say that again! Jim kept his job, I continued the summer swim school, and we all put in long hours. The children became our best workers when school allowed, but employee turnover was a 24-hour headache. The etiquette school fell by the wayside after we opened the Wesleyan Station shop that next year. Disillusionment lurked, but we were too busy to take an analytical breath in those early years, and our home life, very obvious to Ernest, was suffering."

"The work was hard on all of you, wasn't it?" Olivia said.

"At times, it really was. I tried to explain to him about the pressures of franchising and how Jim was really pushing me with all of this, too. I admitted that we may have gotten into more than we planned, but there was no pulling out. He just sat, shaking his head, and seemed sorry for us. He passed away about six weeks after that."

"He loves you and Jim so much," Olivia said quietly. "He wants you to know."

"He told us. His big heart started most of those frank discussions," I said. Talking about him stirred regret for time lost with him. I missed our talks, especially during drives to his beloved hometown, Pinehurst, in Dooly County, or to his big brother Jack's veterinary clinic in Monroe, near Athens. Their father, Taylor, had been the Dooly County veterinarian. Family pride was Ernest's core and he loved his seven siblings.

"Well, honey, he's having a ball with these grandsons! And he wants you to know *that*, too," Olivia said happily. "Had he already passed when his other grandson died?"

"Yes, two years earlier," I said. "It would have broken his heart to have been here for that—he did love those three boys. I'm sure they're entertaining heaven with wild tales of fishing and hunting trips."

"He's pulling his energy back now," she said. "He insisted I call you immediately; maybe it's because y'all's soap opera was on."

"Impatience was a part of who he was, too," I said affectionately. "He was quite a man. Even when he was frail, that deep radio voice got action. Do you think he'd come through like this again, Olivia? I'd love for Jim to have heard this. He was surprised there was no mention of his dad Monday night."

"I bet he would," she said, "if Jim wanted it. I don't know if I told you, but he wasn't the only one who didn't get heard. I'll do a better job of controlling side conversations next time."

"Me, too," I promised. "Thanks so much for calling with this."

Lucy scratched the glass door to the screened porch as we hung up, and I stood on the porch with her, allowing a pleasant summer memory to take shape. It was from when I was pregnant with Taylor and teaching swimming at the American Legion Pool Club on Riverside Drive, across from Macon's first Kmart.

Ernest, the classic extroverted salesman, sold radio commercials, an outside job that allowed free range for mixing pleasure with business. He took special interest in our late-life baby, our first to have his gender confirmed by ultrasound, so he would be named for Ernest's father, Taylor. Knowing there were now three grandsons to balance his three granddaughters gave him additional purpose and patriarchal pride. Despite declining health, he often came by the pool on his way home to lunch to check on me. He sweated miserably, fussing about my being in such heat, hinting that I might better consider its effects on the baby's welfare, if not my own. But since he usually found me happily involved with a class of excited children, splashing in cool water, it began to energize him the way it's always done me. Before long he was there to check on the progress of a class instead of to warn me of the sun's ravages. He adored children and sensed the reward I got, better than income and outweighing discomfort. He rarely passed up a chance to derail a class, telling them to listen to their great teacher, *Miss Julie*. He became my number one fan.

I love remembering the summers there with the three older kids and their friends passing through their teen years, working the snack bar and lifeguard stand, dropping quarters into a loud jukebox, and showing off with their baby brother, Tate, the swimming star. We ran it from 1974 through '88, until we built our home pool.

I hadn't noticed that my sister, Margaret, had arrived until I got back to the kitchen and saw her at the table with Mother. We'd talked about Olivia the night before. Some of her friends had been in group readings with her, but Margaret hadn't been interested herself. I'd never heard of group readings, and maybe I was wrong, but it seemed like some of the spiritual impact of our experience could be lost in a group. I replaced the phone, clicked off the TV, and fixed iced tea, dying to tell them about Ernest, but not wanting to worry Mother.

"Who in the world was that windy so-and-so?" she asked.

"That was Olivia," I said nonchalantly, placing glasses on the table.

"A group of my friends have met with somebody like her," Margaret said cheerily, before Mom could stir up gypsy warnings. "Sounds like a real hoot."

"What she called about was a real hoot," I said, grateful for her levity. I described how Ernest, with the purple peas, seemed to Olivia.

"Wow," said Margaret, "just like she knew him."

"Like I told you, Annie Moore seemed to be in charge of running Monday night's show," I said. "It seems Ernest got his feelings hurt because nobody gave him a chance to speak."

Mother laughed. "Well, nobody could say she didn't like to take charge. But Ernest wasn't one to sit in the background, either." Maybe Mom still resented her bossy sister-in-law; and my jovial father-in-law had been one of those rare people who might've been able to upstage my mother in a roomful of people.

"There's the dryer buzzer," I said, jumping at the chance to clear my thoughts. "I told Earlene I'd listen for those towels—I'll be right back." It was easy to expect people to appreciate what a profound source of hope these talks with Olivia were for my family and me. But I knew that others could not have included such a rarified gift as hers in their daily prayers for us. But neither would they have second-guessed a physician's advice for an antidepressant; in fact, they'd probably have preferred it. I went back downstairs with a stack of folded dishtowels.

The subject changed to talk of my disrupted swim school, which still had dozens of tuition checks to refund. The long list was another reminder of loss, and I hadn't been able to face it. Margaret said she'd help this weekend. She didn't speak of what a strain this tragedy brought to her real-estate business. I don't know how she managed hours of chatting with clients about good or bad houses, while holding her own pain. She had been here on Saturday to help us deal with the heart-wrenching arrival of Brax's things, which Brax's landlord, Mick, had packed and brought to us. She helped settle the monkeys in the kitchen. We'd needed her diesel-powered energy to get us this far.

It always lightened the mood when she told how Brax would swing open the main door to her building, yell, "Hey, Marge!" and continue along Vineville Avenue to Jim Shaw's. I pictured him, curly dark hair air-drying from a last-minute shower, sauntering along with his Walkman, wearing his much-loved, chocolate-brown leather jacket. It had been part of the wardrobe for *Rich Man's Wife*, which Colleen, from Charleston, had worked on. The "rich man's" murderer had worn it in the movie.

"I meant to tell you," I said, "I didn't see Brax's leather jacket last Saturday."

"Neither did I," she said. "It wasn't with things we hung upstairs." She referred to his closet, which we'd have to agonize over someday.

"Maybe a friend has it," I said, "though I doubt it. Jim let everybody know that of all Brax's things, he wants that jacket. I hope we find it—and that it fits him."

"He probably left it at somebody's house," said Mother, "I bet it'll show up when cold weather comes."

"Oh," I said, "did I tell y'all that Susie's definitely going to move in with us while Tommy works on her house? She and Annie plan to come Saturday morning to haul away stuff they left behind—as everybody does after high school—so we can free up some closet space for her and the kids."

"That's a great idea," said Margaret. "It shouldn't take too long. Most of it is stuff they don't want anyway. Need more hands?"

"Always," I said. "They plan to load the truck and give the youth group anything they can use in a yard sale."

"Sounds like a busy weekend," said Mother, encouraged by our return to more concrete ways of dealing with this heartbreaking time.

"About the swim school work," I said, "how about late Sunday afternoon?" I reminded them that Jim's sister, Carolyn, was coming with her grown daughter, Melinda, to visit Richie, Jim's mom, for the weekend. "They'll be working on their own thank-you notes, but I know we'll get together before they leave on Sunday."

What I didn't say then was that as soon as they left, I would be calling Carolyn to tell her about her dad's special visit today. And I wasn't sure, but I suspected that once Jim heard about it, he and Carolyn might like to arrange to meet Olivia themselves, maybe while Carolyn was in town.

10.

❧

Pensive Sky

Jim's mother lived only a few miles from us, but she needed solitude and quiet to deal with this catastrophe, which had now befallen both her children. We knew it was painful for her to come here. She was especially close to Brax and Tate, who had been devoted to her. Brax got his driver's license in '87, the year Ernest died, two years before Eric's death, and the pair of them dropped by her house regularly. Later, when Brax was at Mercer, Grandma cooked and did his laundry while they chatted about books he would bring her. Tate liked to practice there, so she enjoyed the perk of having financed most of his guitar lessons with the teacher he'd been so happy with.

Her long-time friends and neighbors, accustomed to supporting each other through life's crises, kept close watch on her. We were happily surprised when she agreed to join Carolyn, Melinda, and Jim for a meeting with Olivia, which we were able to set for Friday evening, but only if she could just watch.

Friday afternoon I walked to the Browns' garden, half a mile away, hoping for more zinnias for our white vase and for a chance to give Dot a report on Olivia's first visit. She was one of the few friends who knew of it.

So many lives had been interrupted by our tragedy on that July 4th weekend. It made my heart ache to think of how it affected others, especially the Browns. On the night of the accident, when things had calmed down a bit, I had called their house and left a terse message for Dot to call me. When she hadn't called by 8:30 Sunday morning I tried again. Her husband, Phil, answered and reminded me that the rest of the family had left

Saturday morning for a week on St. Simons Island. He would join them in a few hours. Mangling words, trying to control crying, I told him what had happened. "Would you tell Dot for me; I hate for her to hear it this way."

"Sure, Julie, I'll tell her...and I'm so-o sorry." I couldn't respond at all and he seemed at a loss for words, too, so we just said goodbye. Instantly the phone rang.

"Julie!" Phil said. "Did you say your dogs had been killed? I couldn't tell what you were saying. You know I can't hear worth a darn anyway, but *who* died?"

I told him, with clearer voice this time.

"Oh, my God!" he said. "I'll be right there...but let me think. I'm supposed to speak at a Sunday school class at 9:30." There was no time to cancel; he came here before leaving to join the family. Stephen, their 14-year old, was at a music camp in Brevard, North Carolina. He and Tate, our late-life babies, had been friends all his life. Soon Dot, daughter Katey, who was visiting from New York, son Phillip, and his wife closed up the beach rental and headed back to Macon while Phil drove into the night to Brevard to retrieve Stephen.

Dot looked up from picking end-of-summer squash and tomatoes and waved as I jogged along their driveway. It had been her striking premature white hair and the way it enhanced her youthful appearance that had inspired me to let my own hair go natural. This was the end of her second week back at teaching art in a big, old public high school. I don't know why Georgia schools crank up fall quarter in early August—older buildings weren't equipped for these humid high-90-degree days—it had to have been a rough week.

She laid a basket of vegetables on the ground and we hugged. She compared her dragging energy to mine, remarking that I seemed so upbeat.

"Well, I promised a report from Olivia's visit last Monday. I guess you could say it revitalized me."

"Yes! Tell me," she said. "Did she tell you more from Brax and Tate?"

"Oh, Lord, Dot, you wouldn't believe all the people she talked about. It was like that old TV show *This Is Your Life!*—she was Ralph Edwards."

"Really? Who else?"

"Did you ever meet Uncle Vernon's wife?"

"No, she had died before we met him."

"Well, she came through. And even Kat! Oh, and she told us about the vase—that it had been *shattered*. That's it, though. She couldn't say how it arrived."

"Let's go in where it's cool and get some iced tea," she said. "I want to hear it all."

"I can't stay—Jim's mom and sister are bringing Fresh Air barbeque for supper, so I need to set the table. I was hoping for a few zinnias."

She collected a colorful bunch while I rushed through a few more highlights. "Maybe we can walk in the morning," I said, "I'll tell you whatever she says tonight."

"She's coming back?"

"Yes, for supper. Carolyn wants to talk to her, too."

"And Jim's mother?" she asked, her brown eyes widening.

"Well, she's probably just being cooperative. Melinda's coming, though."

Phil drove into their graveled drive, stopped at the garden gate, left his jacket and tie on his car seat, and walked over to speak. His imposing 6-foot height, deep voice, and crown of white hair initially connote power, which could eclipse the approachable nature of the man.

"Well, hello, Miss Julie," he said, slipping his arm across my shoulders as he pecked Dot's cheek. "Whatcha up to?"

"You wouldn't believe it," I said.

"Try me," he said, smiling.

"A medium has visited us," I blurted.

"A medium *what*?"

"A psychic medium, Phil," Dot said, glancing protectively in my direction.

"She came to our house this past Monday," I explained, "to talk about the boys. It was an amazing experience."

"What's that again?" he asked, raising bushy white brows. Phil, a superior court judge, seasoned skeptic of wild stories, probably, like Jim, takes advantage of his hearing loss to extract more information. Regardless, I knew it would require a sales pitch on my part to get the positive reaction I hoped for.

"I wish I had more time," I said. "Maybe one of these days I'll tell you all about it."

He smiled then, patting my shoulder, "I sure hope you will."

Dot shrugged, her grin implying he may have already filed this conversation in that folder all husbands have: "Stuff My Wife Talks About." I gave her a hug, told them goodbye, and hurried home, one hand full of flowers and the other holding the scooped-up hem of my t-shirt as a pouch for four big red tomatoes.

Melinda, Jim's niece, was a year older than Brax, and three years older than her brother, Eric. She lives in McDonough, nearer to us than her mom, Carolyn, so she arrived before her, just as Olivia's jeep pulled in our driveway. Olivia was brimming with messages for her, so Jim, Susie, and I went to the screened porch to give them privacy.

Melinda told us that Olivia had warned of an unnoticed problem with her right cornea. She also mentioned the baby girl Melinda had miscarried earlier, along with the little one she saw playing around Melinda's feet in the future. Eric had several things to say, including that he was around her whenever she saw a scarecrow. Melinda linked that to a favorite Halloween in Yardley, Pennsylvania, where they spent their first ten years, when he wore a scarecrow costume and she wore her "timid lion" costume from a Wizard of Oz ballet recital. Later on, by Christmas, when the first symptoms began to appear, she saw the doctor about her eye problem. Payton, a darling baby girl, was born two years later.

When Carolyn and Richie arrived, Olivia suggested we go to our front room and begin. "With seven of us, we might be crowded," she said, "but I feel comfortable in there." We arranged seating in a half circle around her rolling desk chair. We had no time to wonder if anything would happen like before, because Olivia began as soon as we sat down.

"I recognize *this* man from the other day," she said. "Jim, your father has come to be with us—he really is a big man."

That got Jim's attention, but before he could comment she formed a steeple with her hands. "It looks like he's trying to squeeze into a little tent," she said. "He's saying, 'Tell them I'm just ranting from the rafters.' He's having to be loud, as though he's far away, or could he be upset?"

"Oops," she said, "I shouldn't have said upset—'Don't say I'm upset,' he's saying, 'I'm just way up here—in the rafters.'"

"I can picture it," I said, "literally under rafters, like in an attic maybe."

"Why would Papa be in an attic?" Melinda asked.

"Three lamps...," Olivia went on. "He's glad you finally did something with those three lamps. Were some lamps in an attic?"

"My alabaster lamps!" Carolyn exclaimed. "Remember, Jim, those we found in your garage with all the stuff from Mom's attic after the flood. But I only found the two I kept. I finally had them rewired, just last month."

I explained to Olivia that Richie's house was ruined by the '94 flood. "Ernest had died several years earlier and left tons of stuff. After the flood Tommy helped Jim and Tate clear it out, even from her attic. They filled our garage with anything that seemed savable."

"That must be where those antique lamps came from," Carolyn said. "They look so good now with new gold fringed shades."

"He's obviously glad," Olivia said.

"Jim!" I exclaimed, "That might explain why there's a hole drilled in that handmade pottery vase we found—I bet he planned to wire it as a third lamp."

"That vase dictated our whole color scheme last winter," Jim said. "Julie worked with the kitchen and den paint until it exactly matched the blue green in that vase."

"*Pensive Sky*," I said. "I love it."

"Sounds like he knows, Daddy," Susie said.

"And I use my dresser lamps every night," said Carolyn.

For the forty-plus years Carolyn's parents were married, two storage sheds couldn't contain all the treasures her dad brought home. It was bad enough to be thought of as a junk collector, but it was added insult when his finds were banished to their attic. It felt good to think he knew about these rescues.

"Carolyn," Olivia said, "he saw you just this morning—were you shopping for jewelry very early today?"

"Yes, I was," Carolyn answered, her blue eyes sparkling with surprise. "I promised a friend I'd stop by her fundraiser on my way to work." Jim's sister was an education executive in Atlanta, and her long days started with a forty-mile drive to her south Fulton County office. To make time for anything else before work would require real effort, but something she'd do for a friend's cause.

"You were looking at a dragonfly pin?" Olivia asked.

Carolyn nodded, mesmerized.

"Your dad says, 'Go back and get that dragonfly pin you wanted.' You must have looked at two? He's saying 'And don't get the cheap one!'"

"How about that!" Carolyn exclaimed. "I did like the tiny one but hated to pay more for it. There was a big, cheaper one, but I decided not to get one at all."

"He knows. Go back. Get the one you want. It'll remind you of him when you wear it." Olivia rolled her chair to look directly at Richie, "And he wants you to learn to let people give you things when they want to."

"I don't know what you mean," Richie demurred. Olivia smiled, inched closer, and placed a hand on Richie's. "He says you do." She looked at the rest of us and winked. "Doesn't that sound like a husband? Wait a second," her words came gently, like a teacher's coaxing more from a bashful child, "I need to ask about a friend who wants to give you a bracelet, but you won't accept it."

"Yes," Richie said, quietly. "I believe Vivian wants to give me one." We all knew this friend. Even in retirement they maintained a bond that began from working together at the phone company for more than forty years. Vivian was in assisted living now, and they checked on each other every night at bedtime. She wanted to give her dear friend this bracelet as a token of love, but Richie didn't want to accept it.

"Well, Ernest says for you to take it; it hurts her feelings when you won't," Olivia said, conveying his persuasive tone.

"That's right, Mom," Jim said. "You always give but don't like receiving."

I thought of all the stylish clothes Ernest bought for her. Nobody had more unabashed appreciation for a pretty woman, and he had truly adored this one.

"Uh-oh," said Olivia, "he's asking if he has to *cuss* to make you understand." She laughed then. "He likes to tease, doesn't he? Did someone say he got worked up, trying to make a point?" While we weighed that loaded question, she turned serious. "Did he die once before?"

Richie nodded.

"'My ticker stopped,' he says. Was he revived?"

"Yes," said Richie.

"How amazing—when was that?"

"In 1982," Carolyn said. "He had congestive heart failure because of emphysema. The EMTs revived him; Mother was there."

"He says he lived five more years."

"That's right," said Melinda. "He did."

"He chose to return—because he loves all of you. Hard years," he says. "But he was willing for more time to teach everybody to communicate better. That's what he's saying. This is hard," she said, as if she wasn't sure how we'd take his next thoughts, "but he's not sure he was able to do that."

That didn't surprise me. I knew we'd all been so busy his final years that we missed chances to connect in the open-hearted way he loved. The implication that he might be disappointed was hard to hear but gave us something to work on. We were lost in thought for only a minute when Olivia broke in, cheerier than before.

"He loves all of you very much. He just had to grab this chance for one of his lectures." She chuckled. "I bet that sounds like him, too." She rolled the chair around to look into each face. "He is so happy being with those three boys, his parents, and..." She stopped in front of me and added, "with your daddy. Remember—they're all in a...let me get it right...a wunnerful place."

II.

༄

Elizabeth

Olivia, still in front of our piano bench, looked from Jim to me, deciding her next clue was mine. "Julie, was your father a teacher?"

"Well, he taught me a lot, but he wasn't a teacher—he sold insurance."

"Hmm, somebody, who's a teacher, looks just like your father."

"Uncle Vernon—Daddy's big brother! People often confused them. He was a college professor, married to Annie Moore, my aunt who wanted to direct your visit the other night."

"He says he was here that night, too, 'but not heard then.' He has a foreign accent; where was he from?"

"That's rich," I said, and laughed. "They were all from Charleston, but he taught Spanish at Mercer. He'd left teaching before I was born but helped my friends and me with high school Spanish. He gave up on my reading his Spanish thesis. He died eight years ago."

"He's a polished gentleman with a cane," she said. "'Devoted to Julie,' he says. He wants you to know he loves you all very much."

"He was a vital part of our lives," I said. "A year after his wife died we lost Daddy; they'd talked every night at nine o'clock for years. After that he called me every night and ate with us on Sundays until he was bedridden. He was like a grandfather to the kids."

"Brax's first car came from Uncle Vernon," said Susie. Everyone chuckled at the memory of that old blue Chevy Bel Air and the mortification Brax endured, parking it with the others at Stratford Academy. No amount of rubbing compound could tone down its scars from years of scraping an iron rail along Vernon's steep driveway.

"But Brax solved his problem of that sagging roof liner," said Susie. "It kept hanging on his head, so he stabbed loose fabric to the roof with sharpened pencils."

"His next car was a Mustang convertible," Jim said. "He deserved it."

"After Vernon graduated from Mercer," I continued, "he was dean of Brewton Parker College—they called him Prof. Wallace. Fifty years later the school tapped him for their Hall of Fame, citing his integrity and optimism as a reason for the school's surviving the Depression. His barter system for farm boys whose families couldn't afford tuition supplied labor for his Victory Garden and meat and vegetables for their dining hall. He was 86 when we drove him to Mt. Vernon, Georgia, to accept the award. Ernestine, his beloved housekeeper, went with us."

That pleasant afternoon in 1987 shot through my mind like one of the family's old 8-mm home movies. Uncle Vernon, sporting a new charcoal-gray suit, became a strong-voiced orator, whose brown eyes twinkled as he declined the mic and began, in his smooth Charlestonian brogue, his unwritten acceptance speech. One charming tale after another, accented by his waving stick, brought applause from the packed audience, some of whom had been his students sixty years earlier. I loved his misty-eyed reference to my dad, his ten-year-younger brother, a student under his wing: "I'm afraid I was a little hard on the lad, though," he said. When the emcee apologetically had to create a detour in Vernon's walk down memory lane, there was a standing ovation. He basked in that honor for the rest of his life. He was 89 when he died, four years later.

Just thinking of this community of souls residing somewhere together again made my heart swell with joy.

"Your friend Elizabeth has been waiting for you," Olivia said, before rolling her chair away from me. "Do you have an older friend named Elizabeth?"

"We call her Beth," I said, referring to my friend in the Catskills ashram. "She's who sent us the story about Michael—a boy who came to his father through a medium."

"But is she a very old lady—from years before you were born?"

"Well, no," I said, "but we've known each other since first grade."

"This lady seems to be well over 100," Olivia said, gazing into her private screen behind us. "She says she's seen you go through this sad thing, and she '*understands your sorrow more than most.*'"

"There's Sister Elizabeth," suggested Susie. "Doesn't she still live in town? She must be nearly a hundred by now."

"That's right," I said. "She was our high school Spanish teacher, from Charleston—but she's probably not the one either, right?"

"I don't think so," said Olivia. "But this Elizabeth wants to give you something. Perhaps, if you visit the nun—because this very old lady says she can't bring it to you."

"I can go visit her," I said. "She's in the local retirement convent near Mount de Sales."

"Wait," Olivia said. "Someone has already tried to get this gift to you." She dabbed at her forehead with a Kleenex. "It's hard to describe this unusual-looking thing. It's hand-hewn, I can see the grain of a wide log...maybe a statue, or a monument?"

Jim and I looked at each other. He thought of Macon's future river trail. "Maybe a marker with the boys' names on it?" he guessed. Olivia didn't have an answer.

"I can't imagine Sister Elizabeth having such a thing," I said, "but a visit to her will be nice anyway. I don't know why she would say she understands my sorrow more than most, though—I wonder if she lost brothers."

"Well, be ready," Olivia said, "because you will be hearing more about this. Our sweet old lady says a lady named *Doll* will be her messenger. Do you know a lady who goes by the name of Doll?"

I shook my head in confusion.

"Well, *Doll* will tell you about another gift, too—a smaller one."

"Ohh-kay," I said. "We'll take your word for it, but I'm so curious."

"Your dad is still here, Jim," Olivia said. "He says, 'Take care of that hearing.' Do you have trouble with your hearing?"

"Yes," chorused everyone. Jim nodded.

"Well, he says there'll be something that might help your right ear. He wants you to stay on top of that."

"That's my good ear," Jim said, "the one that still works, but it's about shot, too." His present hearing aid, there had been several, was a nuisance but helped a little, so it was encouraging to think progress was possible.

104

Richie, herself a veteran of imperfect hearing aids, perked up at this. "Jim, do that," she said. "Take care of your hearing. It interferes with everything if you can't hear what's going on."

"Your dad agrees," Olivia said. "He says, 'Spend that money!'"

We all laughed. "I see he's still a good salesman," I said.

Olivia stood to stretch when something above the hall doorway caught her gaze. "Your boys are over there, Jim—on a mountaintop—waving black-and-white flags for you, like this..." She closed her hands around invisible sticks, elbows bent, and waved her hands in X's in front of her chest. "Waving checkered flags at the finish line—for Pop!" We saw exactly what she meant. "Are you about to retire?"

"I haven't really given it much thought," he answered.

"Well, your boys are cheering you at a finish line. Retirement may not be far off—within about a year, maybe? Think about that." She sat, fanning herself with the tissue.

I thought of Jim's retirement as a positive thing. Having to plan for Taylor's college years had meant it would be at least six years away. But now, with that plan so sadly devoid of purpose, after thirty years at the school bus plant, Jim could consider it. But I knew it would take more than this to change his plan.

Olivia rolled her chair toward him again. "They're showing me an angel—he's big—makes me think of Michael the Archangel. 'You've read about him,' they say, and they seem happy that you did."

Jim looked blank—he wasn't into reading about angels.

"Maybe not an *angel* exactly," she went on. "That was for me—to help connect you to a name like Michael—have you read about someone with a name like that?"

"That book, Daddy!" said Susie. "The one about the boy who died in a wreck—remember? We read it at the beach—his name was Michael."

"Oh, yeah—an attorney wrote it," he said to Olivia. "He was able to hear from his son through a psychic medium."

"Okay," said Olivia. "They must think it made an impression on you. They say maybe read it again."

"Well, I don't care about reading it again; but it did make me think something like that might be possible—it was a true story."

"There you go—they like that you read it, especially *'when'* you read it."

Whatever she next saw above Jim made her eyes pop; she drew back, impressed by it. "Are you interested in Indian stuff, Jim?"

"Pretty much, I guess," he said, agreeably.

"Why would you think a big Indian is standing behind you?" she asked. "I'd say he must be a chief, by his headdress."

Jim looked amused—he had clearly joined this game, but I know he hadn't counted on attracting so much attention. "Maybe it has to do with a trail they're going to create along the river."

"No, I don't think it's about a river," she maintained. "It's more like artifacts. Do you have a collection of Indian artifacts?"

"A few arrowheads," he said. "Not much more."

"We have that long beaded tobacco bag," I said, "and the pipe that was with it. Aunt Anne referred to *them* as artifacts."

"Oh, right—we have those," he said.

"My aunt's husband, Bob Brennan, had an ancestor from Pottsville, Pennsylvania, who was the government agent who signed a peace treaty with the Indians in one of the western states. The chief gave them to him; Aunt Anne got them from her attic years ago. She and Uncle Bob had no children, so she gave them to our boys. She thought they might be valuable someday."

"Sounds like it," she said. "I think they're reminding Jim of it."

"She said it might help with college one day. But they loved them—we wouldn't have sold them; in fact, I can't remember where I hid that long pipe." I laughed at my maternal paranoia. "Truthfully, I didn't want them tempted to try smoking anything in it."

"I wonder how we could find out what it's worth," Susie said.

"We could begin by finding where Julie hid the pipe," Jim stated wryly.

"Maybe they're suggesting we sell it now," I mused. "Maybe it's about retirement, or something? Do you think that's what they're trying to tell us?"

"I wish I knew," Olivia said, looking sort of wrung-out.

"Why can't these guys just say what they mean?" Susie asked. "It sure would make things easier. They just throw out these cryptic clues—then we have to work so hard to decipher them."

Melinda agreed. "Does it have to be so complicated?"

"It's nearly always that way," Olivia said. "Though if it's too complicated and you can't connect it to anything, I feel like I haven't given it to you correctly." She had the look of a storyteller who'd closed her book. When everybody stood, Melinda went to the kitchen with her grandmother to warm our barbeque supper.

"It must be exhausting for you," Carolyn said. "Like nonstop charades. But it's fascinating to us."

"I admit," Olivia said, chuckling, "I've had a good workout tonight. But Julie's good at finding something in most of it, which makes it satisfying."

"We're so grateful to you," I said. "You're going to eat with us now, aren't you? You must be starving."

She said she and her teenaged son would be babysitting for her infant granddaughter and she was anxious to get home for a quiet evening with them. Carolyn fixed a barbecue take-out.

I followed Olivia to her car. As she was closing her door, she said, "You know you can always call me if you need to talk, Julie. I'll let you know when I hear anything new. I'm enjoying this, too."

It was hard to fall asleep that night. I wished I could remember where in the world I could've hidden that long red Pipestone pipe when Brax was a teenager. We realized it was lost when Taylor had wanted to take both pieces to show his American history teacher last fall. His teacher said it was a sacrilege for the beaded bag, a museum piece, to ride around on a truck seat instead of being in a protective box. He urged Taylor to look for the peace pipe since the bag lost value without it.

Peace pipe. The smoking pipe had been passed around when treaties were signed, pledging peace and an end of strife. Maybe these sons, who brought us more enjoyment than any serious strife, could see how lost we were in this new world without them and were trying to help us restore peace.

The next morning Margaret, Annie, Susie, Anna, and I plunged into the job of closet cleaning. Two closets in the girls' old room would make plenty of storage for Anna and Rob, and there was no escaping the need to clear out Brax's room, too, since it would give space for Susie's winter things. Just thinking of going through more of his things made me weak, but having these girls to keep it moving would be a prop.

It turned out that his was our first area of attack. We gave it a whirl-wind treatment, beginning with his chest of drawers and then his closet. Most of what he'd left behind were childhood things from when he'd left for the first time—outgrown clothes and toys. We felt less protective of them now. It wasn't so heartbreaking to handle things made of cloth, paper, and plastic, given our new perspective; things that had served Brax during his life with us were completely useless to his life now. And we were con-vinced that he was proud of us for seeing things in that light. He and Tate had made it clear that they had very wonderful, if different, lives now. They had reminded us that *memories*, not objects themselves, would serve us all.

Of course we had known this before, in theory, but the thought of go-ing through my sons' rooms had crippled me. I had regarded anything they had touched as extensions of them. But this morning, despite our strong attachments to some things, we had the choice to keep special items and disengage from others without turning everything into sacred, tear-jerking relics. This gave us energy to go on.

The three generations of women with me—my sister, my daughters, and my granddaughter—went out of their way to honor my maternal wish-es as we plundered through. We had boxes of stuff for Goodwill, for family and friends, for tossing, and for keeping. And the process—separating from these physical things, a requisite step for learning to let go of precious peo-ple—was moving us along.

Brax's letters, postcards, photos, and anything he'd written were put into a wooden box; Annie would pass them along to Kirby and Russell. His collection of little boxes was doled out to his sisters. His drawer of early electronic games (baseball, football, Pac-Man) was pared down. Sports tro-phies went into a "save" box. I would dismantle them (as Tate and I had done with his), stacking marble bases as bookends, topped by one small sports figure and his nameplate. Jim had requested the well-organized box of baseball cards and the boys' matchbook collection, so they stayed on the closet shelf, along with a grand old Royal typewriter. Tons of books stayed, temporarily. Susie planned to create nameplates with her brothers' names before we donated them to Friends of the Library. Most clothes went to Goodwill. We treasured special favorites like his travel-worn Doc Martens and woven Turkish hat, but we'd have to keep looking for his beloved leather jacket.

As we caught our breath, feeling strong from having dived into this pool of memories, which had not been without tears of real anguish, I sat on Brax's bed sipping a Diet Coke, watching Margaret stand on a dresser to dust the top of his long, triple-sectioned book case.

"What in the world is this thing?" she said over her shoulder, as her hand bumped something hard. A long, hollow wooden handle hit the ceiling as she raised it out of the recessed top of the cabinet, then she handed down a T-shaped piece of hollow red Pipestone.

"Oh, my lord, Margaret, you've found the peace pipe! We haven't seen it in over ten years—thank you, thank you! It's the Indian thing Olivia told us to look for."

She was still perched on the dresser, confused by my manic reaction, when I ran for the stairs. "I'll tell you all about it, but first I have to show this to Jim."

Jim was at the lower edge of our yard, out of earshot, patting soil around a freshly planted shrub. Tommy, kneeling beside him, held a shovel, and Rob waited nearby with a water hose.

"Tommy," I yelled, "tell Jim we've located the pipe!" I put the pipe's tip to my mouth and exhaled imaginary smoke. He laughed as he relayed to Jim, "She says she found a pipe, and man, it's really something!" Jim looked up, gave a muddy thumbs-up, and went back to the shrub.

It went without saying that we weren't setting foot in Taylor's room. None of us could bear the thought of disturbing it, looking exactly as it did when he was still here.

Instead, the girls progressed to their old room across the hall. I leaned against a doorjamb, watching the windstorm of taffeta prom dresses, all manner of girlish clothes, shoes, boots, and hats as they went into big plastic bags. They knew instantly which things were of no value to them—some of which I defended—and they allowed me to keep some precious remnants of their childhood, which had vanished in a whirl. Their determination, fortified by my sister's energy, propelled every bag, box, and trashcan straight to the pickup parked at our front porch steps. Our church youth planned a garage sale next month, and what they couldn't use, Goodwill would take.

Tomorrow Tommy would help Susie and her kids bring her bed, dresser, and clothes to the poolhouse, advancing her plan to put her house on the market. That meant Anna and Rob would have to go through their things at home, following the model set here today. They planned Labor Day as their goal for having all boxes into their garage so inside painting could begin.

Margaret and I spent Sunday afternoon writing refund checks for swim school tuitions, content that another regrettable project was behind us, while Susie's group set up her waterbed in the poolhouse.

That evening, when things were settled for bedtime, with Susie in her poolhouse/studio apartment, the kids and I used a connecting intercom to tell her goodnight, like we had done in the days of our young family's bed-times. Back then, during the seventies, our favorite TV show was *The Waltons*. It was so relevant to 5-year-old Brax that his lifetime of plaid flannel shirts, which eventually passed down to Tate, were known as "Jim-Bob" shirts. The show always ended with bedtime and most of the day's problems solved. As credits rolled, their large family began a litany of goodnights to each other, their ritual for peaceful slumber. It had been only natural for our family to do the same.

"Goodnight, John-Boy," we said to Susie through the intercom in the kitchen.

"G'night, Mama. G'night, Mary Ellen. G'night, Jim-Bob," came her response.

110

12.

❧

Call-Waiting

On Monday morning, I read an email from Sue Burch, the wife of my Atlanta cousin, Jack, saying how much they enjoyed being at the Rookery for
the memorial concert in late July. It was a wonderful night, full of mixed
emotions, she said, and she was deeply touched by the reputation of our
boys. She also expected that we hadn't heard the last from Bragg Jam.

She mentioned having come across a little thing of her mother-in-law,
Beverly's, the middle of my dad's three older sisters, that she wanted me to
have. *She actually seemed to speak to me, Julie. I know she wants this to be a
"comfort gift for Julie,"* Sue wrote. She hoped to bring this to me right away.
She and Jack kept an impressive travel calendar throughout their thirty-two
year marriage, and she wanted to squeeze in a trip to Macon before a family
trip to California, followed by a bike tour in France—by the end of September.

When they were here for the funeral, and three weeks later for the
Bragg Jam concert, we all noticed Sue's weight loss and thinning hair. She
mentioned fatigue and an upcoming physical. Goodbyes that Sunday after
the concert were emotional as she hugged me tight, saying how much she'd
learned during the past month as we dealt with this tragedy; our peaceful
endurance had inspired her. I reminded her that she had been my role model thirteen years ago when she showed such courage and optimism during
double mastectomies and implants. Tears spilled from her big brown eyes
when she spoke of having seen how someone can survive even the death of
children. She said she really wasn't afraid of facing death anymore.

The mention of a little gift from my Aunt Beverly intrigued me. I wanted to call Sue but knew that she, a psychologist, and Jack, a lawyer, would be at work. Of course, shiny earrings came to mind, but her email was a teaser and I'd just wait to see what she came across. Later that night I remembered the day had been Jack's birthday and I'd never mailed his card. I doubted he'd fool with an e-card, so I would call him tomorrow.

The next day, Tuesday, August 24, was granddaughter Anna's fourteenth birthday. She exercised her right to choose a spot for her birthday supper—it would be Olive Garden again. We'd gone there last year, so she said the boys would know where to find us. I'd already picked up Mylar balloons that morning and would run other errands that afternoon, but first I wanted to leave a cheery, belated birthday message on Jack's home phone. It was a little after one o'clock when I dialed their number. It was answered on the first ring.

"Sue!" I said, "I thought you'd be at work. I was going to leave a belated birthday wish for Jack—you must be on your lunch break."

"Actually I've just finished a delicious lunch that a sweet friend dropped by for me," she said, a little too brightly, as though her friend were nearby.

"Nice! I'll let you get back to her. Tell Jack I'm sorry I didn't get a card off, but I had good intentions."

"No, don't hang up," she said. "My friend is just leaving—we're in the driveway now saying bye." I heard barking, a car engine, and footsteps on concrete. "I'm walking to the mailbox while we talk."

"When are you going to Bev's?" I asked, referring to their plans to go to Oakland to celebrate Jack's birthday with his sister and her family.

"Oh-h, I'm not sure, Julie," she said, strangely wistful and a bit breathless.

"Are you feeling okay?" I asked.

"Well, I'm just so short of breath. It's been bothering me. You know I told you I had a check-up scheduled."

"I remember. Did you get it?"

"I did, last Friday." Again a pause and quick breathing. "I may as well just tell you—the doctor extracted some fluid from my lungs."

"Fluid? Oh, Sue. What does he think?"

"Well, that's why I'm keeping the phone with me. I'm waiting for his office to call with biopsy results. Julie, I'm so scared. It could be *bad...*"

Of course we were both thinking of how breast cancer can follow a metastatic track to a woman's lungs...but it had been thirteen years.

"I wish I were there so I could sit with you," I said. "We should probably free up your phone."

"No, I've got call-waiting—I'll know. Let's just talk. Tell me something good."

"Okay," I said. "Well, I got Sunday's email; actually, we've been so busy I just saw it yesterday, and I think I've guessed what you decided Aunt Beverly wants you to give me. How about *that*?" I teased.

"You do?" she said. "I don't think I even mentioned it to Jack."

"You'd never believe who told me, Sue. So much strange stuff has happened here lately. I wish I could tell you—but it's too long a story to start today."

"Strange stuff? You know I love strange stuff—tell me." And then her phone clicked. "Hold on..." She was gone, but only for a second.

"Was that your doctor?"

"No, a friend. They're all waiting to hear from me. So tell me, what's this strange stuff that's been going on in Macon?" I could tell she was climbing porch steps now.

"I may as well just say it—a medium came to see us last Monday night." I gave her a second, then went on, "And, Sue, she told us so many wonderful little stories—about the boys, Daddy, Annie Moore, and lots of others."

"A medium? Julie!" she exclaimed, sounding more delighted than shocked. "You've had a reading with a medium?"

I'm not sure if Sue or Jack were regular churchgoers, but ancestors from his mom's and my dad's side of the family were devout Southern Baptists who would've had little tolerance for this sort of talk.

"Yes, she came to us. It was one of those wild coincidences. And I've learned there's much more spiritual depth to her gift than most people think. Someday I'm going to have to tell you the surprising, hopeful things we've learned. I am not afraid of death anymore, I can tell you that."

"Well, tell me." I heard the door close behind her. "I'm just going to sit down now so you can tell me all you've learned from your medium." I could picture her apple-green den, walled with big windows overlooking a stacked rock wall around the tree-shaded terrace in her white house in Buckhead.

"I'm not kidding," I said defensively.

"Me, either," she said, chuckling. "Seriously, I want to hear everything."

So I started with Olivia's arrival, when she mentioned our Rottweiler. Then Grandfather's wounded, gloved hand. She laughed at the boys' knowing about my shower-time idea of writing short stories. Annie Moore's appearance, seated among satin pillows, ringing the cowbell for Ernestine touched her funny bone, too.

"Olivia's tone of voice and facial expression helped us recognize whose energy she seemed to channel," I said. "I think that's the right word for it."

"Tell me more."

"When Annie Moore asked, a bit sarcastically, if we received flowers we didn't like, I immediately thought of that white vase. It made me wonder if she could've had something to do with it." Sue had seen our vase.

"Hold on again," she said.

I reflexively made the sign of the cross as I sat down by our desk, waiting for her to come back on the line.

"Okay, I'm back—another friend. So, Olivia said Annie Moore sent the vase?"

"No, it confused her, too; she said we'd find out one day. A lot of it was like that—she'd say to wait for confirmation later."

"Did you ask her about that man you saw by your mailbox?" she asked. Sue sits for hours as a therapist, encouraging people to share their stories. Her talent for convincing them she takes is all seriously must be a real gift.

"We did," I said. "She told us his name is Matthew, one of Brax's oldest friends. She called him an angel. We were scared that meant he'd die young, too, but it just means he can be used as God's helper—even for out-of-body travel."

"Astral projection," Sue said. "I've heard of it...I can believe it. It's time travel or remote viewing. So, have you talked to this friend?"

"No, he lives in Seattle; he was in grad school at Cornell the last time Brax visited him. Olivia said he'll be ringing our doorbell in three months though."

"November," she said. "Well, what else? Oops, phone—be right back."

My tense right hand made the sign of the cross again. She was back in a few seconds. "Another friend?" I asked.

"No, Jack; I feel bad for him. I'm so glad I'm not just sitting here waiting."

"Me, too. Did you tell him I called to wish him a happy birthday?"

"Yeah," and she laughed. "He said you're late—it was yesterday. So, did she know what the young man was doing in your yard that afternoon?"

"She said he met the boys at the scene of the accident and was escorting them here to see that we would survive."

"You thought he was talking to somebody—so she thinks it was your boys?"

"That's what it seems like to her."

"Well, it makes sense," as though she were notating a client's file.

"Sue, I wonder what somebody would think if they could hear this conversation!"

"Who cares?" she answered with typical oomph. After hearing about Eric, she supplied the clinical name for his thinned eyelashes. "Trichotillomania—a stress disorder—pulling out one's own hair, bless his heart. I'm not sure if that applies to eyelashes, though." She was amazed to hear about his flip-flops. "Oh, that's convincing, Julie. No one could've known."

"I know," I said, "It almost makes me jealous to think how happy they sound while we're so miserable."

"Well, one day we'll get there...hold on again." She sounded like someone who was going to pick up a travel folder.

This time my sign of the cross hit with such force, I literally slapped my own forehead. "Sue, my head may start bleeding from the way I'm hitting it with the sign of the cross every time you leave."

"You're making the sign of the cross? Because you're so afraid for me?"

"I can't help it—more like a prayer for good news. I so want you to get good news; but either way you will have a good life. You *are* having a good life."

"I am," she agreed quietly.

"Are you sure you want to stay on the phone?" I asked.

"Yes—there's more, isn't there?"

"Good Lord, yes." I said. I told her about Taylor's metronome and the time-box in our old playhouse.

"Promise me you'll go look for that," she said.

Then I told her about the gigolo monkeys. "It was like a climax to everything, the way we were offered that cute reminder of their presence—to cheer us when they seem furthest away." Sue already knew of our family's symbol of ivy. "The monkeys can be our Plan B. We can turn to them when we lose hope in Plan A and galvanize our faith."

"So Plan A is your faith in an afterlife?"

"Right. But even Jesus knew his friends would need something tangible—like bread. So when we crave a sign, we've got the monkeys."

"Being Catholic's made that easy for you, hasn't it?" she said.

"It has," I said. "But I doubt the Church would sanction my spin on certain doctrines—I may go to hell for suggesting that bread and wine are Plan B; but, you're right—most of what we believe centers around spirit life."

"Oh, Julie, let's not think of a hell," she said.

"Okay, so you want to hear what happened on Wednesday?" I asked.

"Sure—what happened Wednesday?"

"Olivia called during *As the World Turns,* thinking I could identify a big, well-dressed man she visualized at her house—shelling peas. He asked her to call me."

"Why didn't she know him?"

"She doesn't, until somebody decrypts clues. After that she can remember them."

"Oh, he was a new vision—so who was he?"

"Jim's dad."

Sue's phone clicked. "Hold on..."

I walked to our kitchen for water. By the time she came back I had swapped the low-battery portable for a corded desk phone.

"That was Jack again, a little irritated," she said. "He can't believe we're still on the phone. I guess he thinks I don't know how worried he is. He's coming home."

"Good," I said.

"Okay, so Jim's dad—Ernest—is in her living room, shelling peas—why did he say to call you?"

"To tell me he was here that first night, but nobody let him get a word in edgewise," I said, and we both laughed.

"How long was that first night?"

"Until nearly two in the morning."

"Gee, Julie, I can tell it was good for you, though. Who was with you?"

"Just the girls; Jim wanted to wait for a written report. But I didn't tell you—she came again on Friday night."

"Honey, you don't mean it! Did Jim change his mind?"

"He did. His mom, sister, and niece were here, too. Ernest came through again."

"It's convincing—about this not being all there is," she said. "Sounds like life is pretty busy on the other side."

"No joke. Let's just say that either way we live; either way we win." I heard the sound of ice clinking into a glass. We'd been talking for over an hour.

"Did the lady tell you what my little gift is? Is that why you think you know?"

"Not exactly, but something she said that first night made me think of something of Aunt Beverly's that I'd like—and when I read your email I thought I might be right."

"Well, you couldn't possibly know," she said, "and since you sound excited, I'm sure it's not what you think." She chuckled. "This is a little thing."

I laughed. "What I'm thinking about *is* little."

Her phone clicked again. "Stay there," she said. This time the sign of the cross came slower and my folded hands stayed on my lap. She came back instantly, her voice frightened, "It's him—I've got to go."

"We love you, Sue. Remember: either way, you win."

"Love you, too." She inhaled deeply and added bravely, "And either way, I win."

We hung up. I wandered through our downstairs, praying that Jack would be home soon, knowing God would hold them both. It seemed natural to call Olivia, to let her know what hopeful diversion her readings had been for my cousin just now. I had just explained the reason for my call when there was a knock on our glass door by the screened porch. I hadn't seen the purple flower truck and was shocked when a man handed me a huge bouquet of sunflowers.

"Are these for me?" I asked, then laughed to think how many times he'd heard that cliché. I read the card to Olivia. "Merry and Tim Potts are thinking of me...how sweet is that! He sang Brax's songs at the concert last month. I'm going to think of these as flowers for Sue, too. I hate it, but she's in trouble, isn't she, Olivia?"

"I think she is whole," Olivia answered quietly, "she'll be fine. It's a great time to receive flowers—when you're worried about your cousin. How old is she?"

"Fifty-two, so full of life. We better free up the phone, she may try to call back. Pray for her." The phone rang just as the school bus stopped out front. It was Jack.

"I'm so sorry y'all have to go through this," I told him. "I can't bear to ask what her doctor said."

"Well, Sue is standing right here," he said, "and she wants to tell you herself." I couldn't tell if that was relief in his voice or pride for his wife's courage.

"Julie," Sue said. "It's bad...I have metastatic breast cancer."

"Oh, Sue," I cried. "I hate it. Do you know what the next step will be?"

"We'll go see him tomorrow and discuss all of it. Jack walked in as I said hello to the doctor. I've told him how you entertained me while I waited—it was such a help."

"How about if I make some calls for you? Let me do something real."

"That *was* real; but it would help if you tell the Macon family," she said wearily.

"I will," I said. "Most of them will be at Anna's birthday dinner this evening. We'll pray for you."

It had been hard to muster enthusiasm for birthdays that summer. Jim and I planned to ignore ours when they rolled around just a few days after the July concert. But Susie convinced us that her brothers would expect us to cling to the family tradition of honoring birthdays, especially Jim's and mine. He and I were born a few hours apart—me on July 27th, he a few hours later on the 28th—in the Macon Hospital, our mothers attended by the same doctor, our fathers acquainted through my dad's brother, Vernon. That was the foundation for our family fable. We met fourteen years later and married seven years after that.

So we had decided to gather at the boys' favorite place, El Sombrero, at the Baconsfield Shopping Center, a few doors from where we had run the third frozen yogurt shop. Our group of eighteen, determined smiles and puffy eyes—even the Mylar balloons were drooping—barely three weeks after the funeral, rewound fun memories of being here, at "the Hat," as we called it, with Brax and Tate. It had been the gathering spot on so many Sunday afternoons for friends to wander in and join Brax, and their pal Jose Cuervo, in a group effort to conquer the New York Times' crossword puzzle.

"We miss Brax," the owner of the Mexican place said to us, as he set up our long table in a back room. "We still keep his big book of words, his dictionary, behind our bar. Many Sunday afternoons he sat with his guys, working his puzzle and playing guitars—at this very table. His little brother was often with them—but, of course, we served him only his Mountain Dew."

My only wish, as Jim and I blew out our candles, had been to come up with some way to keep memories like these from being lost.

13.

∽

Knowing-Kindness

St. Joseph's Church is where I was baptized as an infant, received all the early sacraments, sang in the children's choir, and processed with young classmates to lay May flowers at the feet of Mary's statue. In 1960, our senior class of twenty-seven convent schoolgirls received diplomas there.

Four years later, Jim and I were married in the beautiful old place, and the next year we brought our firstborn, Susie, home from Florence, Alabama, to be baptized. After eight years, while Jim's work took us on to Monroe, Louisiana, and to Marietta, Georgia, we moved back home to Macon, having added Annie and Brax to our family by then.

My strict parochial foundation, with its exclusive claim to salvation, shifted as I matured, and as a teenager I began to resent misguided implications that I pray for the salvation of my tolerant Baptist churchgoing daddy. I spent most of my thirties as a nomadic Christian—learning about, visiting, and basically resisting most organized religions. It wasn't a bad time, and it may have led our children to think about God in a less dogmatic, more universal way, too.

Eventually, however, especially once our girls were attending my now-coed alma mater, Mount de Sales Academy, I felt we would all benefit from a deeper church involvement. When the three kids and I asked Jim, a dormant Methodist, if he wanted to attend Father John Cuddy's three-month Inquirer's class in 1980, he came along and became a convert. We enjoyed the recommitment and regarded Taylor's birth the following year as karmic affirmation. I joined the choir thirteen years later.

Thinking of Father Cuddy, his keen mind, gentle humor, and peaceful acceptance, made me want to discuss our experiences of the past two weeks with him. We hadn't talked since he had called to check on us after the funeral, just before he left for his annual month in Europe, nearly seven weeks before.

I first met him in the fifties during his routine trips to Macon from his Savannah office, where he was superintendent of Diocesan schools. His cheerful visits, despite his dire warnings of exams he would be sending our way, endeared him to our all-female student body, most of whom had a crush on the good-looking young priest from Connecticut. Since 1974, for twenty-five years as the pastor of our 1,400-family parish, his sensitive heart had been involved in others' life-and-death dramas. Even knowing he had precious little free time, I wanted his feedback. That morning, once Earlene began her housekeeping routine, I dialed the rectory.

"Julie, it's so good to hear from you," he said when his secretary connected us. "How are things going?"

"Better than I'd have imagined, Father. I hope you had a good trip."

"It was a good trip, and I prayed for all of you each day." A priest's itinerary usually includes offering daily Mass, either privately or as a guest of a local church. I was sure he'd carried our burden with him.

"I prayed for you, too," I replied. "I'm calling to tell you about some amazing things we've learned—unusual things that have energized us. I can hardly wait to talk to you about it."

"I am happy to hear the lift in your voice, Julie—let's do talk. Do you want to come in this morning? I have time at ten."

I looked at the clock on the stove. "That gives me an hour. I'll be there." I packed a cloth bag with a few show-and-tell props, including my notes, Tate's metronome, and a sketch of the white vase, and dashed upstairs to take a shower.

Earlene seemed happy to hear where I was headed—that is, until she noticed the gorillas that I dropped into the bag on my way out. "You sure you want to tell your pastor about all that?" she asked.

"I'd like to hear what he thinks," I said. "And besides, I doubt it'll give him much of a shock." I pointed to a check near her purse and said, "Thanks, Earlene. If I'm not back before you have to leave, I'll see you next Wednesday."

Father Cuddy was standing in the hall with Betty, the church secretary, when I got there. "Betty just told me that my 11:00 appointment canceled," he said, smiling. "So now we have two whole hours to talk."

"Well, we all know that wouldn't be hard for me, don't we?" I said. "But especially not today, because I have so much to tell you." I followed him, barely a head taller than me, down the hall to his office. In his seventies, dressed in black pants and shirt, he still had the casual walk of a slim, slightly bowlegged cowboy.

The small office was crammed with mementos from his travels. Sunlight bathed his desk in rainbow colors from a high rose window, the only remnant of a chapel which had occupied that side of the rectory for its first sixty years, before the business of running a parish required more personnel and office space. An impressive rock, shell, and coin collection impinged on a small work area in the center of his desk, and several bookshelves overflowed. There was no room for a computer, had he wanted one.

"Do you ever give tours in here?" I asked. "I'd love to hear the story on some of these things."

"I could, but I'd rather hear about you," he said. "I'm glad to see you looking so well. What a heartbreaking thing you are going through."

"Well, time is helping," I assured him. "But there's a reason we feel an extra lift, Father. In addition to prayers and help from every direction, a woman has come from out of the blue, and she's told us amazing things. She's able to channel messages from the other side—from spirits of our loved ones."

"From spirits...," he said. "I have heard of people who can do that. Where did you say this woman came from?"

"We became acquainted with her through Annie two weeks ago, when she was in Annie's downtown salon getting a haircut. She lives here and may go to St. Joseph's; at least her daughter does. She asked Annie if she could share some information about her brothers—that's how we found out that she's a medium."

"Oh, so she implied that she had *current* information from them?" he asked without condescension, then surmised, "I think that's what you are about to tell me." He made an adjustment to his hearing aid, brown eyes smiling above black-rimmed glasses on the tip of his nose, and added, "I hope."

"Well, of course—that's mainly what I want to talk to you about, Father. It's the most astonishing experience I've ever had. And you may learn some things, too. It's been such an affirmation of life after death."

"Tell me about it," he said. He settled back in his chair and gave me a confessor-like nod. "Clearly something has given you some peace, and I am thankful for that, too."

After my uninterrupted run through the stories, using notes and props, he asked, "And you say you've never seen her before?"

I shook my head.

"Well, her accuracy with details is amazing, isn't it?" he said. "Each message full of love and hope, too. I find it substantiates Jesus' message about not fearing death, but to believe in the next life."

"I feel the same way. Things are clearer now, Father. This whole experience has moved me a few rungs higher in my ladder of searching."

"Your ladder?"

"Right; I have come to think we're climbers on a perpetual ladder throughout life, grasping onto various rungs, like beliefs, toward truth and God. Sometimes it feels safest with both hands tightly on side rails, each foot squarely in the middle of every rung, no matter how narrow. In fact, it may feel safer when rungs *are* narrow—less chance of misstep. But at other times we can loosen our grip, holding with only one hand to lean out to the very edge of a wide rung, or thought—to look beyond."

I was touched by his respectful listening, heartening me to continue.

"Most of the climb, which might even continue into our next life, is carefree, requiring little thought. But some rungs are so scary that we need to retreat to calmer ones. And maybe we can, for a while. Fear of new ideas can be paralyzing, but the exciting thing is being free to choose how we maneuver the climb. Even if we stay on a linear path all our lives, we can still explore laterally from time to time. Dedication to the process is the deal, don't you think? To not lose sight of the light at the top."

"I can agree," he said. It occurred to me then that priests must weary of people's needs to justify belief systems, but this gentle man gave no sign.

"I've been trying to read a difficult German book," he went on. "It uses a ladder as a metaphor. I bought it in Amsterdam last month. I'm finding it to be very negative." He explained that the writer used a ladder as a way of going in a direction away from God. I felt sure the book was written in German, too.

"I guess that happens," I said.

"I like thinking of a more positive analogy, though," he added.

"This rung I'm on now—about death—is the widest one yet," I said. "There's so much to think about. Not only how to survive the grief, but also to ponder the mysteries of the supernatural. It makes me shudder, but, at the same time, it's like dangling a foot out to touch a cloud. I may be on this one for years."

Our time was nearly over. He had seemed impressed with Olivia's many accurate details and glad it had been an uplifting experience for us. He didn't warn me of evil spirits or demons, like some others had, but I hadn't really expected him to. As we stood, he thanked me for sharing my experience and for allowing him to see how much it helped our healing process. I thanked him for listening. After a prayer, we hugged, causing his hearing aid to react with a squeal.

Near the outer door, Betty, along with Cathy, the youth director, stepped into the hall to express sympathy. That led to a discussion of how a congregation can best help someone deal with a family tragedy.

"Should we mention it," Betty asked, "even when you seem to be so grounded?"

"It's fine—it's all I *can* talk about," I said. "That and my amazement that we do seem to be surviving this horrible thing. Energy and grace come from every direction."

"You must be thinking about it every minute—no matter how peaceful you seem on the surface."

"It's like ashen coals," I said, "always flammable. Making an allowance for the constant crying has required one of the biggest adjustments. Grief has a real energy—it builds up pressure on oceans of tears. If it's not released regularly it can cause a tsunami, wiping you out for days." They nodded, eyes glistening.

"I can't think of anything that cuts the heart as deep as this," I said. "Diseases seem more like challenges now, with options, but it's hard to make it through this without losing all hope, and it's hard to know how to ask for help." The familiar pressure was rising, but I breathed it down and opened the rectory door. "I had a strange dream years ago, about a certain quality we need for sharing another's pain."

"What quality is it?" asked Cathy.

"*Knowing-kindness.* A person gifted with it can truly empathize and intuit the right way to help someone; but without it, despite a desire to help, it can stir up such shocking fear to witness the black hole of someone else's grief that even closest friends might need to back away. Make sense?"

"It does. We'll work on our *knowing-kindness*, won't we?" Betty said, an arm across Cathy's shoulder.

"Don't worry—y'all have it already," I said as I stepped onto the porch. "I'm meeting Annie for lunch while I'm downtown and choir rehearsal starts tonight—although I'm not sure I can make it." As soon as I closed my car door the dam burst.

It had been five years ago, during a hospital stay for cancer surgery, when I'd had that dream. In it, my girls and I, together with hordes of happy faces, mostly children's, were being propelled inches above a lush, endless green meadow of wildflowers.

When others ran to join us we could sense by looking at them whether they had some intuitive quality or not; then we floated on, with or without them. We paused at a house where Jim and two young men were repairing a high porch roof, unaware of our parade floating below. I guessed Jim, at least, would want to join us. But we could hear him griping to the others, who patted his arm good-naturedly, about his wife, who, he said, was *like most women*—exaggerating everything—and how glad he'd be when *she got through this stage.* Our girls assured me he just needed time to recover from something, and they shoved me along. It was a nightmare. I awoke in tears, feeling so alone, certain that it predicted some terrible thing in our future. My eyes teared up whenever I spoke of it, and I could never attach a name to that special quality—as with most dreams, our conversations had been purely subliminal.

That winter I went with friends Trisha Barfield and Beth McKinnon for a weekend at Beth's cabin in Highlands, North Carolina. I was midway in the six-month chemo treatment and facing another scary biopsy, which turned out negative. Beth was in midst of a divorce and had driven from her temporary home in the New York ashram to move some things into storage in Atlanta. We marveled at how we always received enough support to survive life's traumas. It was when I told them about my disturbing dream that I could finally recall the name of that quality: it was *knowing-kindness*.

On my drive to practice that evening, I pondered the hard aspects of returning to what had been such a joy as singing with a choral group, which I'd done all through school, even in college. The comfort of a lifetime of memories notwithstanding, I wasn't sure I could endure hymns that spoke so tenderly of our tie with God, or resist being overcome by the group's sympathy, or even more so by watching altar boys serve Mass on the altar below. It could cause a general meltdown.

I'd seen parishioners return to Mass after the deaths of loved ones, or after their own close calls, or even public scandals, but a most wrenching sight was the family making its way back, minus the child who had sat in the pew beside them. Now, by remaining in our choir, I might be just as sad a distraction. But I could at least go and thank friends for their extraordinary gift of performing at the funeral.

When I joined them, the group treated me normally, as they do anyone recovering from trauma. I was fine until a friend from Taylor's folk-music group told me about a memorial they planned for him at next Sunday's evening Mass. We cried together as she spoke of how they missed him, his talent and humor. It would take strong hearts, but I knew we would be there.

After rehearsal I felt at peace with my decision to continue with the choir. I would count on Nelda, our director, and these friends, with their keen sense of *knowing-kindness*, to overlook my fragile attention span and guide me back to the central joy of choral singing. Church choir members everywhere know the benefits of the adage: he who sings prays twice. I enjoyed the choir connection for ten more years.

Our wedding day, June 6, 1964.

Our young family at Mexico Beach, Florida, 1982.

Tate and Brax on the beach in Charleston, South Carolina, 1984.

Tate and Papa (Ernest Bragg) on the swing, October 29, 1982.
(Tate's first birthday.)

Jim and Julie Bragg with children Anne, Susie, Brax, and Taylor, 1995.

Family portrait including our mothers, Peggie Wallace and Richie Bragg, and grandchildren, Julianna and Rob Slocumb, 1995.

Tate and Brax playing chess in the pool house, Mother's Day, 1999.
A month before their road trip, this was the last time most of the
family ever saw them. *(Courtesy Margaret Wallace)*

Brax and Tate preparing to leave Los Angeles, July 2, 1999. This is the
last photo taken of them as they left Jim Morris' apartment, bound for
New Orleans, then home to Macon. *(Courtesy Jim Morris)*

This vase appeared on our piano within the hour after the sheriff and chaplain, who brought us the tragic news at 4:30 p.m. on July 3, 1999, had gone. A dozen family and friends were gathered for my 6:14 p.m. phone call with the Texas Trooper who had worked the accident scene, when the white vase seemed to glow. No one had brought the vase.

Plaque by the pool to commemorate the mass said by Fr. Tim McKeown, July 10, 1999 (also the birthday of Ernest, Jim's dad). The image of the plaque was used on the first Bragg Jam t-shirt. The verse was printed on funeral thank-you notes. *Courtesy Jim Messer*

"The Monkeys," a stocking-stuffer to Brax in 1997, were brought back home to us on August 14, 1999 by Mick Allen after cleaning out Brax's apartment. The following Monday, Olivia *channeled* Brax and Tate, "Tell Mama—go look at the monkeys!" They then called these gorillas (your) Gigolo Monkeys.

Cemetery plaque dedicated October, 1999.

Brax's leather jacket, a gift to him from Colleen Kelsall in 1996, was lost from June 1999 though September 2002.

Rock labyrinth laid on July 4, 2000, for a sacred garden.

Labyrinth painting by Claudia Hartley, 2008.

Ms. Julie with granddaughter Taylor, 2008,
on Taylor's second birthday.

Our home.

Granddaughter, Taylor (age 7) and great-grandson, Logan (age 2) at
the Ocmulgee Heritage Trail memorial overlook, 2012.

Julie with great-great-grandmother Elizabeth's antique lapboard.

14.

❧

Cereal-Eating Contest

Brax's Australian friend, Mick Allen, called the next morning, wanting to bring pictures from his recent trip in the Outback, which is where he had been on July 3rd. He said he had an urging to contact his mates in Macon around that time, but ten days passed before he could finally reach Russell, who, like Brax, was also a renter in his rambling house. He said his next two weeks, while he traveled on the bottom of the globe, were cold and wretched. It was nearly a month after the funeral when we wept together at our back door. Soon afterward, he made it his job to pack up Brax's things from the downstairs apartment and bring them home. He was here when we decided on the spot for the monkeys, two days before Olivia's first visit. He and I talked about the visit later in the week.

Susie and I were chatting with Dot Brown and her son, Stephen, in our den when Mick's vintage VW van pulled up. We were soon engrossed in his photos and uproarious tales of adventure. He spoke of dark storms and raging rivers, and we told him about own impressive storms—on the funeral night and on the day the freight line delivered the boys' belongings from Texas.

"And don't forget about that beach storm," said Susie, "when we had to eat by candlelight."

"*Those* pink candles!" we said in unison.

"No wonder my episode on our back deck fell so flat," I said, "it was *that* night they wanted us to remember, wasn't it?"

"At least now we know to be patient," said Susie. "Clues will clear up and it'll be worth it." She explained how that clue had confused us for all these days.

"It didn't make any sense," I said, "until just this minute."

We walked into the dining room, where piles of photographs still covered the oval table. Mick touched one of Brax toasting someone with a tall glass of beer, looking exuberantly alive and happy. "Look at this, Julie," he said. "The lady mentioned a photo of a bloke with a blue tie, toasting his mates—well, here's ol' Brax, raising his glass high. His leather jacket blocks most of it, but see how the shirt's blue design passes for a tie?"

"She said we'd see a picture like this," I said excitedly as I passed it to Dot. "Merrie Potts gave us this picture at Bragg Jam."

"So like him," she said. "And that does look like a blue tie."

Mick lingered a while after the Browns left.

"Would it be okay if I go to the memorial on Sunday evening?" he asked. "I'd like to pray for my mates in a church—maybe it will help."

"Of course," I said, "we'll support each other."

For me, it was an extra chance—who knew if there would be others—to honor the boys, especially our precious Tate. Jim went with me to the mall, a rare occasion in itself, to shop for a dress. We went in a nature store there, hoping to find figures of black gorillas. I'd already found out there were no more at the museum and the girls wanted their own. Luckily, we found some miniatures.

Shopping was getting easier than it had been in those earliest days, when grocery trips had been excruciating. Counting ears of corn or pork chops, once mindless activities, were fresh slices to my heart, only emphasizing an absence of plates at our table. On my first venture into a store I rushed out in tears, leaving groceries in the buggy. Friends escorted me after that, for *baby steps* through stores, where ambushes loomed in every aisle. Once, when Cile lost track of me at Publix, she found me slumped over my buggy in the toothpaste aisle, crushed because I no longer needed to buy Tate's favorite, Aqua Fresh. Department stores could present a warzone, too, with endless displays of masculine back-to-school clothes and racks of big running shoes. In addition, there were well-meaning swim students' families who popped up everywhere, surprised to see me with dry hair and street clothes. Anyone who wants to play the role of shopping-guard for a friend in the early stage of mourning must possess a strong amount of *knowing-kindness*—there will be crying.

On Sunday we went to six o'clock Mass as a family, hoping for strength in numbers. The folk group, comprised of about ten adults and teens, played and sang. A woman read her lovely poem about Taylor, the beautiful flower, gone from the garden too soon. Father's sermon focused on the value of a life well lived, speaking of both brothers, especially of Taylor. Our hearts quaked but stayed intact. Mick wept for his friends—the service, with keyboards and guitars, gave him the funeral he had missed.

Kirby Griffin taped the memorial for us. He and Mick, like mature bookends to Brax's younger, mostly college-aged musician friends, were like magnetic poles balancing the group's energy. Mick, the partier, with guitars, beer, and burgers, could rev the group for an all-nighter while it took Kirby to remind them that *practice* makes music perfect. Brax, on his own for years, had talked about these friends with whom he spent great times, and we'd met a few of them, but our collective suffering made them part of our family now. Time would soon bring more changes cascading like dominoes through this group of carefree bachelors.

Later, as we thanked the musicians, Father Cuddy walked up. "For your collection," I said, slipping a pair of tiny gorillas into his hand. "I hope they'll remind you of the boys." He gave me a hug and put them in his cassock pocket. There would never be another more beloved or humble priest than John Cuddy. He received the honor of being named a monsignor the year before he retired in 2004, after sixty years in the priesthood. When he passed away thirteen years later, he was 88 years old.

I thought a lot about the little time-box Olivia mentioned when she held Tate's metronome that first night. I had no idea who was living in the house I grew up in, but one day I decided to stop by there. Our playhouse was still standing but no one was home. The camellia bush Mama gave Daddy the year after my baby sister, Margaret, was born on his birthday was as tall as the house. Showy red flowers always lit up the shrub like a Christmas tree for their New Year's Eve birthday. A gray mockingbird hopped along with me, from tree to tree, tweeting his repertoire of various birdcalls—it felt like being in the yard with my dad, whose whistling sounded so like a bird's warbling. The bird stayed close as I headed down the short alley toward the street behind us, past our garage, where Daddy and I built a lean-to for Stardust, the old white horse I loved when my friends and I were horse-crazy teens. Before the horse, there had been a series of chickens, rabbits, ducks, and goats. Our short street of fourteen homes had over forty kids. We skated, biked, and paraded together; there were always players for croquet, badminton, and hide-and-seek until dusk, when adult voices began the roll call for supper. Our dad was the only one with a piercing whistle, though. Our adults had cookouts, bridge parties, and they sang together. I loved falling asleep on open-windowed summer nights hearing banjoes and happy voices in our front yard.

Mary and Dave Ennis, the only neighbors still around, happened to be in their yard at the end of the alley, and it was delightful to reminisce with them. They would soon make a point, they said, to meet the young couple living in our house.

Having been reminded to search for my time-box, probably in rusty ruins by now, helped me rediscover my real cornerstone—and I hadn't needed a chainsaw for that!

Taylor's class began their senior year at Mount de Sales with an article about him in the school paper, written by friends who found it hard to begin it without him. I heard that the school chorus sang Clapton's "Tears in Heaven" at the first PTA meeting, which, after twenty-eight years, I no longer had reason to attend.

His closest buddies tried to carry on our home's open-door policy, which included having full access to our fridge, sometimes late at night. On a weeknight, shortly before Susie moved in, Michael Stramiello had called to ask if some guys could come visit us in the poolhouse the next night and have, of all things, a cereal-eating contest.

"Of course!" I said, doubting the seriousness of the cereal. But next night five carloads of boys pulled into our driveway. They hauled ice chests of milk jugs, boxes of Frosted Flakes, and disposable bowls into the poolhouse, where Jim, Anna, Rob, and I sat with them in a big circle of chairs, catching up on school news and sharing memories. When we ran out of things to talk about, Jim shook hands all around and headed up to the house, and I began to wonder if the contest had been an endearing ploy to camouflage young grief.

But interest was revived and Anna, Rob, and I were recruited as score-keepers. We provided spoons, portion control, and a swim school t-shirt, since they'd forgotten to factor in a winner's prize. Contestants sat at three round glass-top tables, bowls were filled and refilled until groaning replaced laughter, and one by one the boys flopped on the lawn behind the pool-house, holding their bellies. Michael, the gorger of eleven bowls of soggy Frosted Flakes, won the t-shirt.

It was a school night with homework for Anna and Rob, so we left these young men—who would become scientists, lawyers, teachers, and fathers—to digest their latest test of manhood. They turned up the outside stereo speakers and sat around the pool for another hour, none seeming to feel like swimming.

In bed, hearing achingly familiar sounds, as though time had been re-wound, I was sad to hear the cars drive away. Young lives, marked by a trag-edy, the first for most of them, had charmingly shown *knowing-kindness* by bringing this light-hearted evening to us.

15.

❧

Lady Named "Doll"

Labor Day weekend, the first Friday in September, marked the end of summer and our second month of warped, depressing time. Jim and I, slowly emerging from shock, were settling into a pattern of avoidance when it came to speaking of our misery. A child's death can disturb a marriage that way, as parents become the walking wounded, unwilling to excoriate another's injury by seeking sympathy. If I grumbled about wanting to sell the place and move away, he, instead of exposing his own sadness, questioned my loyalty in running from reality and memories. I doubt if he realized how his blue eyes, guarded by moats of unshed tears, betrayed his stoic facade.

I couldn't remind him of memories around our place that were torturing me—he had his own—but for me, a whiff of mown grass brought the image of a boy bobbing on a mower, singing along with Radiohead, the last cassette tape in Tate's Walkman. I wondered if it saddened Jim to think of falling leaves as erasers of our sons' footsteps. My view from the kitchen sink needed to include Brax's dark curls as he lay on the sofa reading, and the aroma of sautéed onions triggered memories of guitar strains, drifting from our dining room, where Taylor practiced while I cooked supper. Sushi, his black Persian, lulled into pleasant dreams, used to doze on her back in the plush red lining of the guitar case at his feet. She pined for him, too, as she brushed back and forth against the scarred case leaning idly in the corner.

The inadequacy of language left Jim and me unable to talk to each other about the pain, nor did we cry together. As a mother, I was mourning for the role I lost as the woman in my sons' lives. I expected my ranking to be downgraded eventually, but I was looking forward to their futures. I think a father, in losing sons, the bearers of his family name, could feel that his own future is shattered. In the past week he had sold our pontoon boat, and before that, the four-wheeler, which Taylor loved to ride though our woods. Next would be his tractor, his fishing boat, and hunting rifles. He was back to driving the boys' old green truck, since his SUV was gone, and I couldn't ask how he endured it, nor could I say how my heart lurched whenever it came in our driveway. I prayed that his office staff realized how he needed privacy, but we didn't ask each other how to deal with those unexpected spasms, which feel like heart attacks, whenever we remember...

We developed ways of coping with the approach of nightfall. He would stop for a drink at his mom's on his way home, where it may have been safer to speak of the boys, the accident, and the losses, softening his home landing. My safety net was having long conversations with our girls or special friends, reinforcing our belief in a divine plan; but beneath all comforting ideologies lay a trapdoor into the dark.

During my most despondent moods I had the advantage of being able to wander around our rural property, away from neighbors, noticed only by our two dogs, and surrender to it. At night, while the others slept, Sculley would follow me out to our wailing wall—a cinder block retainer along the driveway at the far side of our garage—where he leaned his heavy black fur against my pajamas to lick my tears. I wondered if his pure spirit felt as far away from his mother as I did from my sons. The moon waxed and waned high behind giant trees, which morphed into skeletons as fall nights became cold wintry ones.

We realized the good fortune of having Susie and her children with us. Their routines required the structure of chores and meal planning, forced optimism and humor, and kept me from losing myself in loneliness and lack of purpose. Jim and I were jolted from TV one night by a rare but loud slamming from the kitchen. Susie was rummaging through cabinets, searching for another thing that had been misplaced by helpers who swarmed over the place during that sad week. "It would just be better if all *this* hadn't happened!" she roared. We had to laugh. From then on, *"You know what Susie would say"* brought levity to our moods.

On Monday, Labor Day, the Browns invited us to join them for a picnic at Lake Juliette, north of us on Highway 87. In the past, we had used this weekend as a last chance for a quick trip to the beach or for camping at one of Georgia's state parks. This year we had no plans, so when Dot said there would be only their family and a couple friends and that they were taking canoes, I found her invitation irresistible. Susie's children were at their dad's, and I couldn't convince her or Jim to join me, so I loaded a folding chair and small ice chest into the truck and went alone.

Once off the highway, I drove along a winding gravel road connecting shady shoreline campsites until I located their group: Dot, Phil, their two sons, daughter-in-law, and another couple with a little girl, her hair in blond ponytails. Dark green waves lapped at two canoes bumping into the red clay at the water's edge. Their picnic covered a concrete table under a pine tree. I walked up with my chair and cooler to the welcoming sight of this intact family, enjoying normal life. I was glad I had come.

When Dot introduced the other couple I recognized Richard Keil, a highly respected former priest who had come south decades ago to dedicate years of his life to working with the local African American community. In the early eighties he founded the Harriet Tubman Museum. The cute little girl was the granddaughter of his wife, Sandra.

The group took turns canoeing on the sunny lake. As it worked out, Richard and I were left together while the others were on the water. Having lived amid deprivation and sadness, he understood grief well. I'm sure there had been torment in needing to turn away from that life as well. Having to let go of early dreams in order to survive was a life lesson we shared. He was happy to point out that his present life was a generous counterbalance, and I offered that even in our worst days, there were spells of optimism that gave us hope that our lives might be restored to balance one day, too.

Mother called one morning a few days after that as I was about to go for a run. She had just opened her mail.

"I don't know why these people send me an invitation to their family reunions," she said. "I don't remember who they are; they must be from Bob's side. They started mailing these cards last year—surely they know he's been gone more than sixteen years."

"Whose name is on the card?" I reached under the sink for yellow rubber gloves to do breakfast dishes while we talked. "Maybe we should call and ask them to take your name off their list."

"That's a good idea," she said. "Let me look; it says the reunion is October 16."

I rinsed coffee cups and began loading the dishwasher.

"Here it is," she said, "*Rowell Family*. They've gotten so fancy, they even sent out email addresses this year."

"Well, that'll be easier—I can just send an email to one of the addresses. They'll understand. I wonder how we're related to them."

"It says they're descendants of Elizabeth Rowell. I think she was your daddy's distant cousin or something."

"I don't think so," I said. "Remember that stack of old pictures Uncle Vernon copied for nieces and nephews one Christmas? I helped him label them—I think she had higher rank that just a cousin."

"Whatever. Here's the email address: *D O L L,* a little encircled *a*, then *A O L...*"

"Oh, my gosh!" I interrupted her, looking around for something to write with as I peeled off the gloves. "DOLL! Olivia told us I was going to hear from a lady named *Doll*! What's her phone number—I think I'd rather just call her."

"Olivia told you *what*? This is her email, not her name."

"I know it sounds crazy, but we heard that a lady was going to contact me about a strange gift from a lady named Elizabeth. Is her number long distance?"

"No, she lives in Warner Robins and her name is Helen, not Doll. They have the reunions at a Camp Eunice in Roberta. What's this about a gift?"

"You're not going to want to hear this, Mom, but Olivia told us that a very old lady named Elizabeth was trying to get a strange wooden gift to me. She even described it, but I have no idea what she was talking about. She mentioned a smaller gift, too."

Mom had heard enough on this subject, so we chatted on about our plans for the day. She had, as usual, been to eight o'clock Mass, checking in with her cronies who met there each morning. Though she never said it, I'm sure they prayed for me, asking the Blessed Mother to continue sending me peace and strength. This other talk would only worry her, causing her to think I was toying with the ways of gypsies or worse. There was no point in bringing it up again.

I postponed my run and dialed the number. Helen Manning was genuinely pleased to hear from someone on our side of the big Rowell family and especially to learn that I was Annie Wellons Wallace's granddaughter.

"Can you give me a brief rundown of our connection?" I asked.

"Sure," she said. "Elizabeth Rowell, born in 1816, married William Shelley Wellons. They were parents to Edward Shelley Wellons, who was father to your grandmother, Annie. That makes Elizabeth Rowell your great-great-grandmother!"

I was speechless. Here was my *Elizabeth* who has loved me for over 100 years.

"I hope you can come to the reunion next month," she went on. I explained that I doubted if any of us would be there this time due to our recent tragedy, which she had been saddened to read about in the paper, even with no idea of our connection.

"We're still in such a state of mourning," I said, "that I can't face meeting all those people and having to explain our situation."

"I completely understand," she said, "but we'd love to have you. Last year there was such a nice surprise for everybody. Bill and Nell Chapman, from Missouri, shared a book of letters they had published. Our reunions would never have gotten back on track without the Chapmans. Once he began his family ancestry work, Nell went right along beside him. We lost dear Bill in March."

"I'm sorry to hear that. Whose letters were they?"

"The title is *Annie's Trove*," she said. "They were written by Annie Wellons and her father, Shelley, while she was at college in LaGrange, Georgia, during the late 1800s. Gracious, that would be your grandmother's letters—there are even some from her husband-to-be from Charleston, John Vernon Wallace."

"A book of my grandmother's letters!" I exclaimed, "Oh, I'd love to see that."

"Well, you ought to have a copy, for sure," she said. "I'll email Nell and ask her to send you one as a little gift."

"By the way," I said. "I love your email address—where's it from?"

"I've been a doll collector forever," she said. "Guess what Nell's email handle is."

"Tell me," I said.

"Stone cypher—from searching tombstones and cemetery records. Perfect, isn't it?"

"Really!" I said.

"Wait, I just remembered," she said. "There's another thing that was your grandmother's, which you may not want but you ought to at least see."

"What is that?"

"Well, let me see if I can describe it. Bill brought *it* to the reunion last year, too. Somebody in Atlanta passed it on to him during his genealogy work with the Wellons side; they brought it here in their motor home. It's a bulky kind of wooden thing…"

"Would you say it's hand-hewn?" I interrupted, "the grain of a log exposed?"

"Oh, you've already seen it?"

"Well, no, but I've heard about it."

"How in the world did you hear about that?" she asked.

"Well," I said, chuckling, "I'm just going to risk that you aren't afraid of this kind of thing when I tell you, Helen, but a lady who is a medium told me about it a couple of weeks ago." I had decided to avoid the term *psychic*—it usually conveyed a disrespectful image, very unlike the one we had from our own experience with Olivia.

"A lady who's *what?*"

"A person who can intuit messages from spirits on the other side—you know, from people who've passed away," I said.

"Oh," she said, "You mean like a psychic. I've always wondered how it would be to go to one," she admitted, "but the opportunity just never presented itself."

I described the sensitive way Olivia had channeled Elizabeth's words a couple weeks ago. "But I had no idea who Elizabeth was," I said, "only that she was well over a hundred years old and knew my sorrow more than most. I was told to wait for a message from a lady named Doll, too—can you believe that?"

"I'm not doubting a thing you've said—it must have meant so much to you."

"It's been an amazing comfort," I said. "I wish more people could have questions about death answered the way we have."

"Is it okay if I tell Nell about this?" she asked. "We're counting on her coming next month. I wish you were, too, so you could meet."

"Sure, and who knows, I may end up coming," I said. "I'm getting real curious about the wooden thing—what would you say it is?"

"Why, it was your grandmother's writing desk," she said. "More a lap-board, really. It used to have some way of coming down over the shoulders, I think—like a tray. Last I heard, Bill left it with the Crawford County library for a genealogy display. Elizabeth's father had it made for her as a child, by a slave. She's the person we all descend from, you know. She passed it down to her first granddaughter."

"I'd like to learn more about her," I said.

"She had a real sad life," Helen said. "Her two sons died young—one as a toddler and the other one was killed in the War Between the States. He was 28 when he was killed at the Battle of Seven Pines. He was a teacher before the war. She was a widow, living on what little he sent her."

She understands your sorrow more than most. As only she could, I thought.

My head was spinning. There was no doubt that my ancestors were aware of me now that my sons had entered their celestial world, nor that their love connected me with gifts to distract me from my sorrow, with which my long-deceased great-great-grandmother was all too familiar. My eyes filled with tears. "I guess I better get my run in before it gets so hot," I said. "I was headed out when Mother called about the invite."

"Well, I know I don't get enough exercise," she admitted, "but this body of mine is way past being in shape to run."

"I hope we have a chance to meet," I said, "I've loved talking to you, Helen, and I learned a lot."

Running could wait—I had to call Olivia. I knew she'd like feedback on this mystery. Once she heard my voice on her answering machine, she picked up.

"Olivia, the coolest thing just happened! There *is* a lady named Doll—I just talked to her." It took a minute for her to unscramble the cast of characters that had traveled through her brain recently.

"Oh, so you did know someone named Doll, after all."

"Not exactly—that's a woman's email address," I replied. "Can you believe it? And the century-old Elizabeth was my great-great-grandmother." I told her about the reunion, the book, and the wooden gift. "She said some-one will send me the book of my grandmother's letters, but I'm not too optimistic about the wooden thing."

"Your energy sounds so high, Julie," she said. "It does me good to know that it all meant something. I can see purple and gold all around you—wisdom and vitality."

"Really? Like an aura?" Then I looked down at my running clothes and laughed. Purple shorts and halter and a gold tank top.

16.

⊷

Either Way, We Win

Concern for cousin Sue Burch mounted as lab results—positive in the most negative sense—came back. Breast cancer, dismissed long ago, had been running a stealth course through her body. Chemotherapy, thought unnecessary thirteen years before, was being offered as a token for buying time. The prognosis held precious little hope—it was devastating.

Friends, clients, and Atlanta neighbors surrounded her and Jack. They kept their plan to go with their grown sons, Jake and Andy, to visit Jack's sister Bev's family at their Northern California beach house in mid-September. Sue would begin her chemo in Atlanta a week later.

As a child of the fifties, I often rode the Nancy Hanks to Atlanta to visit my Burch relatives. The passenger train, named for a racehorse whose namesake had been Abe Lincoln's wife, made a daily run from Savannah to Atlanta and back, stopping briefly in Macon. During my visits I was awakened by raucous blue jays flocking in tall pines around the Burch home on East Wesley Road. I wrote to Aunt Beverly, my father's middle sister, in her last birthday card, that I loved the blue-jay call because it reminded me of her house and my first trips without my parents. At her funeral in 1997, I told her daughter, Bev, that the blue jay would always be my Burch Bird, though they rarely visited our yard.

The next winter we got our first computer and my joy of letter writing went on overdrive. Our far-flung families could connect with a click of the *send* button. Bev and I renewed our kinship with emails. She wrote of sitting on her Oakland patio, honoring her mother's birthday, rereading years of their letters, when a big scrub jay dropped onto the arm of a chair beside her and watched as she read.

Aunt Beverly had adored her spunky daughter-in-law, Sue. During our long phone conversation a few weeks ago, my gaze often settled on a nearby lampshade finial—a bisque blue jay—which I'd bought because it reminded me of my aunt. After that, I sent one to Sue to remind her that many angels watched over her. She said it was in their mailbox on their return from California, where they saw many jays, and that Jack had already attached it to their bedroom floor lamp for her to see while she recuperated. She went for her first treatment on Wednesday, September 22nd, and boated with friends on nearby Lake Lanier that Saturday. When I talked to Jack's secretary early Monday morning, she said she was waiting for Jack's report and would keep me posted with any news.

Late Monday afternoon, September 27, we joined a group for the exciting groundbreaking of Ocmulgee Heritage Greenway. Under a canopy of colorful umbrellas bumping together along the muddy riverbank, we applauded Chris Sheridan, who represented the civic leaders who had dedicated years to get to this point. He mentioned their heartfelt connection with the newly formed Bragg Jam group.

We were stunned that evening to hear from Jack's secretary that Sue was in ICU, in unrelenting abdominal pain from septic shock. When I reached poor Jack, who was so perplexed that nothing relieved her pain, but still clinging to hope, he said things had gone too fast for him to make calls. I told him I'd call Bev for him and be there next morning. At midnight their neighbor called with the terrible news that Sue had died.

Next morning, as I packed to leave, a flock of boisterous jays gathered around our house, their racket impossible to ignore. The sound doubled when I opened a bedroom window, and when I called Jim at work he heard them, too. As soon as we hung up, my cousin John Lert, who had also come for the Macon concert in late July, called. He and his brother had grown up near the Burches, their mothers being sisters; he said they'd arrive in Atlanta by evening.

"I just talked to Jack," John said. "He wants to know when you're coming."

"I'll give him a call," I said. "Are you able to hear those loud blue jays?"

"Yes—you must be outside."

"No, flocks of them are circling our house, clattering like that for the last thirty minutes. We hardly ever hear them around here, but there were so many at Aunt Beverly's that I always called them the Burch Birds—it's probably no coincidence."

"Well, call Jack," he said. "Maybe it'll cheer him up."

The grating birdcalls did seem to lighten the mood when Jack and I talked. We imagined what it must be like for Sue—greeted by so many loved ones; and then we noticed the quiet. "I'll be there in a few hours, Jack," I said. "I'm heartbroken."

"I still can't believe it," he said. "By the way, tell Susie she's right."

"About what?"

"That it would be better if all *this* hadn't happened," he said dryly. "She sure is right about that."

My sister, Margaret, and I stayed in a neighbor's guest cottage for a couple nights, and the rest of our family joined us in Atlanta for Sue's funeral. Bev, Jack's sister, planned an extended visit to help him and his sons begin the long process of adjusting to the sudden shock of life without Sue.

The night after her funeral Jack invited us to select something from Sue's jewelry boxes, which she kept in their dressing room upstairs. As Margaret and I dug through an amazing collection of earrings, I gave up expecting to find Aunt Beverly's antique diamond studs among all those hoops, parrots, flowers, cats, palm trees, straw hats, elephants, and pearls. I'd let my imagination run wild to think Sue had implied that her mother-in-law's intended *comfort gift* for me was her diamond earrings.

Jack met me in the hall. "Did you find something you wanted in there?" he asked.

"Well," I said, "Sue wrote last month that she had come across something of your mom's that she wanted to bring me as a comfort gift. It was very sweet but mysterious—she said she could almost hear your mom speak to her. My first guess was crazy, but I wondered if it might've been a pair of your mom's earrings. Sue said it was small and she wanted to deliver it, so I guessed it was valuable."

"Sue had a hundred earrings—you didn't see any you wanted?"

"Not really, but I found this Victorian rose-gold cross in a little side box—I'd much rather have it. I remember seeing it on Grandmother Annie's lapel—probably mourning jewelry, from when Grandfather died. Your mom probably passed it to Sue."

"Sure. But I wish I knew what she was thinking of," Jack said, entering their bedroom. He poked around the dresser top, mantel, and shelves for a little box or a note from her. "She never mentioned it to me—maybe it *was* this cross."

"Well it sure is fitting—I'll always see it that way," I said, as we hugged. "But enough of this. There's a houseful of folks downstairs and you look like you're asleep on your feet. Last thing I need is another pair of earrings—these I have on are the only ones I ever wear anyway." He was on his way to the stairs when I felt the chills on my arms. Why had I not thought of it before? These gold earrings that I got at Sam's that day, at near the exact time my sons left this world—my aunt was right! These *were* meant to be a gift—but not from her. Some part of myself must have felt it when I said to Susie and the clerk that I'll think of them as a traveler's gift from my sons. Every time I wear them I'm reminded of the boys and of how nice the world was before we knew.

Sue's funeral, so soon after our boys', had an unexpected effect on me. She was in the world of energy and wisdom that my children and lost loved ones inhabited, and I thought of her as the lucky one. Within just fifty-two days of one another, we had each received our life sentences, and now, in barely a month, her suffering had passed. I imagined her tall, thin frame, her radiant face, listening, ever the therapist, to my grudging congratulations on her getting there before me. She'd smile, I know she would, and jab my shoulder, and then she'd whisper, "Julie, honey, we're feeling a little jealous, aren't we? Don't worry, you'll be here soon enough—and I guarantee it'll be worth waiting for. Don't forget what we used to say, 'Either way, we win!'"

17.

❧

Hauling Rocks

I returned to my world on Friday, the first of October, Taylor's birthday month, where the air had become heavier with melancholy. Fall was covering every trace of our sons with a patchwork of leaves—velvety yellow plate-sized mulberry and crisp multicolored varieties—along with sweet-gum balls, acorns, and twigs. Even decaying grass clippings, the last to ever be piled by their hands at the edge of our woods, tore at my heart. Anything they had touched became fragile shrines, and I was obsessed with wanting some kind of permanent memorial at home. For weeks, on my daily run, I had passed tons of granite rocks recently blasted to the surface for a new waterline on our rural street. Being a lifelong rock fanatic, I rejoiced at this convenient bonanza and began parking an empty wheelbarrow at the start of a run so that, on my return, I could push a heavy load of rocks over the 500 feet back to our yard. I had no plan for using them yet; but *hauling rocks* was the perfect metaphor for my dreary mood. Before long, a mound the size of a Volkswagen was piled around gnarled roots of an ancient oak tree.

Every October our public schools are given a holiday—primarily as a day for teachers to confer with parents, or in our case, grandparents. Anna, Rob, and I were headed for our teachers' conferences one morning when we were surprised to discover noisy land-moving equipment at my rock mine across the street. A long yellow dinosaur neck moved clumsily over the steep right-of-way, scooping up rocks as big as refrigerators in its jaws and dropping them like potatoes into the bed of a giant yellow dump truck. I had dreamed of being able to move some of these boulders.

I stopped my car in the middle of the road and rushed over to the startled driver, who paused his machine in midair. "Will you still be working here in about an hour?" I yelled through the megaphone of my cupped hands.

He smiled, removed his backwards, yellow baseball cap, which read "Caterpillar," and nodded tentatively.

"When we get back," I shouted, "could you possibly move a few of these really big rocks over to my yard? We won't be gone very long."

"Where's your yard?" he yelled back.

"Oh, just back there." I said, and pointed behind me to our driveway.

"Sure, that won't take us but a minute."

"Wonderful!" I said. "And there's one other place I'd like to put some, too—to surprise my neighbors."

"Surprise your neighbors?" He powered down his engine, letting its big bucket rest halfway up the red clay slope into the woods above. I hoped he wasn't rethinking his generosity.

"I want to repay them for their kindness to our family," I explained. "They just live across the highway there..." I pointed vaguely toward the Browns' house. "I've imagined how fine a sculpture these rocks could make—I have their permission."

By now the dump truck driver leaned out of his window, waiting for us to conclude our chat, which was drowned out by the roar of idling motors. As soon as I explained why I wanted to create such a memorial in both yards, the first driver's pleasant face softened. He removed his yellow cap again to wave it at the pickup.

"We understand," he said, nodding his head in that direction. "That's my brother. We lost our brother last year—it nearly killed our mom." He signed a thumbs-up to his brother and lifted the head of his yellow monster. "We'll be here til afternoon and happy to oblige," he said. "In fact, we might take a nice one with us for Mom's yard."

An hour later, the kids and I followed his huge backhoe across Riverside Drive and watched from my car as the men carefully positioned three bathtub-size granite rocks into a bench-like sculpture beneath longleaf pines at the edge of the Browns' yard. Bronze needles and golden leaves fluttered around it as the giant toy plodded its way back across the highway. The brothers then arranged three oval shaped boulders under an old cedar tree in our yard, too.

"That's an impressive collection there," one of them said, admiring my big pile of hefty rocks. "You did all that with a wheelbarrow? Want us to drop a couple loads on it."

"No, thanks," I said. "There's something about hauling them that actually serves me these days—but I may have just about enough now. I still haven't figured out what I'm going to do with them, anyway."

18.

⤳

Pisces on the High Seas

For the past eight years I had made fall visits to my childhood friend Gina Hersh's home in Annandale, Virginia, close to DC. Our tradition began when she dropped her son, Cass, off at Auburn, drove on to Macon to her mother's, and then talked me into riding home with her. We managed to turn a normal ten-hour drive into a two-day excursion by stopping whenever we felt like it—outlet centers, antique shops, apple stands—like liberated women. We even detoured west toward Gatlinburg just so we could eat at a place where she and Dave had eaten on their honeymoon twenty-one years earlier. It wasn't until our first motel stop that I noticed that I'd forgotten my suitcase. When I phoned the boys to ask them to put it on a Greyhound Bus the next morning, I asked them not to tell their dad. After ten days I rode home in a tiny overnight Amtrak sleeper, so pleased with my first solo getaway; but I could hardly wait to see Jim at the Peachtree Station in Atlanta and plan Tate's tenth birthday.

He rode with us two years later to have Thanksgiving with the Hershes and their two sons. Brax unexpectedly worked it out to join us and drove up in the truck. He took Tate sightseeing, including to the new Holocaust Museum, and thus they began their road-trip tradition on the ride home together. They were 22 and 12.

In 1995, round-trip tickets to Gina's were my early Christmas gifts for Anna (10), Rob (7), and Tate (14). It was the younger kids' first flight. They learned to maneuver airports, the metro, tour-mobiles, and the Smithsonian. Dave, a former Navy pilot, gave us a hands-on tour of the Air and Space Museum. The entire experience is one of my favorite memories. Taylor took his guitar, and I saw in Gina's kitchen how much my talented son loved playing for an audience.

Those trips were perfect transitions from hectic summers, but I couldn't bear to leave home again after just returning from Sue's funeral, so Gina planned to come to her mother's the first Wednesday in October. She coordinated with our friend Beth in New York, whose plane would land in Atlanta three hours after hers. That gave Gina and me time to drive out to Buckhead for lunch with my cousin Bev before she wrapped up her visit at Jack's. He was back at his law practice and his sons were hardly ever home, so her sisterly duty had run its course and she needed to get home to her family and neglected family-therapy practice in Oakland.

An unusual thing happened before I left to meet Gina's plane that morning. Susie had a vacation day to transfer some things from the pool-house up to Brax's room so as to leave the poolhouse ready for Beth—she no longer had family in Macon. Otherwise, the house was ready for company because Earlene had come a day earlier than usual. An hour before leaving, I was headed toward the shower when the phone rang.

It was Olivia, seeming troubled. She said her daughter, hostess at a sports grill, had been upset last night by snarky remarks from a fellow who had been a pal of Brax's. He had heard his friends talk about having met Olivia at our house when Brax's steady girl, Christina Cellie, his muse during their Mercer years, had been in town visiting her relatives. Russell Walker also had a reading while she was here and had been amazed that Olivia mentioned "steam-roller music," which he and Brax called the music they wrote together. The fellow's diatribes were aimed at Olivia and that gathering here. She was right to call.

"I wouldn't take this too seriously," I said, "everybody knows how he is—probably just jealous; but I think there's a big heart under his brashness. I'm sorry, though, knowing it hurt your daughter—or you."

"Well, she was more mad than hurt," she said. "She may be too protective of me, but she respects what I do, and I know you do, too."

"More than I can say."

"But I'm convinced it ticked Brax off, too," she said, chuckling.

"How do you mean?"

"Because I can hear him repeating, 'The mutt, the mutt,'" she said. "I think he's calling this young man a *mutt*."

"That doesn't sound right," I said. "His insults weren't that tame." We laughed.

"Well, that's what it seems like he's saying—only odd, more like moyt—*the moyt, the moyt.*"

"Still, I don't get it," I said. "Lord, the time!" I exclaimed, seeing the red digits on the vanity clock. "I'm supposed to be getting ready to meet friends at the airport—one from Virginia and another from New York. I'll think about this, though. There's no reason for anybody to slander our friendship—he probably just had too much to drink."

"Well, it's over with," she said. "I thought you should know, though—mother to mother. Enjoy your drive and have a wonderful time with your friends. We'll just leave this business of the *mutt* to Brax."

I walked down the hall to his old room. I so missed him. With Susie's laptop and little TV, the room had a new look. On his dresser was a small black book with shiny gold *Pisces* embossed on its cover. Though I knew he preferred spiral notebooks to trendy journals like this, I had given this one to him, my March-born dreamer. He used it once, several years ago, on a boat trip with his Aussie friend, Mick.

Brax had still been an undergrad at Mercer, living in a tiny upstairs apartment on College Street, when they cooked up that plan for an Atlantic voyage from West Palm Beach to the Bahamas. It required a five-hour cruise for a large ship, but they expected to make good time in Mick's boat. The idea scared me, but Brax convinced us that this older friend, whom we had yet to meet, was an accomplished seaman, and although no one described it to me, I assumed his boat was at least a cabin cruiser stored somewhere in South Florida. I insisted on being at Brax's apartment so I could meet this friend. Despite their efforts to assure me that folks made the trip every day in boats like Mick's, I had strong reservations as they drove merrily away.

It turned out that Mick's boat was an 18-foot fishing boat. Motor problems sent them back to shore on their first day out, and they also got stranded the second day—only this time they were about twenty miles out in the Atlantic. Huge cruise ships traversed choppy water where Mick bobbed in a life jacket, a spark plug clinched in his teeth, behind his little boat, working on its outboard motor.

That cruise was the only subject of Brax's scribbling in his black Pisces journal. He filled two pages while he waited out those hours, *within sight of the Grand Bahama Island, in stunning cobalt water, the perfect blue, for my Captain to repair our vessel. Meanwhile, we're drifting off to sea on the Gulf Stream. Panic has yet to set in.* Further in the book was Mick's typically cheerful poem, after rejoicing at the sight of food. I would reread all that one day.

I had lathered my hair, thinking sadly about how Brax didn't get to hear his song about a *Pisces on the high seas*, sung so sweetly by his friends at the memorial concert, when Susie came to my shower door with the phone.

"It's Mick," she said. "He needs to talk to you before you leave." I shut off the water, extended a dripping arm to the towel rack, and took the receiver.

"Hello, Mick," I said. "I was just thinking about the first time I met you, when you and Brax went on that ocean cruise."

"G'day, Julie," he said. "Yes, that was quite a lark. Look, I apologize for intruding, but I felt I had to have a quick word—it's about Brax's leather jacket."

"Oh, great! You found it?"

"No, Julie. That's why I'm calling. I feel so bad about the jacket, and I am not satisfied that you're convinced it's not still here someplace. I just wanted to assure you it's not. I've looked everywhere, and I know it's logical that it be somewhere in this house—but I promise it's not."

I had sent an email to all their friends with a plea for news of the jacket, which Jim really wanted. Mick had already told us, early on, that he hadn't seen it when he emptied Brax's apartment.

"Mick, I know it's not there; I should have excluded you in that last group email. But isn't it a mystery? Nobody has a clue."

"Well, that's all I wanted to tell you," he said. "I just didn't want any doubt remaining that it might be here."

"Thanks, Mick, but there's no doubt. It'll turn up somewhere. Are you still remodeling the house?"

"Yes, we are planning to get going with some work on the roof," he said, "as soon as my helper shows up."

It had been several years since Mick bought his old white house with red tin-shingled roof in Macon's historic Vineville district. It needed painting and all manner of remodeling in order to update its five apartments, including one over the garage. Russell, whose apartment was above Brax's, was miserable with grief and would soon be moving to escape the depressing loneliness.

Mick mentioned that his helper, the same fellow who was bashing Olivia the night before, was running late. I didn't have time or reason to mention the coincidence. "I better get going, too," I said. "I'm off to meet friends at the airport. Thanks, again, for calling me, and please be careful on that roof, Mick!"

"Susie told me about your visitors—goodonya', sweetheart."

I turned the water back on, thinking about Brax's and Mick's friendship, and smiled, remembering Brax's exaggerated Aussie accent whenever he referred to his friend, his mate—his *moyt*.

I had to resist the urge, while I threw on clothes, to call Olivia and explain that it wasn't mutt she heard, but *mate*, but I felt like I had to call Mick. I dialed the number, previously Brax's, relieved for Mick's instant pick-up; he hadn't wanted to replace Brax's outgoing message, and I was glad to avoid the sadness of hearing it. I rushed through the gist of Olivia's call while I applied makeup.

"Brax was talking about *you*, Mick—he wouldn't refer to anybody else as the mate. Maybe it's a warning of some kind—maybe you shouldn't be on that roof today. Is your helper there yet?"

"No, he's not," he said. "I was just ready to give him a call."

"Be sure he's got insurance," I said, as soon as it popped into mind. "If not, there's a liability risk, you know—maybe that could be the warning."

"I understand," he said, "completely."

"I'm just saying what's running through my head, Mick, but does it make sense that Brax may have wanted to pass on a warning in connection with his friend?"

"Actually, Julie, it does," he said quietly. "We've talked about liability and insurance. I actually advanced money for the bloke to buy a policy." I could hear a door close. "I plan to follow up on that, and some other things, too—I'd thought of it before."

"Well, don't worry," I said, chuckling. "Just don't assume from this that I'm trying to be a medium myself."

With no time to dry my hair, I yelled goodbye to Susie as I rushed through the kitchen and out the door. I phoned Olivia as soon as I was within the stream of interstate traffic. She felt better for having brought me into the unpleasant energy now that it might have had a purpose, and I felt new confidence from responding to intuition. Like most people, I usually confuse intuition with imagination, letting self-doubt cancel what might actually be valid, extrasensory perception. Mick told me later that Brax's reminder of their friendship touched him deeply, and he did postpone the roof work.

It was a fine day for an hour's drive, with steady, sane airport traffic. My mind drifted to Mick, his red-roofed house on Rogers Avenue, near Vineville, where one of my darling boys last lived, and a comic memory from his time there.

It went back to a time before Brax and Russell moved in, back to when Mick, broke from buying the old place, had needed a second mortgage to update apartments in order to generate sorely needed rental income. Clearly, a bank inspection of the shabby, near-vacant place could be a problem, so Mick recruited his mates for a little charade to enhance prospects of its already being a viable revenue-generator.

Before his lovely next-door neighbor, a well-known interior designer, left town for the weekend, she handed Mick her house key, offering to loan whatever props he needed for the staging. For the next few hours, he and his five mates hauled all manner of her fine furniture, paintings, and rugs across the shared driveway and set up models of full rentals.

Books were open on casually rumpled spreads and breakfast dishes were left in kitchenette sinks. A toilet was hauled in from the garage and bolted to the floor of a hall closet, which would soon to be plumbed as a bathroom, trusting an appraiser not to test it or the sink hanging on the wall beside it. On cue, a pretty girl, her head turbaned in a towel, exited the closet and darted to her pretend room. Cars were parked under huge pecan trees in back, and two guys lounged on the wrap-around porch. There was even mail in four black boxes on the peeling clapboard siding. The scene was convincing, the loan approved, and soon funds would flow to bring the makeover to reality. Before ink dried on the approval form, and after a round of beers and high-fives, Ms. Katherine's fine trappings began their return trip across the driveway. Knowing Mick, there was loud celebrating that night. No doubt his loyal friends were rewarded with a frosty keg and piles of meat smoking on the barbie, but I bet that Ms. Katherine missed a fine night of guitar serenading that night. I loved hearing the guys tell about it.

19.

❧

Abraham

Gina's plane arrived on time, we squeezed in our lunch visit with Bev, met Beth's plane, and headed back to Macon. It is a unique comfort to be around these friends whom I'd known for over fifty years. With email and online chatting, there's hardly a lag in news flow, so we always pick up where we've left off.

Three days before they were leaving, there was a call from the cemetery office to tell us the bronze plaque, ordered in late July, would be in place and ready for inspection the next day. It had taken all these weeks to create exactly what we wanted, with ivy as an embellishment—no bibles, folded hands, pinecones, or crosses—only *ivy*, as was our family pact.

It would help to have these friends, who couldn't be here for the funeral, be with us to face this hallmark of permanence. It would be Mother's first trip to the grave, since she'd gone directly from the church to greet visitors at our house. I sent a group email to others who might want to join us. We set the time for six o'clock so Jim could drive from his Blue Bird office in Fort Valley and Richard Keil, the former priest, who graciously agreed to lead us in prayer, could leave his financial consultant office early.

Gina, whose parents had owned Casson Flowers, was our floral director for the plaque's dedication. Dr. Hudspeth, a veterinarian known for his clinic's rose garden, gathered sacks of open blooms early that morning, and my friends filled a white wicker basket with fragrant petals. They cut long runners of our Biltmore ivy, aptly named when my dad secreted a sprig of it in his coat pocket while touring Vanderbilt Estate in North Carolina. Decades later, we rooted our prolific spread of ivy from his backyard.

About a dozen cars were already at Macon Memorial Park when we got there. We spread pine straw over freshly broken red clay around the plaque and sprinkled rose petals over the brown straw. Merrie and Tim Potts, Brax's friends, had brought yellow roses, which Gina entwined with our ivy and arranged in the plaque's bronze vase. Margaret took a Polaroid picture of the grave, with its petal halo of pink, white, and red. Someone hung a bracket on the thick pine towering over the shady slope, where I could hang a wind chime of copper moons and suns, which had been a gift from Jim's sister. She would see it when she visited Eric's grave, just up the hill, beside her dad's.

The burnished brass marker itself looked fine with its two-line epitaph—*We had music, we had love, we had life, the best gift is my brother.* It was attached to a base of polished granite and, according to the cemetery covenant, it lay flat on the ground. It was a dignified resting place for our sons' combined ashes. There was room in the plot for our ashes to be buried beside them one day.

When Jim arrived, he told us about a bizarre thing that happened on his drive. When he left work in the old truck, with only thirty minutes to spare, its fuel gauge was on empty. He doubted if he should pass the up-coming station, the only one on the road leading to the interstate, when all of the sudden the needle on the gauge began to climb upward—all the way to *full*. He was totally shocked but decided to trust it as a sign that he was okay with whatever gas there was—so he passed the station. After that, the needle dropped back to empty. In his earlier days, Jim would never have seen that weird behavior as anything but a malfunction, and never would have passed up a last chance to refuel, but that day none of us, he least of all, doubted that he had truly seen a sign.

When Richard suggested we begin, we passed candles around and he led us in prayer. Standing in this place, wrapped in the coral glow of an autumn sunset, I'm sure I wasn't the only one whose mind returned to what we had done here a hundred days ago.

I had been awake since daybreak that Tuesday morning, July 6th, obsessed with finding our four children's white baptismal candles. There was no rationale to my mission, but I went downstairs, straight to our dining room sideboard for them, then back upstairs to Taylor's dresser drawer, where he kept his match collection in a metal box. The first matchbook I touched had a grotesque mask on its cover, from the Vortex, a heavy-metal place in Atlanta's Little Five Points where he and Brax liked to go. I placed it into a zip-locked bag with the candles, which were embossed with red liturgical symbols, and left it on the kitchen counter. Then I took my first cup of coffee to the back deck. Bright morning sun washed over two white market umbrellas that dear friends had brought from their home the day before. Like an enormous pair of angel wings they stood as sentinels over our home.

The house filled with family and friends as we waited for mortuary cars. Earlene was there to keep things organized while we were gone. Jim passed around a cut-glass bowl full of foreign coins, offering folks to select one in memory of our boys. The coins were mostly from Brax's travels: from Ireland, Spain, Holland, France, Italy, Canada, and the Baltics. The little sugar bowl had been a gift to me from the lady hotel owner in Dinard, on France's Brittany coast, where the boys and I spent a long weekend during our glorious trip in August '97.

Before climbing into one of three black limos in our driveway, I handed the bag of candles to Carolyn's son-in-law, Melinda's husband. "I'll let you know when I'm ready for these," I said, as he put them unquestioningly into his blazer pocket. "I'm not sure why, but something tells me to take them. I hope they don't melt."

After the long funeral and fifteen-minute cortege to the cemetery, we pulled up to our plot, selected just two days before. A huge crowd stood in blazing noon sun since a green canopy installed for the family took up most of the shade from the tall pine. Plush artificial turf did its best to disguise ruptured clay, and a five-gallon cargo bottle of water sweated on a metal rack beside a tray of tented paper cups.

Father Tim McKeown was there to greet us since Father Cuddy would soon be leaving for Europe. The family exited the cool limos and filed in a slowly moving chain of linked hands into rows of green-draped chairs under the canopy. I remembered the candles and motioned for Keith to pass the plastic bag to Father Tim, whose look of surprise at my idea was so fleeting that I knew he understood. He set the bag beside his bible on a podium and began the burial ceremony by sprinkling holy water over the mahogany box-shaped urn of precious ashes. In the stillness that followed prayers and Scripture readings, he prepared us for the candles.

"When a Catholic is baptized," he began, "a special candle is used. Godparents light the candle and vow to walk beside the new Christian, whose life is now dedicated to the glory of God." A thought consoled me— *Taylor and his godfather are still together.*

"The Braggs have brought their children's baptismal candles," Father continued, "and want me to light them now as a continuance of that pledge to walk beside their children in accordance with God's plan." He whispered to me, "Do you want to stand?" We stood. He opened the matchbook, struck a black match, lit each candle, and handed them, in turn, to Susie and Annie, and passed the boys' to Jim and me. Then we returned to our seats. There was not a hint of breeze, and the pleasant scent of warm wax mingled with organic smells of pine and Georgia clay.

"Julie told me they will now, as a family, extinguish Brax's and Taylor's candles," Father said. He looked at me, speaking softly, "Was there anything you wanted to say?"

Looking into flames, with Jim on my right and the girls on our left, I said, in as audible a voice as I could muster, "I want to say that we now give our sons back to God. We realize what we're losing, and we'll always be grateful for having these people in our lives, but we must accept His plan." Then we leaned in and blew the boys' candles out. Susie and Annie looked from their own flames to us for a clue. "For God's sake," I whispered, "don't blow them out now!" Bless them, they managed a weak smile at that.

We have a photo of cousin Sue Burch, eyes glistening, one hand to her lips, her other hand with Jack's, engrossed in our uncommon candle ritual. We talked about that unforgettable, simple episode many times—about how it allowed us to feel more a part of this letting-go of our loved ones and less like powerless victims. I'm glad my heart hadn't sent its strange inspiration to my head right away, but to my feet instead, or this powerful experience might have been rejected as something unnatural and brutal.

Because of it, as I reread the stunning Old Testament story of Abraham, I've come to think more kindly of him. An image of him, wielding a knife over his docile son, had always been repulsive to me, eclipsing any symbolism. I'd figured the old man was insane. But my perspective of his story has softened.

I wonder now if his love for his child had become so intense that it frightened him. Could he have feared that God could be jealous of such love as a parent has for a child? Maybe the obsessed father was willing to go to such outrageous extreme to prove his loyalty to his fearsome Creator. Or maybe he thought God had warned him that a parent must exhibit his ability to detach from beloved children, who never belonged to him in the first place, in order to liberate himself, along with them. Maybe the message he received, just before striking his boy, convinced him that we are all facets of that powerful Creator, and our connections with Him and with each other are unshakable.

20.

❧

Annie's Trove

It seemed like my girlfriends had just gotten here when local lifelong friends, Trisha and Cile, arrived on Friday to drive them to the airport. As they were loading suitcases into Trisha's car trunk, Bart Stephens, Brax's friend from New Orleans, drove into our parking area. The joy of seeing him buffered the blow of my friends' leaving, even though we knew he was here to report on the sad pilgrimage he had just completed. He had duplicated the boys' trip from New Orleans to Los Angeles. After spending time with his college buddy James Morris, with whom our boys had stayed, he proceeded on to Ozona, Texas.

There, he met with Junior Bilano, the Texas trooper who had talked to me. Bart had photos from the scene on Highway 10, where he had left a letter in an amber beer bottle, which he tied to a nearby mesquite tree as a memorial. I still have a small white rock, spattered with yellow marking paint, which he picked up there. Bart had been our lamb, enduring this agonizing experience for us—we would never forget that.

He had been at McKibbon Lane elementary with Brax and Matthew Davis. Their sixth-grade gifted-class teacher, Marie Sears, our neighbor, liked retelling her favorite memory of them. Her assignment had been to create a business, complete with its mission statement, business plan, and a presentation, for the class. She noticed the three big shots moving along tables of stressed-out 11-year-olds, offering last-minute buyouts. Some, in despair over their own models, caved—creating easy conglomerates for the hustlers. "You had to admire the rascals," she'd say, "but it made me mad to see others tossing in the towel so quickly." I suspect that was the year the three got bitten by wanderlust, because Mrs. Sears's love of travel was contagious. She also instilled a value of setting long-range goals.

Bart, with brown eyes and a quicksilver mind, smallest of the trio, was their usual ringleader, a ranking never fully accepted by Brax. Matthew, blond, with blue-gray eyes, quieter, like Tate, seemed more at ease with his intelligence and with the world in general. All four boys, in response to Duke University's talent search, did well on their SATs when they were in seventh grade. The older ones entered public middle school together, but Bart's family moved away, and we later transferred Brax to Stratford Academy. Matthew graduated from Central, the public high school, where he was valedictorian.

Brax loved his life back then. He began journaling as a youngster, probably inspired by Mrs. Sears, though we weren't invited to read any of it. Russell Walker located the following excerpt from one of Brax's journals in time to read it at the Monday night memorial and again at church the next morning. It exemplified Brax's happy perspective on life at nearly 20 years old.

January 9, 1991: I love January 9. I remember in 1980 realizing in class that on January 9, you could simply write the date as 1980—1/9/80. And I always do that on the ninth day of each year. It's especially weird because today I picked my brother up from school—McKibbon Lane—the same elementary school where I went—and today I went inside and looked around. Tate's in the third grade, the same grade I was in when I noticed this neat calendrical phenomenon. So you see, ten years does an awful lot, and yet I can remember so clearly so much about that year and all of those years. All the little games in my head that I entertained myself with, my emergence as a pubescent sports hero, fascination with the 30's gangsters, with snakes first and then sharks, my extensive biographical readings on sports stars and especially boxers, the games of baseball and football that I played alone in the front yard out here in the country, my complete honesty and bashfulness behind a brash surface, my lip-synching, hunting and target shooting with Papa, hitting Dad's hands with gloves on when he got home from work, my easy grades, being big for my age, collecting matches and discovering my urge for travel, beginning to fall in love with girls but keeping this a secret, my love of the woods, playing director and staging fights, and starting my own Mad Magazine.

Now as men, Bart, his brown hair showing a little pate, and Matthew were still close friends. They had a recent visit in New Orleans when Matthew's employer sent him from Seattle to deliver a talk on water reclamation.

While we waited for Jim, Bart and I drank a beer at the wrought-iron table on our shady back deck, watching black-capped chickadees and purple finches sling seeds from two feeders that hung on the side of the house. The late afternoon was quiet except for raspy cawing from two lanky black crows high in a hickory tree near the pool. He told me that Matthew had become engaged to Betsy, a Boston girl he met in Seattle.

"Were you able to bring up the subject of Olivia?" I asked, hoping he had risked it. "I can't imagine being able to seriously ask someone if he had ever been a time-traveling angel, though."

"I did—mostly what you had told me on the phone," he said.

"Really? How did he react?"

"He was cool with it," Bart said, and smiled. "Apparently, talk of angels doesn't unsettle Matt like it might some people. He's anxious to see you and Jim. He said to tell you he'll be coming to visit his mom in a couple weeks and wants to drop by. I expect he'll talk to you about it."

"Did I tell you that she said that very thing in August—that he would be here in less than three months?"

"You did," he said, "We'd liked to have been here at the same time."

Bart's degree from the University of New Orleans was film making. He had talked Brax into spending several months in New Orleans in 1995 to star in a student film, which Bart wrote and directed. I flew there for a weekend myself for a cameo role as a convenience store clerk. That fall Tate and I had a fantastic weekend at the New Orleans' Film Festival, where Bart's film was an award-winner, with an incentivizing grant. The video, with its close-ups of Brax's precious face, is a bittersweet thing to watch now.

Bart's film work remained a serious passion, but his bread-and-butter job as a croupier on a Mississippi gambling boat meant he would have to report for work by tomorrow night. He had hoped to meet Olivia this evening.

"You know," he said, watching the big birds move noisily to an oak nearer the driveway, "whenever I hear crows, it reminds me of Brax and Tate—we listened to the Black Crows all the time."

Susie drove up in her silver Nissan about that time and had just sat with us when the kitchen phone rang. "I bet that's Olivia," I told them, as I hurried inside. "She said she would try to come over."

"I'll only come for a minute," Olivia said. "My daughter has to work, so I'll need to babysit. But I can't wait to tell you what happened last night at Publix."

"Tell me," I said, "it sounds like a good thing."

"I was there with my teenage son, walking from the check-out toward the door," she said, "when I heard, '*If you want to know what I look like, look at the one in front of you.*' I was sure it was Brax's voice."

"Are you serious?" I asked. I wondered how she got through a day in the real world. "I guess the one in front of you was a guy," I said. "How did he look?"

"A Greek god," she said, chuckling. "He walked out ahead of us, head full of dark curls, wearing shorts, showing his tanned legs."

"Sounds like him," I said. "He had a healthy ego." I laughed, wondering how long he had waited for the ideal doppelganger to stroll by. "Could you see his face?"

"Yes—beautiful. Smooth skin would hardly need shaving, and the bluest eyes!"

"One of these days you'll have to see their pictures, Olivia. Susie just got home and Bart's here, hoping to meet you—they'll want to hear about this. Would you say they're with you a lot, like that?"

"It surprises me sometimes," she said, "to discover when they're near. They're helping me so much, Julie. Seriously, they encourage me to follow my heart in a way that's never happened. I don't want to disappoint them. I feel their gratitude in many ways. They probably wondered if I would ever take a chance to connect with you."

"I can imagine what a dreadful state we'd still be in if you hadn't," I said. "We're grateful, too." As soon as we hung up I told Susie and Bart what she'd told me.

"Why can't they ever talk to *us* that way," Susie complained. "It makes me feel left out to hear they're always telling Olivia stuff—even at Publix.

Why don't they give us a chance to hear anything direct—without needing someone who never even knew them?"

"Maybe they've tried," Bart and I said together.

Since some of Bart's local friends would be joining us and I hadn't cooked a thing, I left them to visit while I drove into town for fried chicken. I waved to Anna and Rob, who were stepping off the yellow Blue Bird bus at our driveway.

On my way home I passed a serious wreck in the opposite, south-bound lane of I-75. Jim would see flashing lights, ambulances, scattered belongings along the median, and the traffic jam on his way home, too. Never again would I pass a wreck without feeling empathy for the people involved or without reminders of my own children's last moments. Maybe one day I could do it without crying.

Olivia's jeep was in our driveway when I got home. I left my packages in the kitchen, where Susie was making iced tea, and met up with Bart and Olivia, who were coming in from the screened porch. The trailing aroma of fried chicken lured Anna and Rob in from the basketball hoop in the drive-way.

"Before I do another thing," Olivia said, "I have a message for Susie." She led Susie into the hall by our front door. Suddenly we heard Susie's outcry.

"What happened, Mama?" Anna called, running to see.

"Olivia just said Taylor had a message for me," she said, her voice muffled in a Kleenex. "She said he knows *I'm feeling left out.* Can you believe it—my exact words?!"

"Gosh, they must hear everything," Anna said.

"That was just an hour ago—he had to have been with us on the deck," Susie said, in awe, appearing consoled by the idea. "Thanks for telling me that, Olivia."

Jim came home and a few more young friends drifted in, but Olivia needed to leave after introductions. Before going, she asked if I could take her to see Brax's room. We left the others, climbed the hall stairs, and went into the room that had been his.

"I see such pain in your face," she said. "I just wanted to have a quiet minute to talk. Please don't dwell on thoughts of their suffering."

"I try not to imagine it, but I can't stop images from creeping in," I said. "I passed a bad wreck on my way in from town just now. It breaks my heart—for those people, for the police, for all of us."

"Your boys want you to know that there *was* no suffering. They were here and then...," she snapped her fingers, "they were gone—just like that. It was their time, Julie." She put her arms around me then.

"I pray for that all the time, Olivia," I said, letting tears flow.

"Please remember that my main obligation is to *you*, Julie," she said, as we headed downstairs. "I've promised them I will continue to help you any way I can whenever they try to convey their love—they so want to lessen the pain this has caused you all. Do you understand what I'm trying to say?"

"I do," I said. I was beginning to realize that I may have crossed the line by being so eager to promote her amazing gift.

The young people had lots of catching up to do. Russell and Kirby were there and glad for Bart's help in rounding up more bits of Brax's writing. Timmy Potts sang the soulful song he'd written about Brax. Criss Strain and his fiancée, Kate Dodson, were here, too. She and Brax had been literary confidants since high school, spending hours on the phone sharing their teenage writings.

When Kate was in her twenties, during the fall of '96, she and I attended an Artist's Way class together. The pastor of a small country church near the river had asked our neighbor Dot Brown to lead a group of adults in the twelve-week course, designed by artist/author Julia Cameron. Dot's weekly assignments were intended to free our inner artists so that we could share resulting creativity with each other. Ten years of owning yogurt shops had sent my inner artist into hibernation, but maybe I could coax some creativity if I first cleared a path of order though our neglected house.

I hoped that my pleasure from clean closets, shampooed carpets, organized cabinets, and a new but short-lived habit of writing *morning pages* might offset my lack of poems, essays, or drawings, which the others produced that winter. Above all else, I treasured my firsthand experience of my friend's inspired teaching, along with a chance to get to know Kate as the lovely, sensitive poet she had become.

At our house that evening, she and Criss talked about their future. She was thinking of starting law school, following in her father's footsteps.

They, like the rest, had a keener grasp of life's brevity and were resetting vital goals to make each day count. I envied their optimism.

None of us could have imagined how intact Brax's special bond still remained with his friend Kate. Maybe Olivia could have enlightened us, had she had been able to read for Kate that night. Or maybe, had either of them known of two mind-blowing surprises that lie ahead, it might have innocently upset a plot for their unveiling.

The next morning was Saturday, October 16th, and I headed for Camp Eunice in Roberta, an hour away. I had decided to have lunch with my daddy's distant kinfolk at the Rowell reunion. When I signed in at the welcome table, there were Helen and Nell, aka *Doll* and *Stone Cypher*, hugging folks and passing out nametags. Long tables groaning, as Mother would say, with enough home-cooked food for an army were at the far end of a crowded rustic building set deep within a local church's wooded campground. Nell, bravely filling shoes left empty by her late husband, Bill, had come from Kansas City to be Mistress of Ceremony. Before presenting me with the navy-blue soft-cover book of *Annie's Trove*, the little gift I'd been promised by the spirit of my great-great-grandmother, Nell introduced me to the large clan. As Annie Wellons Wallace's granddaughter, I was the only representative from our side.

Before I left she reminded me to check on the pine lapboard, which Bill had left at the Crawford County library last year. Later, after phone calls with the county historian, I learned that an old scratched, 30-inch pine board, its implicit value obscure, was known to be buried in a closet in the court house, which was undergoing a major restoration. I doubted if I'd ever see it.

But how comforting to believe that Elizabeth wanted me to know of this thing which she and her granddaughter, *my* grandmother, touched so often in their lives. I believe my strong women wanted me to be inspired by this witness to their life stories. But I wonder how impressed they'd be with my modern version of their lapboard—my amazing laptop. Probably not much. After all, their waves of energy, faster than Wi-Fi or flying fingers, convey thoughts through centuries, creating bridges to eternity. The only tool they need is to locate a channel into our open hearts and minds.

Annie's Trove is a window into Grandmother's life as a young woman at LaGrange Female College, in Troup County, Georgia. I feel the wisdom and love of a father for his eldest of five daughters, whose features are stamped upon my own. I become a time traveler through their letters and those with her fiancé, my grandfather John Vernon Wallace, as they meet, fall in love, and prepare to move into the home he had waiting for them in Charleston, in 1901.

Like me, her life was setting up to be absolutely perfect. She didn't know it then, but there would be five wonderful children, a fine three-story house, servants, a family piano store, and her husband, a handsome, respected member of the South Carolina legislature—all before she was 44 years old. And, like her own grandmother Elizabeth, and also like me, it was better that she hadn't known how abruptly so much could be lost.

One fall day in 2008, my sister Margaret's daughter, Shelley, our family historian, coordinated an ancestry search trip to Crawford County, where I finally got a chance to meet up with my great-great-grandmother's lapboard—a 34-inch by 18-inch oval pine board with numerals, words, and alphabet scratched into its smooth, worn surface. It has since been included in a display at the Crawford County Pottery Museum.

My daddy's memories of having watched his mother use this lapboard must have been his inspiration for the lapboard he made for me before I left for Georgia State College for Women in nearby Milledgeville. I stuck the odd-shaped piece of sanded plywood in the back of my dorm closet right away, but my friends and I soon discovered how handy it was as a lapboard, especially on long choir-concert bus trips. I've kept it all these years but until recently I had no idea that it had a remote connection with my maternal ancestors.

21.

❧

Yoburt

October days moved tortuously toward the 29th—Taylor's birthday—a day
we had always joyfully prepared for. He would have been 18. Dealing with
the notion that we'd suffocate from an approaching avalanche of sadness
was exhausting.

Running continued to be a valve for releasing pressure. There were
days, though, more than I should admit, that a dark fantasy lurked at the
busy intersection down the street. Riverside Drive, where 40-ton gravel
trucks roared to and from a mountainous rock quarry, could quickly bring
an end to my suffering. Even though I would never have carried out my
part in such a drama, just by refusing such an option seemed to give me
strength. I was anchored by my belief that if we choose items from the
world's menu of self-destruction, the universe could subject us to a shameful playback of its recording.

During the third week in October, I was almost back to our driveway
at the end of a run—I'd made it to a grassy shoulder at the edge of our
property—when the weight of grief became too heavy for one more step.
Just below the roadbed was an old outbuilding, part of the original homestead built on our land in the 1800s, with its rusted corrugated roof, which
had been the target when Brax had taught his little brother to chunk small
rocks. I could see Tate's denim overalls and new cowboy boots as he sat in
their red Radio Flyer, Brax kneeling beside it, arming the toddler with one
rock after another. I could almost hear happy outbursts after every clattering
hit. Turk, their huge white German shepherd sidekick, would have been
barking cheerily.

As I stood there, doubled-over from crying, Phil Brown drove by. Given my appearance and the fact that I barely looked up when he tapped his horn in passing, his car immediately reversed. He stretched an arm through his window to touch my hand and introduced a person riding with him. "I can imagine what must be wrong, Julie," he said, "but is there anything I can do? Let us take you home."

"Tate's birthday is a week from tomorrow," I stammered. "I don't think I can stand it. I just need to stay here awhile; there's nothing anybody can do." I turned back to the shack, waving off his offer, covering my face with my other hand. They drove slowly away.

There was another reason I wanted to stay outside that day. Annie's Mexican housekeeper was deep cleaning our house. Even though Earlene had been here the day before, Annie hoped to cheer me by leaving Luella, a highly energized lady who spoke little English, with me for the day. She was the mother of two sons and had met both of ours, so her empathetic soft brown eyes and her way of tiptoeing around me only made me sadder; running had been my escape.

I dried my face with my shirttail and went inside, calling to her as I headed upstairs to shower. I reached inside the linen closet, which is in our laundry room, to the right of Tate's now-open bedroom door. With a bath towel hanging on my shoulder, I stepped inside for a look around.

Bed linens had been changed, the carpet vacuumed, and his furniture was gleaming. A familiar cardboard box of books, which he and I had packed for possible tossing months ago, was still under the window by a guitar stand near his bookshelf. On his music stand was the last composition he had worked on. Out of impulse, I slid a frayed, black loose-leaf notebook, which I'd seen a hundred times, out of the box and opened it. Tucked in its front cover pocket were two unfolded pages of Tate's typewriter-tiny handwriting—clearly a letter—from May 1998. His greeting jumped off the loose pages in my hand and the notebook fell to the carpet.

Mom and Dad,

Our childhood is often something that we take for granted. We rarely take the time in our busy, everyday lives to reminisce about our years growing up and the things that our parents have provided for us. We all have old memories in the back of our minds of special family moments, whether they are good or bad.

I think that time should be taken to remember how we made it through those bad times and to remember those that were good. There is nothing in the world that can replace time spent together as a family.

Luella must've heard my outcry as I realized what I had found, and I ran with it to our bedroom, to the far side of our poster bed, where I slid to the floor to sit, leaning against the bedrail, to continue reading.

When I think back to the early years of my life, dozens of memories come to mind. I can remember all the baseball games you got me to, and how you would both stay and cheer on the team. Whenever I came up to bat you would always stand up and cheer.

I can remember the fishing trips that you and I took, dad, and how you always knew where the fish were. Whenever you hooked a big fish you would hand the pole to me so that I could reel it in.

I can remember the family trips to the beach that we took and the miserable, hot hours we spent driving all the way to Mexico Beach, Florida. Once we got to the beach, though, all the trouble of getting there faded away. The first thing my brother and I would do was to run down to the beach and play in the sand. It was like a magical experience to go to the beach as a child. I was mesmerized by the hot, white sand, the salty water that rolled gently across the shore, and the taste of the ocean in the air. Something I always looked forward to at the beach was the food that we cooked together. We would go to the seafood market and plan out a special meal for the night and then after supper we would take a walk on the moonlit beach.

Each of his sweet memories brought heaving sobs. Only when she touched the top of my head did I know Luella was beside me. "Misses Julie—ohhh, what is it?"

I pointed to the pages in my left hand then patted my heart. "I've found a letter from Taylor—a precious gift from my *bambino*—for us on his birthday."

"Oh, I so sorry, so sad, too," she said, stroking my shoulder. When she disappeared around the foot of the bed, it crossed my mind that she might be going to call Annie, her boss, to report that Miss Anne's poor mother had collapsed on the floor, having a breakdown, but I read on:

Some of the most cherished memories I have of my childhood, though, are the birthday parties that you gave me. You would rent the clubhouse at Grannie's apartments and, since my birthday is close to Halloween, everyone would come in costume. You made invitations so that my whole class would come and you organized games like "pin the tail on the donkey" and treasure hunts for us to do. Sometimes you would try to scare us with a story about a dungeon below the clubhouse. You would convince someone to go down to the basement and my brother would jump out from a hiding spot and scare them and then everybody else would scream. Those are some of the happiest times I can remember.

What sticks out more than anything else in mind about my parents is that no matter what, the family always stuck together and that problems, no matter how serious, always seemed to work out sooner or later. Throughout my life you have given me everything that I needed and wanted and you have taught me countless lessons about life. The only way I can try to express my gratitude for all you have done for me is to say thank you and I love you."

The pages lay on my legs while I sat in a haze, like in a recovery room, where distant voices insist you're doing fine—but remind you again how to use the attached morphine pump—when the staggering pain of having lost this boy struck again and took my breath away. Eventually I got to my feet, placed the letter on our bedspread, thinking how much Jim needed to know about it. But I was in no shape to call him, nor could he hear about it over the phone—he would need solitude for this letter.

I retrieved my towel from the hall floor, put the book back in the box, and stepped into the shower, hoping to be transported from this dismal state. When the first thing that popped into my tired head was a corny bath-salts commercial from the seventies—"Calgon, take me away!"—I began to feel the mood lifting. Soon, hot water began to unblock a flow of comforting memories—the happier side of our boys' birthdays.

I felt a twinge of guilt when I realized that Tate hadn't written a word about his sixteenth birthday, the one preceding his letter. Maybe he wanted to forget about that major milestone in '97. Brax's return from Europe, where Tate and I had left him that August, had been scheduled around this sixteenth birthday. He had enlisted Colleen Kelsall, his English friend who had moved from Charleston to Macon by then, as part of the production.

Brax's memory of his own sixteenth was what planted his resolve—his kid brother must endure a certain rite of passage.

Back then, in March 1987, our frozen-yogurt shops were in full swing. I had bought a huge Waffle-Cone-Man costume, "Yoburt," for marketing purposes. Though he came at a high price—over $750—Yoburt earned his keep. I'd worn the cumbersome thing myself to kindergartens and first-grade classrooms when children were learning to write "y," which stood for "yogurt," which I carried, along with coupons, as treats for "Y.O.U." Various employees strutted Yoburt in parades, and he spent sunny afternoons waving at passing cars from sidewalks in front of shopping centers where we had a store.

Yoburt was an 8-feet tall waffle cone—from his white faux-leather spats to the perky curl on his thick imitation-fur swirl of pink yogurt. Twinkling pie-sized satin eyes, a raised satin nose, and a huge black smile created his charming innocence. The furry swirl was velcroed to a waist-to-floor quilted-fabric brown waffle cone. Encased inside this giant dessert would be a good-natured human, wearing black-and-white-striped satin pants and shirt, and white gloves. When Yoburt walked, his heavy cone swayed behind the striped legs like an alligator tail.

A black mesh window was sewn into his wide, permanent smile, allowing limited vision for the person inside, who, despite a tiny, useless battery-run fan droning in his ears, was drenched in sweat. Yoburt was occasionally overly friendly with his admirers, relieving stress by hugging them too roughly into his large pink furry face.

Brax was attending Stratford Academy, a private school within short driving distance from our Forsyth Road shop, on March 10, 1987, when Yoburt shuffled into the crowded lunchroom, shiny Mylar birthday balloons bobbing on ribbons alongside his tall pink swirl. Our uniformed store manager, a personable young man sporting a green straw hat and waving a white cane, announced their arrival by shouting, "A singing telegram for *Brax Br-agg*!"

Startled students froze as the waffle cone galumphed his way around a labyrinth of lunch tables to reach red-faced, fuming Brax. The entire room erupted in singing "Happy Birthday" before a teacher ushered Yoburt and his escort back to the parking lot. Brax didn't realize that it had been Annie inside the costume, since he'd deflected all hugging attempts from those waving arms. He later said he only wished he could run away. I hadn't been able to go because someone had to mind the store, and Yoburt's quick exit left no time for photos anyway, but the episode kept us laughing forever.

Ten years later, two days before Halloween in 1997, Tate's time had come. That morning I had called the office at Mount de Sales Academy, where he was a sophomore, but Patty, the secretary, couldn't give permission for Yoburt to make an inside visit.

"It's just as well," I said. "He'd probably never speak to us again if we walked in with this costume. Brax will be so disappointed, though."

"You know this is Spirit Week, don't you?" she reminded me. "That's the reason for daily dress-code themes, like today's Western one. Homecoming's this weekend."

"Right," I said. "I helped Tate with his cowboy get-up."

"I guess he told you that parents are invited to have lunch outside with students today—no rule against his brother joining you."

"No! He never mentioned that part," I said. "He was acting nervous this morning. Now I know why," I said, laughing. "I figured it was because it's one of our last days that he'd need me to ride shotgun—Jim's taking him to get his license on Friday—but he even said I didn't have to come back because he already had a ride home."

"Probably teenaged paranoia," she said, as a mother of a son herself.

"Well, thanks for this information!" I said, and we hung up.

Tate hadn't been happy about having to wear Jim's oversized, dorky corduroy cowboy hat with his jeans and plaid shirt, but he couldn't find his sleek black felt hat that we got on a family trip to Arizona. He knew the whole family would gather in the poolhouse that night for his birthday chili, but he was clearly not himself—probably feeling his day was a risk all around.

I retrieved Yoburt from the garage, dusted him off, and left him with the rest of his costume on the porch for Brax. Our plan was for us to drive Yoburt in the pickup and meet Colleen at the campus gate at lunchtime. Colleen, the Hollywood wardrobe artist, wore denim jeans and shirt, black boots, a fringed suede vest that matched her long, curly copper hair, and Taylor's sleek black cowboy hat, which I'd shamelessly hidden in my car trunk the night before. She was a striking cowgirl. And Brax, as Yoburt, strapped a festive white wide-brimmed Mexican hat with red-sequin trim atop his faded, now-wilted pink swirl. Yoburt was a tad dowdy with age, but Brax's high-stepping in those striped satin pants did a lot to rejuvenate the formerly dapper celebrity.

Tate's friends saw us coming through the crowd, with Mylar balloons sparkling the sunrays like flashbulbs above our heads, and must have tipped him off. Colleen stopped a group of bubbly cowgirls, and asked, in lyrical Brit form, "Could you please tell us where the birthday boy Taylor Bragg might be?" A posse of curious teenagers followed behind them as she held hands with the waddling giant cone. I trailed along as proud mom with my camera.

By the time we found Taylor—actually his friends dragged him from hiding behind a lunchroom table—his blistered face looked hostile, making me glad his only weapon was a cap pistol. He had never really glared that way, and with that uncool cowboy hat, it was impossible not to laugh along with the others. I tried to give him a hug and say I was sorry, but he moved away, and through clinched teeth, snarled, "Go A. Way. Mom." He tolerated the camera, but when Yoburt made a clumsy grab to get a hug from Tate, all he got was a slug from one of the smiley-face balloons. After the crowd sang the dreaded birthday song, our little group left. I wondered if he would come home or ever forgive me.

At his chili dinner in the poolhouse that night, I heard him say to Annie, "I guess you heard what Mama and Brax did to me today." When she'd asked if he'd hated it like Brax had, he admitted that he hadn't really hated it all that much. He turned to Rob, though, and warned, "You'll be sixteen in a few years—you better be ready, boy!"

I later learned that a teacher had required Tate's sophomore class to write that letter to their parents. His pals told me that most of them were never shared with their folks. I don't know where this letter had been all that time (seventeen months), but I'm glad he never threw it away. I'm sure the teacher, who had written "80" on top, would give it an A+ today.

The next day was Friday. Jim and Susie were home and had taken turns with Tate's letter. We talked of his tradition, since kindergarten days, of leaving tiny pumpkins and pots of mums on the doorsteps of his grand-

mothers and a few elder friends as his Halloween birthday neared. I thought
it might give me a lift to go to the farmers' market where we'd always
shopped for them. On my way upstairs to change, I detoured into his room
again. Respect for him and disbelief that he was really gone forever still
made me feel like a trespasser for all these weeks. In his top drawer, amid
scout badges, guitar picks, postcards, firecrackers, pocket knives, and other
savables of a boy's life, was a white envelope with his name on it stuffed
with a bundle of cash. Several birthday cards were saved there, too. Tears,
hard to stop since the day before, came again.

I yelled for Susie. "Look at all that birthday money he never spent," I
wailed, as she took the envelope from me.

"I knew you weren't up here changing clothes," she said, reprovingly.
"Mama, you really need to get out of this house for a while."

"What are we supposed to do with that, though?" I asked.

"Think of it as a gift from him," she suggested. "Get something to
cheer you up."

"It's too sad, when we're missing him so."

"Take some of it with you to the farmers' market," she said.

"Maybe so—he'd like that, wouldn't he?" I said. "But there's over a
hundred dollars there."

"Spend the rest on that tape player you've been wanting," she said. "I
know Taylor wants you and Daddy to have something with this, or you
wouldn't have found it today." She sat on my bed while I washed my face.
"Wow!" she said, "I've got news for you—there's nearly two fifty here."

When I neared the farmers' market, panic overtook me. I dialed my
brother Bobby's house, so lost in sadness that I wasn't able to tell Harriet
where I was. She said to spend the afternoon with them, which I did. I resumed the mission on Monday and enjoyed it as much as the folks did who
found the little pumpkin surprises on their doorsteps.

Tuesday morning I thought of calling Terry Cantwell, Tate's guitar
teacher, to include him in whatever birthday thing we did over the weekend. I was too down in the dumps to cook chili, so we would likely go to
the Mexican place. Figuring I'd leave a message for him, since Terry was
also a teacher at Macon State College, I was surprised when he answered.

"So, no one has called you about Saturday night's concert?" he asked,
when I mentioned our weekend plan.

"No," I replied. "Whose concert?"

"Macon Symphony's. Ben Aultman is coming home with his guitar teacher, who's playing with the orchestra," he said. "Ben has the encore piece with him. Your family's invited to the after-party—it was on somebody's list to have called you by now."

Ben also had been a student of Terry's and was Tate's role model. Terry had entered them each in statewide competitions and both had won first place for their respective years. Ben had gone on to Eastman School of Music in Rochester, New York.

"How perfect!" I said. "I'll call and reserve tickets." Then, remembering the stuffed envelope, I said, "You'll love this, Terry: he left a stash of birthday money in his dresser—I found it Friday. We decided he'd want us to use it as a gift for his birthday."

Tate's stash paid for eleven of us to go to Wesleyan College for the symphony featuring Ben's guitar professor, who was the soloist for their performance of "Concierto de Aranjuez," written by Spanish composer Joachim Rodrigo. The second movement, so profoundly sad, is said to have been written after the death of his infant daughter. Ben accompanied his teacher with an encore, which they dedicated to his friend, Taylor.

We later learned of a coincidence. Rodrigo, a favorite of all classical guitarists, had died in Spain at 97 years old, on the sixth of July that year—the same day as the boys' funeral.

22.

A Little Cup

The first quarter of our worst year was ending. Each week we felt more convinced that death is a bridge from this life into an altered but equally vital world, and there were many days when I walked with a foot in each. A film was slowly lifting to allow a clearer view of how nature and universe form a non-dual energy, which we're all part of. Not only did I feel a tie to the boys, but the natural world presented daily reassuring signs of its connection to their world.

Bees, butterflies, and birds came in for a closer check, and two chatty black crows traveled from tree to tree, spurring me through my run. Flowers bloomed out of season and leaves fluttered straight into my hand. Rain clouds seemed to inhale when I set foot for a run, then let go thirty minutes later, making me scramble for cover on my return. Clouds arranged themselves in pairs of elegant, wispy angel wings, and there were rainbows, often in short pairs, even when there had been no rain. Electronic tricks seem to be a favorite pastime of fun-loving, high-frequency spirits. We had lights to answer our questions by one blink for *no* and two for *yes*. Radios turned on or off when we entered a room, and the TV occasionally came back on at night when we shut it down too early. Car door locks startled us by loudly unlocking then relocking in the moving car. Pennies littered parking lots near our car doors, and both back and front doorbells rang themselves. I gathered feathers as signs that angels were near and began finding golf tees in the strangest places—a brown one behind my parked car, a blue one on the beach, several white ones—sure that we were hearing from Tee-Man, the nickname Jim had given Tate. I wondered how long this could continue, but mostly I was enthralled by the notion of brilliant, witty spirit life. I felt safe and connected to our Creator, able to envision His view of me as I plodded along with millions of others on this lovely marble, speeding safely through space.

Days were slipping into routines which were surprisingly comfortable, partly because of Susie and her children, Anna and Rob. With enough time to myself—to be with friends or to wander miserably around our property and have a good cry—an oxymoron that has earned my respect—I also looked forward to chauffeuring the children around after school.

On Thursday after the symphony, Anna needed a ride to a middle-school football game at a stadium on the east side of town. I was to drop her off, pick up Chinese for supper, and Susie would bring her home after work, also on that side of town. I called Susie from the truck—Jim had resorted to using my Acura on most workdays—and asked her where there was a good Chinese place on my route home.

"Watch for Baconsfield Center," she said. "You ought to be passing it in a minute. Remember the restaurant that moved into our old yogurt store?"

"I'd forgotten about that," I said. "Brax took me there once for lunch." I made a sharp right turn at the next light. "I almost passed it. What should I order?" I parked facing the building's rust-brick facade, as I'd done so often during our five years of operating that third yogurt shop, which we opened not long before Jim's dad's death. Even with its vivid red and green Hong Kong Express sign, it hadn't changed enough to erase negative feelings about our final years of dwindling business there.

"See if they have Happy Family," she offered. "That's good."

"Seriously? Happy Family? Is that a menu item or a description of people who run the place?"

"Trust me," she said, chuckling. "Just order that, it'll be plenty. Be sure to specify fried rice—that's better—and some braised wings for the kids. I gotta get back to work. See you at home later, okay?"

It was nearly dark, but a cheery yellow neon OPEN sign brightened the drab sidewalk. Through a wall of windows I saw a dozen or so people in booths or waiting under fluorescent lights at the counter. As I pulled the door open, I was struck by the feeling of someone brushing my shoulder, trying to make it through the door before it closed behind us—barely as strong as a spider web breaking against my shoulder, more like the shifting airspace inside an overcrowded elevator. Stepping through that door took me straight into a lovely memory of the time I had been there with Brax.

It was January 1995. Brax had been living in Seattle since July and had come home for Christmas. He would leave for New Orleans in a few weeks to do editing work with Bart Stephens's student film.

Spring and summer of '94 had brought incessant rain from tropical storm Alberto. Before Brax had left for Seattle on Friday, July 5th, Macon's Ocmulgee River, which flows from Lake Jackson, near Atlanta, along with the Oconee and Altamaha, into the Atlantic, had begun creeping over banks, creating what was to become the hundred-year flood of middle and south Georgia.

Richie, Jim's mom, lived five miles from us on a short street between the river-edged Macon Water Works and I-75. Rain had stopped when she called early that Friday morning, after being awakened by a fireman's frantic knock, ordering her and her neighbors to evacuate until the threat of rising water passed. Luckily, it was Jim's off-day, so he went to help her while Brax finished packing and I taught swim classes. They placed books, photo albums, and electronic things at safer levels in case any water seeped under her door, and she followed in her car with an overnight bag to stay with us for the weekend. By 9:30 that morning, Jim and Brax were on their way north to the Atlanta airport, dodging bridges and low areas that were already waterlogged.

By late afternoon Richie's entire neighborhood was going under; by the next morning over thirty homes had nearly disappeared under ceiling-deep, slimy, rushing brown water. They remained that way for three days until the river finally receded. No one could have predicted that her weekend stay with us would stretch into five months.

Bibb County's water treatment plant, located between her house and the river, was immobilized, meaning the whole city of Macon had to endure nearly a month of July's heat and humidity with no running water. I was able to carry on the swim school because of abundant cold water from our deep well. Daddies from swimmers' families lined up for showers in our poolhouse before heading to work, and everybody left our place with containers of clean water.

Tate helped Jim hook Richie's washing machine to the garden hose in our driveway and it ran constantly. Her friends, unscathed by the flood but with no running water, took home baskets of her wet, clean laundry and provided a nonstop dryer service. Some even did their own laundry in our driveway. Richie's furniture, even upholstered pieces, got power-washed— almost good as new.

In the meantime, my doctor called, disturbed by an unclear result from an April mammogram. He wouldn't hear of waiting till summer's end for a lump-biopsy, so in mid-July, during a lunch break, I was with a surgeon who had to scrub with bottled water before doing an incised biopsy on my left breast. Results would take a few days, so before numbness wore off, I was back in the pool for afternoon classes.

Mother and Richie were here when his next call came. Mom's cheery shout from the back deck didn't fool me. I reached a wet arm into the poolhouse for the long-corded phone while I kept an eye on six three-year-olds perched obediently on my pool steps.

"He wants you to run by for a few minutes," said the nurse casually.

"I have more classes this afternoon," I said. "Can't you just tell me the results?"

"He'd really rather talk in person..." In that instant, a loud thunder-clap, followed by needles of rain, sent squealing kids inside, leaving me no choice but to call it a day at the pool. Richie and Mother made calls to can-cel remaining classes, and I drove to the surgeon's office. He wanted me to drop everything for a lumpectomy, so I arranged to free up a Friday morn-ing and prayed the worst would soon be behind me. Huge silver tankers of fresh water were parked all over town, including in the hospital parking lot outside my window.

By the time that biopsy came back I had cancelled the rest of summer and was miserable, dealing with surgical drain tubes, painful edema, and doctor's orders for a mastectomy. He had made an appointment for me to see a plastic surgeon to plan reconstructive surgery. When I got to the plas-tic surgeon's office, a mental vacuum had so taken my memory that his nurse had to help me look up my home address in their phone book. Six weeks after the hospital stay, I began a six-month round of chemo.

That whole stressful time was exhausting for all of us. Brax had called repeatedly from Seattle, where he was working two boring restaurant jobs, saying he knew he should come home to help his dad and Tate with the demolition of his grandmother's sodden, muddy brick house, and he wanted to be here during my surgery. But we encouraged him to stay put. Volunteers from everywhere had descended upon Macon, and we assured him there'd be plenty for him to do when he got home at Christmas.

Whenever he talked with Taylor about the ordeal at their grandma's house or the progress of my chemotherapy treatment, Brax's homesickness intensified. By Thanksgiving, he and I, each so dejected, held our phones in silence, knowing the other was crying. He was also beginning to feel the clammy chill of Seattle's winter and doubted if his idea of moving there had been a good one. In mid-December he used his round-trip ticket to return to the South.

Brax moved into a downtown apartment with friends and became a walk-in regular at the Mexican place and its neighbor, Hong Kong Express, where I was now having such a pleasant flashback. Our lunch date that January was a prelude to my afternoon chemo treatment, but because my white blood count had been low in December, I'd missed a round, throwing the conclusion of the chemo series closer to my spring start-up of swim school. Anxiety over this one quelled my appetite, but Brax assured me that their wonton soup was as good for the spirit as it was for the body.

"Bring my mama some of that wonton soup," he asked the waiter, who I assumed was the owner, standing behind me. I was facing Brax and a wall of windows to the familiar parking lot as I arranged my jacket on the booth seat beside me.

"Thanks, but I really don't feel like eating," I said to the waiter, shaking my head. "I'll take a cup of tea and some crackers, though."

"No, she's eating," Brax corrected, smiling up at the man, with whom he seemed well acquainted. They discussed the long single-page menu while I was absorbed with the strangeness of being on the customer's side of this place's counter, where I'd felt so much stress as an owner until just two years before. "So?" Brax asked.

"Alright," I agreed, "But just a little cup." I measured about four inches, using my thumb and forefinger. Brax mimicked my gesture, winking at the waiter. "Bring her just that little cup," he said, "and I'll take my usual."

When our food came the *little cup* was a wide, deep bowl of dumplings, filled with delicious chopped meat, floating in steaming, irresistible broth. I ate what I could, with plenty left as a take-out for supper.

Brax took me on to chemo and seemed relieved, as the nurse was attaching a disturbing network of needles and tubes to the back of my hand, to make a quick exit to fetch his brother from nearby Mount de Sales, where he was in seventh grade. They returned only to quickly depart for Golden Bough, their favorite bookstore. Brax shook his head disapprovingly at my paperback, *Crazy in Alabama,* by Mark Childress. "Brax is an insufferable literary snob," I told my nurse Donna, who was the mother of one of Brax's best childhood friends, Matthew Davis.

Tonight, nearly five years later, I looked around at the mural of tall, snow-covered mountain peaks, colorful, flying birds, and Chinese scenery on the wall beside me. Mirrors reflected the view onto the opposite wall so that long-legged birds appeared to sail across the room. I asked the young man behind the counter if he was the owner.

"No, owner my uncle," he answered. "No work tonight."

"We used to have a frozen yogurt store in this building until 1992," I said. "It looks so different now."

"We have no ice cream," he explained. "No frozen yogurt."

"Well, no—I was saying that *we* used to sell frozen yogurt in this very building." Despite his patient face, he probably wished I'd just place my order so people behind me could do the same. "I'd like to order a Happy Family and some braised wings," I said.

"That all?" I nodded, and he rattled Chinese into the handheld microphone.

"Oh, and make that fried rice," I added. He uttered into the mic again, clicked a small calculator, wrote a receipt, and slid it across the counter— the same forest-green Formica countertop from yogurt-shop days.

"My son used to love your restaurant," I said, passing money to him. "He brought me here once." The man focused on his register drawer while I continued talking to the top of his black buzz cut. "That was nearly five years ago."

He smiled directly at me when he gave me my change. "Will be right out," he said and subtly waved his finger to the next customer. I stepped sideways, the wrong way, so that as the customer line moved forward, I was hemmed in by the booth closest to the counter, where a young man, his empty plate shoved aside, was sitting with a book. I was about to ask the waitress for a glass of water when the man in the booth spoke.

"Don't I recognize you from the symphony party Saturday night?" he asked. "I remember—the encore was dedicated to one of your sons."

"Yes, it was—Taylor. How nice of you to speak," I answered, grateful for someone to talk to. He said he had just moved to Macon, and I recognized him then as the first violinist from the symphony—we had spoken at the after-party. As soon as I sat on the edge of the opposite seat, to make way for the line of customers, the Chinese waitress came over with two Styrofoam cups of sweet tea. She said my order was ready so I excused myself and went to the counter.

The owner's nephew had his back to me, filling a bag. When he turned around he handed me a big brown grocery-sized bag with paper handles. I had opened my wallet to pay for the tea, but he shook his head. "Something extra for you," he said, breaking into a broad grin. Then he held up his thumb and forefinger and said, "Just little cup."

"Thank you," I said, barely above a whisper, "I think I know what may be happening here." Holding back tears, I hurried past others to the door, which the violinist was now holding open for me.

"I'll be giving a recital next Tuesday night," he said, handing me his card. "I'd love for your family to come."

"Thank you, that's very nice—we'll try to make it," I said as I dropped his card into my heavy bag. I folded down the top of the bag, its paper handles seeming insufficient, and tucked it securely under my left arm. My cheeks were wet with tears by the time I walked to the dark parking lane and got in the truck.

"I know you were there," I said aloud. "You made him give me that 'little extra' cup of iced tea." Driving home, it dawned on me that the violinist may have felt a nudge from Tate as well.

Jim was looking over mail and Rob was watching TV when I arrived home. We would wait to eat with Susie and Anna and I would share my experience then. I put the big bag on the countertop by the stove and got salad fixings and chardonnay from the fridge. It wasn't long before we were all gathered in our kitchen.

"The sweetest thing happened at the Chinese place tonight," I started, excitedly. "It felt like Brax was in there. But first, you have to hear about a time he took me there for lunch, before a chemo treatment." After a quick recap of that five-year-old scenario, I demonstrated *just a little cup*.

"Well, tonight's man did that same thing with his hand when I tried to pay for the tea, which I hadn't ordered. He said he wanted to give me a little something extra."

"Was he the same waiter from back then?" Anna asked.

"No, this was the owner's nephew."

"I bet Brax made him do it, don't you, Mimi?" Rob said.

"Probably so," I said. "The other man seemed to be Brax's friend when we were there before—this one hardly spoke English."

Susie unloaded lidded trays and square cartons of fried rice. "Do you want to keep this card from...wow!" she exclaimed, as she lifted a tall cardboard cylinder out of the bag. "You went a little overboard with this soup, didn't you, Mama?"

"I didn't order soup," I said, "check the receipt—did I pay for soup?"

"Well, it looks like you really *did* get a little something extra, then." She brought the container to the work counter where I was filling tea glasses. "It's not on the receipt."

"Open it, quick," I said. "What do you bet it's going to be wonton?"

"You're right," she said, laughing. "I think an old soul waited on you in there."

23.

♈

On Eagle's Wings

Matthew Davis, Brax's Seattle friend who was identified through Olivia's reading as the man in my so-called apparition, made his visit within a week or so, on a beautiful fall afternoon, just under three months, as she had thought. He and his mom had lived near us during the boys' early years and they walked to each other's houses constantly. Brax visited him at Cornell before Matthew moved on to Seattle, but I hadn't seen him in years. I'd always been struck by his maturity, and he had transitioned from an easy-going, towheaded boy to this confident man with a relaxed smile and smooth complexion that still blushed easily, his fair hair now darkened to a light brown. He told me on the phone that this detour through Macon, after the New Orleans business trip where he saw Bart, left almost no time for visiting, but I appreciated the chance to see him.

I was filling water glasses to take to our back deck when he asked if he could see Brax's room, where they'd spent so much time as youngsters. "We've made some changes," I said as we went upstairs. "It won't look the same."

"It really takes me back to be in this room," he said. "But it looks so different with the pool down there—what a view."

Blue water sparkled in late afternoon sun, adding to the glare from white concrete that filled the area now. When we'd built our house that whole spot had been left as a steep green slope into woods, so the present view, including the angular black roof of the poolhouse, was quite a change. Also, this room, once a familiar hangout for a motley crew of boys, now had girlish touches from our whirlwind re-do for Susie's move-in.

"We built all that ten years ago," I said, "after Brax's first year away at college. Y'all would've loved it growing up. Can't you just imagine the parties?"

It was hard not to stare at Matthew, given Olivia's interpretation of my apparition. What may've seemed plausible in the abstract now seemed preposterous in reality. I wished he'd be first to broach the subject.

"Maybe your mom told you she was my chemo nurse for six months," I said. "I loved having her to chat with. She's got such a nice way of lightening heavy situations; but it's got to be a hard job."

"She told me; I think she really likes oncology work. I'm glad that's behind you." He trailed his hand along a row of books on the shelf. "She said you did great. Things still okay with that?"

"So far, so good," I said. "It seems like a long time ago now—five years—just a blip, in the big scheme of things. Compared to *this*, it was a walk in the park." We headed downstairs, followed by Lucy, the Boston terrier.

"I really miss Brax," he said. "We hadn't seen each other much lately. I always thought there'd be time to catch up."

"We always think that," I said. "Bart tells me he mentioned the lady named Olivia to you. Can you believe in stuff like that?" I glanced back over my shoulder at him. "I hoped we could talk about it, but you may think I'm crazy."

"He did tell me some of it," he said, "But I'd like to hear it from you. It's fascinating. I've heard of such things, but I don't know how it works—especially if she mentioned me."

We went through our front hall, got the water glasses from the kitchen, and headed to the wooden deck overlooking the pool. Green pots of bright red geraniums hung among four windows behind us; crimson dogwoods lit up a massive backdrop of green and rust foliage. We sat opposite each other at the wrought-iron table.

"So, did Bart tell you some of the other stuff, too?" I asked, hoping for some credible groundwork already.

"He told me she gave some real details about your father and about Brax's cousin Eric. That story of him watching you try on his flip-flops was amazing. But you told *her* about having a vision of a stranger, right? Was that the same night?"

I nodded. "The first night she came. We'd been talking to her about a white vase, and that led to asking her if she could help us interpret a possible apparition."

"The vase? Oh, yeah, Bart mentioned that, too," he said. "That's wild. Any resolution there? You still can't remember who brought it?"

"No. I talked to everybody who was here by 6 P.M. The main thing she could say was that it had been shattered. But she said it came from the boys; that's all she could feel certain of. She said we'd eventually find out more."

"Well, fill me in about this man you saw."

"All I know is that I positively saw the man that Saturday afternoon after the sheriff left. He looked young, had white hair, and was dressed in all white. He was alone, no car in sight, walking around our azaleas and curved bench near that white oak by the street. His head was down, bobbing slowly, and I thought he was talking to himself or on a cell phone. I figured he was a little swim student's daddy, looking for something—a pacifier was actually my guess—that may have been dropped after baby classes the evening before, and I was afraid he would come to the house."

"And this lady said that he was me?" Though his brows were raised, Matthew didn't appear patronizing.

"Yeah, that's what she said." I shrugged, self-conscious at how it sounded now. "Well, actually she said he was 'a friend of ours named Matthew.' We thought of you when she asked us to recall a Matthew who fit the description. Then she said you—*he*—was being used as a messenger and would be ringing our bell in less than three months."

He and I were facing each other, elbows on the black grillwork. Our conversation could hardly be thought of as normal but his face was relaxed. If he suspected I might be on thin ice emotionally, someone who needed humoring, his gray-blue eyes were kindly not showing it. The sun was dropping lower and cast an orangey-pink wash over our putty-colored house; shade from the high roof fell around us.

"Who was with you when she was telling you this?" he asked, jerking backwards, startled by Sushi, our Persian cat, who chose that second to pounce on the table. We watched as she settled herself into a black ball at his right elbow and closed her eyes.

"Only Susie and Annie," I said, "Jim had gone to bed by then. We first thought of Tate's friend Matthew Gray, but he's a brunette. And we were so upset when she said you were an angel who would be ringing our bell—we thought that meant you were going to die soon, too."

"Well, it's been three months," he said. "And here I am; but she may be the first person who ever called me an angel."

"But what do you think about all of this, Matthew? It sounds bizarre to us, but I've thought about it so often, and about all the other things, too, that I'm coming to terms with ideas like this. Now that you're actually here though..."

"It sounds bizarre alright." When he stroked Sushi's head only the tip of her long bushy black tail reacted, in a wave. "The first thing that came to mind when I heard about their wreck was that silver necklace of Brax's, with the big medal on it. You know the one I'm talking about?"

"His Saint Christopher's," I said. "Yeah, he loved that thing. I bought it in an antique store for his sixteenth birthday. That was my standard gift for new 16-year-old drivers—Christopher is the patron saint of safe travel."

"I'd love to see it," he said. "Brax was wearing it whenever we saw each other the last few times. I've been hoping you still had it—I wondered if it had been with them. Bart and I talked about it, but he didn't know."

"No, he'd lost it a few times but gotten it back," I said. "Then he lost it for good during one of his travels. He was sick about it; he figured he might've left it in a shower somewhere in Europe."

The medal, over an inch in diameter, unlike any I'd ever seen, was hollow sterling with a full sunburst on one side and the tall saint, carrying the Christ child on his shoulder, on the reverse, in rich silver relief.

"Our priest told Brax that it was probably Spanish silver. I think the Church demoted Christopher from its roster of saints, but that myth of his safely ferrying the Christ child across a Nordic river is lovely."

"So, he wasn't wearing it..."

"No, and Tate didn't have his either. The rascals..."

Sadness floated up from where it always waited. Sushi stretched her arched back, her pink mouth gaping in a ferocious, toothy yawn, and strolled across the table to butt my chin with her forehead, making us smile.

"One thing I've been curious about all these weeks," I said, "is if you remember what you were doing that day—around the time of their wreck. It would've been around 12:30 your time."

Just then, Jim drove past us in the green truck, coming in from work, and we got up to greet him. Sushi leapt over to a flat wooden rail surrounding the deck, keeping an eye on the dogs, who raced to Jim's door.

"Jim's come a long way—to think along these lines," I said as we walked the gangplank leading to the driveway. "His engineer brain stretches when it has to delve into talk of invisible men and conversations with spirits."

Matthew nodded his head, as if mindful of such a challenge. "But Bart told me he's talked to Olivia, too, right?" By now we'd reached the truck. Lucy danced on her hind legs as Sculley pressed his heavy frame between Jim and her, each vying for a pat from their master.

"Mostly he tries to listen," I said, chuckling. "His hearing aid doesn't help much."

The men were happy to see each other after so many years. Matthew had been a teenager the last time Jim had seen him. I imagined him flinching when I said Matt and I had been talking about my man in white. I guess he thought any young man, especially one looking so like the civil engineer Matt was now, would be uneasy discussing a moonlight job as some angel messenger.

"Oh, really?" he said, smiling. "Crazy stuff, isn't it?" He shook Matthew's hand, brushed my cheek with a peck, and then raised the truck's hood to check the dipstick for oil. The old truck needed oil again, which explained the need for ever-present cans rolling heavily around the passenger-side floorboard.

"Matthew was just about to tell me what he was doing that day, at the time of the wreck," I said, patting Matt's arm, encouraging him to go on. We stood there while Jim poured oil through a funnel and slammed down the hood. Holding a paper napkin and the empty can, he came around to us so he could hear. "That was a holiday weekend—were you in Seattle?" he asked.

"I remember exactly," Matthew said. "I've thought about it a lot. I was on Lopez Island, on the northern edge of Puget Sound, for the weekend. That Saturday morning Betsy and I and two friends took the San Juan Ferry to a farm that belonged to a friend's family. Someone in a pickup met our ferry and drove us to meet a larger group at the farm. I didn't know many of them, so after a while I decided to explore the area on my own, telling Betsy I'd be back for the clambake at lunch."

"So, about what time was that?" Jim asked.

"Around noon, Pacific time," said Matthew. "Julie said that their wreck was at 1:30 Texas time—so it was actually near then."

"And you would've been by yourself at this point," I surmised. "Did you fall asleep?" Instantly I felt foolish, but how else could a person leave his body on an island and have it appear somewhere else, nearly 3,000 miles away, at the same time?

"I was walking," he said. "The farm's on a hillside with a steep slope to the sound in front, so I headed up the hill away from it—toward the forest. The view looking back was great: the farmhouse, folks swinging in a hammock, tall golden grass, smoke from the fire, and water in the distance."

"It was a gorgeous day here," I murmured, remembering cotton clouds in an unusually blue sky.

"There, too." He went on, "Once I got to the woods, where it was shady and cool, it was an easy walk. I hadn't gone very far when I came to a structure made of logs—Brax and I'd have called it a fort, and it would've been a dream place for kids to play in. Adults had obviously built it. It wasn't locked, so I shoved the door open. It was so dark in there I could barely make out a pile of folded black plastic on the floor. It instantly gave me the creeps—I actually felt frightened by it—and I backed out, into the sunlight."

I felt a chill, watching him rub his crossed arms, dealing with this repulsive memory. It was easy to visualize—he casually opens a log door, eyes straining to see in the darkness until he spies a black, mounded form on the floor. The symbolism made me shudder. "I would have run back to the others at that point," I said.

"I did want to get away," he said, "to shake the feeling, so I walked on further into a forest of Douglas firs. The rest of the walk was beautiful—dark woods giving way to bright grassy clearings. I remember startling a rabbit and spying on a doe and her fawn. The best part, though, was trailing an eagle."

"You followed him?" I pictured the big bird with huge wings rising and falling, leading someone up, out of the woods.

"I heard him first. A loud screech with a high pitch at the end. I walked to the edge of the firs, trying to spot him. He called out again from another treetop, so I circled around, and then he called again from above the next meadow, like he knew I was trying to catch up with him. The meadow was full of tall grasses, with wildflowers everywhere. I decided to sit down to wait him out. He'd have to fly eventually; I would see him then."

I was mesmerized, hearing about his calm afternoon from four months ago—such a contrast to our boys'—or was it, I wondered. I couldn't say it then, but maybe it was true, that his perfect afternoon served as framework for a divine bond he had with my sons that day, before the awful truth was delivered to us.

"So you just sat there waiting to hear him again?" I asked. "By now it's been about thirty minutes or so?"

"Probably at least that. My hands fiddled with the tall grass around me. I started braiding pieces of it into a chain, still looking out for the eagle, by bending and pulling green streamers by feel. When I finished one section I started another, and I tied the two braided strands together. That's when I realized I wanted it to be a necklace for someone, so I picked flowers and tucked them into the weaving. It's strange how pleasant the whole experience was—of my waiting in the field for the eagle and of making this necklace. It seemed important that it be a gift for someone." He flushed self-consciously as he mentioned this compulsion, so artless, almost childlike.

"But you were going to give it to your fiancée, of course," I guessed.

"I don't know why exactly, but I didn't feel like it was for her. There was something so special about the experience that I couldn't expect anybody to really appreciate it."

"Did you see the eagle again?" Jim asked.

"I did—just as I was finishing the necklace he took to the air with a huge wingspan." Matthew spread his arms as wide as he could. "I stood up and watched him fly higher and higher, over the woods and away."

"So you went back to the others then?" I asked. He nodded. "Did you take the necklace with you?"

"I handed it to Betsy; she smiled—about the reaction I expected—but it wasn't exactly impressive in that setting. The crowd had grown by then and so had the party," he explained, grinning.

"I think we get the picture," I said, as Jim chuckled. But my heart was touched by the image of this relative newcomer, walking into a crowd of holiday weekenders, their party well under way, with his wilting flower necklace—his show-and-tell for his girlfriend. "But it sounds lovely," I offered, "even if you're not sure who you were meant to give it to."

"It was like a dream," he said.

"We'd love to meet Betsy—maybe we can, next time you're home."

"For sure," he said. He glanced at his watch then leaned down to give me a hug. "I'd better get going; Mom's expecting me for dinner."

"Could you ever write this down for us, Matthew?" I asked. "I hear so much symbolism in what you've told us. It may be good for you to write about it, too. We'd both like to read it."

"I will, I promise," he said. "It occurred to me at the time, but the grief, when I heard what Brax and Tate had gone through about that same time, totally trivialized everything else."

"Don't forget what Olivia told us," I reminded him. "It's mind-boggling, but she said they *had* to see that we would survive before they could pass completely away from us, and they told her that God used *you* to help them. That would make your hour extremely significant."

"It's a lot to process, alright," he agreed, shaking hands with Jim. He walked to his white rental car and we watched him drive away. Jim went on inside, but I lingered in the yard with the dogs, thinking about all we'd talked about, with a fresh awareness of how my childhood education had opened our young minds to ideas like these.

The nuns used to teach us children how to use energy to create spiritual gifts for others. The obvious, easy way was by doing good works, but we learned that we could even offer our suffering—whatever that meant to us protected, well-loved children—to send as rays of grace for someone. Shots, illness, brave visits to the dentist, serious and sad disappointments, even giving up sweets during Lent—any of these qualified as deposits into the universe's spiritual gift account. I figured most of it applied to our debt to Jesus, whom, as we were constantly reminded, we could never repay in full anyway.

We did daily Bible study and researched lives of saints, their sacrifices and extraordinary mystical experiences, and we read of modern miracles and intercessions by Mary into the lives of normal people. We were expected to believe those stories literally. As we matured we learned to offer our energy in the form of prayerful meditation to create a positive force which could telegraph comfort to a troubled spirit, help a body's power to heal, or even bring about world peace. We spent years trying to refine our best intentions.

Maintaining those beliefs into adulthood required some latitude, but the value of prayer, of dispatching energy to aid someone—even strangers on different continents—is still real to me. But never had I seriously day-dreamed about seeing the image of a living person, such as I saw in our yard that day.

I sat on the cinderblock wall to watch the dogs stalk squirrels, thinking back to all the prayers and help that supported us on July 3rd, and ever since. Even from Highway 10 in Ozona, Texas, according to the group of first-responders who wrote to our Macon paper, there had been prayers for the boys and their families. Before any horrible news had even reached us, spiritual energy had been directed to our home in Georgia. It required a wide stretch of faith to believe Olivia's interpretations of what she heard about Matthew; but if it could be true—that our sons were met and, for whatever purpose, ushered to their home place once more before beginning their new life, while allowing me the calming distraction of such a visual—then I am beyond grateful. We did receive the prayed-for peace, which Paul promised to the Philippians, and it has transcended all understanding.

Within a few weeks Matthew's letter arrived from Seattle. His telling of that afternoon was easy-flowing, descriptive prose. We all loved reading it. In the middle of the second typed page he summarized his interpretation of it.

Julie, I don't know what all of this means. But these are the things that I felt and saw at that time without any post factum additions. At the time, I remember thinking what a special, beautiful walk it had been and that I should write it down. If I had written it at that time, it would not be much different from the way that I am describing it now.

When I think back on it, and think about Brax and wonder if there was a connection, the thing that immediately comes to my mind is the necklace that Brax used to always wear—that medallion on a chain. I didn't know that it was Saint Christopher until you told me. Nor did I know that he had lost it. I wondered if he had been wearing it the night [sic] *of the accident. I figured he had, and I wondered if you kept it. That's why I asked you about it when I came to see you. I asked Bart about it when I saw him in New Orleans. For some reason, his necklace kept coming to mind. Now that I look back on that walk—flowers I picked and the necklace I made, and I think about Brax, what I feel is that the necklace that I made was for him. For safe passage, to replace his old.*

I miss Brax. It has been difficult to be so far away from the people who knew and loved him. I hadn't kept in good touch for some time, and I can't tell you how much I regret that. But this pain has taught me a lot—Brax is still teaching me important lessons in life.

24.

☙

Angelfire.com

To avoid the gloom of empty chairs around our Thanksgiving table, our extended family jumped at an invite from Jim's cousins, Barbara and Rick Collins, to join theirs in McDonough. Her dad, Jack, Ernest's veterinarian brother, was still alive then and regaled us with old Bragg stories, and Rick's hayrides around their lake were delightful. Despite the crowd—over thirty—everybody left with plenty of leftovers and new memories that happy day.

During the second week in December, our Artist's Way class had a reunion. Don Welch, former pastor of the little Methodist church on Arkwright Road by the river, was in town with his wife; it had been a year since we were together. Dot, our teacher, was needed at school, but about twelve members of our class met for lunch at Idle Hour Country Club. Kate Dodson sat across the long table from me, and everyone was admiring the engagement ring Criss had recently given her. As usual, conversation drifted into a session for sharing creative activities. There was talk of published articles, poetry, finished artwork, quilts, and new careers. Kate shared her plans to begin law school in New Orleans after an April wedding. We toasted to both plans.

When my turn came, I said my main accomplishment had been to manage our survival, which everybody understood. "That's taken about as much creativity as I could muster," I added. "But we're doing fine, I guess."

"Julie's been writing poetry, everybody," Kate announced. "The Braggs have done a memorial website, and her poetry is so moving. Lots of us have signed the guest book."

Several weeks earlier, Susie and I had begun a memorial for Brax and Tate on Angelfire, a free website. She learned HTML code, created a guest book, scanned photos and letters, and transcribed my efforts at poetry. While she was away at work, I'd pour over the writing—poems as letters to the boys—losing all track of time until I heard her open our back door. "I hope you've been working on something for me today!" she'd yell, passing through the kitchen. Her first good clue would be a stack of crusty breakfast dishes. If she found me still in pajamas, tear-streaked, but with printed paper held high, she'd take over my chair and spend hours encoding text. Titles—*That Innocent Day, The Alarm, Man in White, Independence Day Parade*, and *The Vase*—described our early life-changing days, when we wondered if the boys were watching us cope without them. We hadn't been ready to write about our experiences with Olivia at that point.

"How fine," the pastor said. "Tell us how we can read it. How about writing down the link to it." He slipped a card from his jacket pocket and passed it across to me.

"Sure, if I can remember it," I said, and reached down to my purse on the floor to search for a pen.

"Oh, Julie," Kate said, "I've been meaning to tell you—I can solve your mystery of that white vase you wrote the poem about."

"You can?" I straightened up, pen in hand, instantly forgetting about our long website address.

"Yeah, that was *my* white vase!" she said, beaming. To the others, she explained, "The Braggs didn't remember that I was the one who took a white vase to them after the boys passed away. It created such a mystery that Julie even wrote a poem about it."

"Yes," I said, struggling for words to hide my shock. "We all felt like it was something so special."

"I love that it meant so much to you," she went on, pleased to have given us not only a special gift, but her solution to its mysterious arrival.

"But, Kate," I interrupted, "you weren't there that first day—Saturday. It was after the weekend when you came, wasn't it?"

"Right—we came on Monday. We were by the pool at my folks' house on Tybee Island when Frank Kern called Sunday morning to tell us about

Brax's accident. I cried the rest of the trip—I'll never enjoy another Fourth of July."

"But," I repeated, "the vase was there on *Saturday*—by 6 P.M.—about an hour after the sheriff left. I remember when you, Criss, and the other couple came through our kitchen door a couple days later. Sassy carried a clear, round vase of yard flowers. I remember saying how much I love yard flowers when she handed them to me, and I went straight to the bookshelf by our fireplace with it."

"Exactly, and I was carrying my vase with lilies from *my* yard on Walnut Street. Maybe it wasn't you that I handed it to at the door, like I thought, but by the time we got to your front room I was surprised to see it already on your piano, like in the place of honor." Her greenish-blue eyes were tearing up. I couldn't say it, but I thought her memory of this was a delusion.

Light-hearted conversations hummed around us until eventually chairs were pushed back and the group stood, busying themselves with divisions of the check. Kate and I, engrossed in our conundrum, stood, too, and absently paid our portions. Outside on the leaf-spattered sidewalk, others exchanged good-natured hugs with us and we made usual promises to stay in touch, but Kate and I couldn't go anywhere until we sorted through our conflicting memories.

It was a perfect late fall afternoon. Golfers were on the green behind the antebellum-style brick clubhouse. Kate and I kept talking as we made our way toward the parking area. Her dark brown hair hung loose, kicking up on the shoulders of her rust-colored cardigan. We could clear this up—I'd been waiting five months for a solution, but the timing of the vase's arrival had been the whole core of its mystery. I didn't mention it, but Kate had clearly been in shock when she and her friends came to our house that Monday afternoon.

"From the minute I heard about Brax," she said, "my very first feeling was that *I* was your child, too. Isn't that strange? I instantly wished I could protect you from this pain—like Brax would've done. I loved him like a brother."

"I know."

"I realized on Tybee that as soon as I got home, I needed to give you my vase—it would be the perfect gift. I loved it—I'd painted my kitchen shelf a lime green to showcase that white vase—but I wanted you to have it. I knew exactly which lilies I would pick for it."

"But you weren't returning to your apartment until Monday, right? Truthfully, it was already with us on *Saturday*—we all saw it. And there aren't two of them."

"There's not one on my shelf anymore either—because mine's *on your piano.*"

My mind was swimming, unable to make sense of this. Standing by her car, we both cried, touched by memories of that whole dreadful July weekend. Our conflicting recollections of it made it worse.

"Where had it come from?" I asked.

"I bought it at Goodwill." She smiled at the irony. "I was helping Jackie Waters at her Society Gardener shop during last Christmas when Colleen Kelsall told Jackie and me that she'd seen some really good vases at Goodwill. Colleen and I made a special trip there and bought some of those milk-bottle shaped ones for the garden shop. All of them were clear except for that white one, which I kept. I left the label on it—did you know it was hand-formed, mouth-blown in Poland?"

I nodded. "We saw the little gold label, but Mother washed it off on Wednesday. The flowers were really dead by then, Kate—they were over four days old and there hadn't been enough water to cover their stems."

"That's right, because I planned to hold it in my lap on the way to your house. I meant to tell you to add some water."

Had she dreamed this?

I said, "Can you believe that a vase, exactly like the one you wanted to bring us, with those pinkish striped lilies, was already there by Saturday afternoon though? It showed up on our piano out of nowhere. It actually seemed to be glowing when I was on the phone with the Texas trooper, hearing dreadful details of their wreck. We knew it was bizarre. I tracked down every single person who was in that room by that time—6:14—no one had brought it. That's why I wrote the poem. Six weeks later we were still puzzling over it; we even asked a medium to tell us something about it."

"A medium?" she asked. "The lady who was there when we came to see Bart before he went back to New Orleans?"

"Yes, I wish you could've talked to her that afternoon."

"How did you get to know her?" Kate asked.

"She and Annie happened to meet in August, right after our family's R-and-R trip to Amelia Island—in the downtown salon. Annie called me and I talked to her, too. That first conversation blew us away—she said she had Brax and Tate with her. The girls and I set up a meeting for her to come to our house, and we planned to ask her to touch that vase to see if she felt something, thinking she could tap into its mystery. Back then, before I learned how spiritually true she is, I figured it could be like a touchstone of her credibility."

Kate sniffed into a wadded-up Kleenex before stuffing it in her bag. "What did she tell you about it?"

"Right away she said it had been shattered. That was her word, *shattered*. She couldn't say how it got to us—she asked if I had bought it to replace a shattered one."

"Wow," Kate murmured.

"Yeah, she seemed convinced it was from the boys."

"And I didn't even know they had died until Sunday."

"I know."

"Funny thing," I went on, "When Olivia began her reading for me that first night, she said she could hear a bedridden lady on satin pillows asking what we had thought of some strange flowers. That reminded me of our plan with the vase. The way she described the lady made me think instantly of my aunt, Annie Moore Wallace, in her house in Shirley Hills."

"Mrs. Wallace?!" Kate exclaimed. "I knew her, too; she and her husband lived around the circle from us—they were good friends of my grandparents."

"I remember that now," I said. "Did you know she was married to my dad's brother, Vernon?"

"I knew Mr. Wallace, such a sweet man, but I didn't realize they were your aunt and uncle until I met Brax in tenth grade at Stratford. She used to give prissy tea parties for us little neighborhood girls. I was barely out of kindergarten when Mama used to take me over there to read to her—she called me her little angel."

"Well, that makes two generations of us," I said. "She did the same with my sister and me when we were little."

Kate chuckled. "Mama made me wear a dress and promised something *fun* if I was good at their house, especially after Mrs. Wallace was bedridden. It was years later, when Brax told me his great-uncle had given him that beat-up old blue car, that I told him they were my neighbors. She'd died by then, though."

"Brax had a love/hate relationship with that car," I said. We both laughed, remembering the long sideswipes on that Chevrolet Bel Air from Uncle Vernon's years of skidding along his mailbox at the foot of his steep drive before he finally surrendered his license.

"Driving it around Stratford could've been the ultimate humiliation for most guys," Kate said. "But I think Brax was secretly smug—he was a true minimalist, and they were pretty rare in that parking lot."

"He was that way even as a little boy," I agreed. "Today, we'd call it eccentric."

"I'll never forget," she said, laughing, "how he used pencils to stab that black liner into the roof."

"So creepy," I said. "Tate loved riding around with him, though; I think he paid Tate to clean it out every now and then."

"Well," Kate mused, "the Wallaces sure were sweet to me. By high school, I actually loved my memories of reading with her."

"Same here; every little girl needs someone who makes her feel like a princess."

"So," she said after a pause, "the medium said Mrs. Wallace told her about my vase and flowers? She actually called them strange?"

I began to explain all that we heard about the vase was that it seemed shattered when Kate looked up from her watch and exclaimed, "Uh-oh, I'm supposed to meet my mother on Ingleside Avenue right now. We're working on wedding invitations."

She groped in her bag for keys and we hugged goodbye. Clearly, this discussion hadn't done much to solve our mystery; it was even murkier now. We had to just leave it hanging in our minds. I was weary and more confused than ever as we drove away.

25.

❧

Mission Impossible

On my way home, I thought about the Society Gardener, a charming little upscale, below-street garden shop in Ingleside Village, two blocks from where I grew up. It was close to the print shop where Kate and her mother were meeting.

The Village has thrived for more than fifty years by constant metamorphosis. A random string of basic-needs stores—grocery, drugs, dry cleaners, hardware, bookstore, beauty shop, filling station—is now an array of little antique and art galleries, gift shops and eateries, creating a shopping haven with a chic, new-age flavor.

The fifties' corner drug store, Harrisons Pharmacy, with its penguin sign touting conditioned air, had a soda fountain where we spent many teenage summer afternoons. It was adjoined, by a swinging door, to Bateman's Grocery. The drug store later became a popular pizza parlor with a mural of a happy green dragon walking full-length along its outside wall.

Last Christmas, the garden shop's owner, Jackie, had hired Brax and Tate to play guitars for her shop's open house. In lieu of being paid, they bartered for Christmas gifts for me. Tate decided on a wicker basket of little herb pots, and Brax picked out a large hollow copper butterfly on a chain. Kate had probably helped them. Both gifts from our last Christmas together are treasures. I wish I knew if they had learned about a special blown-glass vase there.

One night, about a week after the luncheon, Jim and I ran into Kate at a party around the corner from Ingleside Village at Mick's house on Rogers Avenue, where Brax had rented his downstairs apartment. The party was a celebration to showcase renovations of the old place. Kate told us that after she and her mother finished their invitation business, she'd gone down to the garden shop to talk over the bizarre puzzle of the vase with her friend, the owner.

"Jackie remembered my vase," Kate said. "The mystery fascinated her. She suggested I talk to her friend—a practicing shaman—to see how *she* would explain things like this."

"A what?" Jim asked.

"A shaman," Kate said. "She's like a medium, or spiritual healer."

"What did she tell you?" he asked. He had already expressed his opinion to me, since my lunch meeting with Kate, that nobody could be expected to believe this crazy, far-out explanation of the vase's origin.

"The shaman believes that all things have energy," Kate said. "She says it's possible that my vase allowed *itself to* be teleported because the boys' spirits willed it. That would mean my spirit knew about their wreck before my ears heard it, and that all our spirits communicated and reacted."

"Like the guy who bends spoons," Jim said, good-naturedly. "I guess she'd say the spoon's spirit allows the bending."

"Probably," Kate said, smiling. "I think that's called *telekinesis*. But she said spirit and energy are interchangeable words."

"I still can't get over your having such a strong memory of it, though," I said.

"Well, she's here somewhere, let's go talk to her," Kate said. She and I went into a hall leading to a bigger room where a small band with big amplifiers was starting up. Jim headed toward the bar in the kitchen. Teresa, the lady we met, was about my height and very regular-looking, with short, curly brown hair and the sturdy, competent look of a head nurse or lady pastor. She introduced her husband before he also went in the direction of the kitchen. It was getting harder to carry on a conversation.

"Kate says you've helped unravel the mystery of a vase that arrived at our house," I said, speaking directly into her left ear.

"Things like that are rare, but they do happen," she said with cheerful confidence. "Spirit energy is in everything—it's just that our Western culture has to relearn how spiritual activity can be so easily coordinated."

"We've sure learned a lot about spiritual activity in the past five months," I nearly shouted over increasing noise. "Would you say the vase is an *apport*?" Then, in answer to Kate's quizzical look, I added, "An apport is a paranormal movement of a material object. I read that they've been recorded for centuries."

"Sounds like it," Teresa said. "You're blessed to have had such an experience, especially at such a terrible time. I'm sure your vase is a real treasure now."

"Absolutely," I said, feeling my eyes water; her empathy was so compelling.

Kate said, "I can't shake my memory of taking it, though—it's so real."

"Didn't you say you weren't in town when you heard about your friends' deaths?"

"Right," Kate said. "I didn't even hear about it until Sunday—the next day. I went into shock then. We got back to town on Monday and went to the Braggs'—I can barely remember the memorial at the funeral home that night."

Noise from the other room had quieted while more players arrived and had to hook up to amplifiers.

"Perhaps emotional energy and shock, along with your desire to carry the vase yourself, created your memory—validated when you saw it at her house," said Teresa.

"So that means my vase was teleported in circular time—in spirit time, that is—on Saturday, after only my spirit knew of the tragedy and understood that Brax needed my vase for his mom—even while I was happy at Tybee Beach, not yet knowing until the next day about the horrible thing."

"Spirits are not confined to our physical time," said the shaman, smiling at Kate's grasp of things.

More time-travel talk! Was I the only one who's never experienced it?

Party noise had resumed, louder than before. Teresa patted my arm, saying, "Your sons were strong spirits; I'm so sorry for your loss. Remember: everything that is, is alive." Before she excused herself to join her husband she said that she hoped I was keeping a journal.

"A lot to think about, Kate," I said while I poured glasses of wine at the bar.

"Sure is," she said. "Our friend Kippy Tift's father-in-law is Dr. Raymond Moody. Once, when he still lived in Macon, I talked to him about circular time. You knew Brax and Tate met him in New York last summer, right?"

"I do," I said, "during their road trip to Montreal. They told me about running into Kippy and Avery on a New York sidewalk and then being invited to go to Alabaster Bookshop for Avery's dad's book signing. Brax came home with an autographed copy of *Life after Life* for Jim's mom—we all read it."

"Don't you wish we could talk to Dr. Moody about this?" Kate asked.

"I wonder what he'd say," I mused. "Some of his patients' experiences gave such positive but incredible evidence of life after death."

"Yeah," she said. "I don't imagine any of yours would seem abnormal to him."

"I feel like I should give that vase back to you, Kate, but I swear it's one of the most special things in our house now."

"No way! I meant for you to have it all along; just never imagined it would cause such interesting commotion."

Neither of us had any idea that there was one more *mission impossible* for her to perform for her friend Brax—it would take two long linear-time years before conditions would be set up for that one.

When I got home that night, knowing I'd never convince anyone about these mind-boggling answers to our vase or apparition mysteries, it was fun to string together my own simplistic version. So here's the perspective I'm stuck with:

Brax and Tate, while entertaining at the garden shop's Christmas open house, notice their friends admiring some new vases, especially an uncommon white one. Later, during their summer road trip, they come across a vase exactly like the most prized one, which Kate had kept for herself, and they buy it for me.

Then, on that Saturday, July 3rd, the spirit of my doting aunt Annie Moore learns of our heartbreaking tragedy, maybe even before we do. No doubt, she, the queen of regifting, would also be aware that a duplicate of my shattered gift, its sticker still intact, stands on a lime-green shelf in her *little angel's* Walnut Street apartment. All she has to do is remotely contact the spirit of Kate, whose body sunbathes on Tybee Beach that beautiful afternoon. Together, the spirits snatch a few of Kate's lilies and teleport the duplicate vase, containing a little water, to our piano. The next day—after

Kate goes into shock from hearing about her dear friend and his little brother—details of her having brought it herself will be implanted in her memory and are substantiated as soon as she sees her vase at our house on Monday.

All this spiritual scurrying takes place during my trance-like spying on a young man, dressed in white, who is in our yard. We learn through a trusted mystic's reading that the man was actually the spirit of Brax's very alive friend Matthew Davis. Although his human form is on a meaningful hike on a Puget Sound island, his spirit has been dispatched to comfort the spirits of our sons, so abruptly jettisoned from their damaged bodies. Matthew's mission is to lead his best friend and the little brother up, away from the darkness of a blinding crash, and eastward over their home place, and then to point them beyond—to spread their wings, as wide as an eagle's, toward the limitless layers of perpetual light. This mesmerizing apparition keeps me from collapsing in grief.

That will have to work for me—at least while I wait to transition into that life of wise, loving spirits myself. I recently came across a famous Einstein quote urging us to loosen our minds from bonds of limited thinking about time: "People like us," he wrote, "who believe in physics, know that the distinction between past, present, and future is only a stubbornly persistent illusion."

26.

❧

A New Year—2000

Christmas plans that first year were simple: we just wanted to survive it. We agreed our poolhouse could no longer be Santa headquarters, with everybody coming for turkey and gifts around our tree—I didn't even do a tree. Susie's kids went to their dad's and she, Jim, and I spent Christmas Eve night at Annie's; Bert's kids were with their mom. A choir friend gave me a ride to Midnight Mass, where the rigors of concentrating on our singing parts allowed for almost no mind-drift, and festive grandeur offset the ache of watching a column of altar boys process solemnly toward the altar below. We welcomed fatigue that helped us sleep in our own beds the next night. New Year's, a day for looking ahead, was even more anticlimactic. But we had passed into the sixth month of our grieving process, trying to live normally, even though nothing could ever be normal again.

I had begun making shrines everywhere. Down a short logging road, across the street from Dot's driveway, I discovered a sapling pinned to earth by a fallen pine log. It formed a graceful arch, which I wrapped with fluttery silver tinsel, creating a frame for the thick log that became my bench. I tied two orange crosses, woven from pine-straw-bailing twine, to its branches. Deer antlers, bleached with age, lay in a rock-bordered bed of moss. I stopped by there on most of my runs.

Further down the street, a life-sized, over-bright statue of Mary, red-haired, blue-eyed, hands steepled in prayer, stood on a green globe beside a backyard playhouse. In memory of my loved ones, I left small rocks by her pinkish toenails along with red dogwood berries for friends facing health issues, like Trisha, one of our lifelong friends, newly diagnosed with breast cancer. I hadn't met Mary's homeowners those first years, but they never moved my little collection.

The cemetery on Thomaston Road held a precious shrine, of course, but visits were mostly for housekeeping and replacing silk flowers—I didn't need to go that far to commune with my boys. Creating a permanent sanctuary at home became my resolve for 2000, and we finally decided on a labyrinth as the perfect sacred garden. I had been amazed by the reverent atmosphere of San Francisco's crowded, famous Chartres design in front of Grace Cathedral years before and felt the same peace when walking a rock-and-brick Cretan-style labyrinth at the little church where we'd had the Artist's Way class. Our neighbors, Dan and Gail Johnston, Macon's labyrinth experts, had one in their yard, and he offered to help us select the spot for ours. We chose a lower terrace where the boys' archery target had stood and would wait for warmer weather and coworkers to lay it. Planning for it gave purpose to rock hauling and enlivened gray days.

When Barbara Collins, our McDonough cousin, and I talked about the fabulous ski trip Tate and I had taken with Annie, Bert, and his kids last February—when the young crowd were great teachers and Tate and I were quick learners—she and I decided that a new version of that Park City trip might be just the escape we four adults could use, even if neither she nor Jim were skiers. So, we set about making arrangements right away for the coming February.

That second trip was like trying to re-whip a soufflé. Jim hated skiing, so only Rick and I skied, and I saw reminders of my young ski buddies everywhere. We were such wet blankets that I don't know how our sweet cousins stood us; we couldn't stand ourselves. We came home more miserable than when we'd left, facing additional sadness because of Brax's approaching birthday on March 10th.

Positivity, which we'd always held for our family's future, had flattened into resignation. Painful disappointment, throbbing angrily, felt like true anger, and we were too numb to tell the difference. Statistics are grim for marriages after a child has died, and our thirty-five-year marriage felt sick with grief. Mid-March was also the deadline for deciding if I was strong enough to operate the swim school for another year. I wasn't hopeful, but I couldn't admit my fear of drowning in this sorry state. Irony aside, it was clear that something had better rescue the lifeguard.

In the mid-eighties I had learned about the Enneagram, a system of self-discovery that helps discern one's true nature, that core quality or gift around which is layered our insulation—our personality—which we feel is needed to survive in our bewildering world. I had almost memorized Don Riso's first book, *Personality Types*, and listened to tapes by Franciscan priest Richard Rohr. I'd learned that my own Type Two, the busy Helper, prefers to solve others' needs and fears rather than to submit to quiet introspection, which exposes personal neediness. The driving fear is of being seen as selfish or weak or even unloving. Maybe a renewed study of the Enneagram could help revive my sense of identity and purpose.

I contacted Enneagram Institute in New York, and by the first week-end in March I was in Philadelphia, immersed in a workshop on "The Wisdom of the Enneagram," taught by Riso himself, along with Russ Hudson, his coauthor. Time spent in self-reflection helped me see that I *was* healing. Being able to help others conquer fear of water had come as a life gift and a reliable sense of purpose. I was reminded that it's not selfish to throw myself a lifeline of *knowing-kindness* whenever I am adrift in a sea of sadness.

I came home recharged, ready to face the rigors of swim school and to celebrate Brax's twenty-ninth birthday, guessing that the timing of this epiphany had his soul-print all over it. We remembered his birthday with Mexican food and a movie the next Friday night and joined a full house at the Rookery on St. Patrick's Day for celebrating and singing. Kirby and Russell made an exciting announcement of their progress with the vast job of compiling Brax's writings. They'd found its title among his papers: *Bullet Proof Bible*.

Labyrinth-building delays were due mainly to winter weather, but one morning I stared at those gray rocks from a different perspective. Blasting had ripped their world apart, left them fractured, scarred, and ugly; they would never be whole again. I could feel their pain but couldn't see them in our sacred garden, our symbol of life, energy, and peace. How had I over-looked tons of aged rocks, so full of history, on our own land?

Settled on the northern outskirts of Macon in a community known as Holton, Georgia, our property had been a homestead for a family of seven children of a Civil War veteran. One of its structures had been the last stagecoach stop en route to the Lewis Ferry, which crossed the Ocmulgee into Jones County. We bought the property from W. D. H. Johnson's descendants in 1976 and named our white shepherd "Turk," after the son who had last lived there. Their two now-demolished cabins, built in 1876 and full of heart pine, much of which was recycled into our new home, had been our favorite hangout—we were weekend pioneers with oil lamps, wood stove, two-seater outhouse, and a cabin filled with young sleepover friends. We played in the creek, tended a herd of Nubian goats, chickens, and eventually a horse, even after we moved into the new house. By 2000, all that remained of the original grounds were two tall, loosely stacked retainer walls of ancient native stones. Right away I hacked a path through the underbrush to begin dismantling those walls and haul heavy *ancestry* rocks over to our future labyrinth site. Later on Jim found a home for my mound of rescued granite—a fellow at work adopted them to create borders around his mobile home.

When the phone began ringing on April 1st and word spread that swim classes were being scheduled, I was relieved and grateful. It had occurred to me that parents might stay away, uneasy about my stability after our tragedy only eight months earlier. When May 8th marked the beginning of the swim school's thirtieth year, I felt, as I rewarded little hands with the famous blue whale stamp imprint, which I'd used since the seventies, that the real reward was mine—more than ever before.

Just before Mother's Day, Olivia called. Our chats were usually more about present life topics than mystical ones those days, but she let me know if there was something specific to tell me.

"The boys want you to know that there'll be a gift for you under the trees," she said. "They show graceful circular shapes in shady woods. It will be their gift to you."

"Gift? Like for Mother's Day? Maybe mobiles or wind chimes in the trees?"

"I don't know exactly when," she said. "It feels more like a big tire or maybe like an air filter, and I don't think it is hanging. I guess you don't know about it?"

"Not yet, but I'll let you know if I figure it out."

"Didn't you tell me that Taylor made things from clay?" she asked.

"He did," I said. "He gave away most things, but we have some unfired pieces he made last spring."

"Well, look through that and see if you don't see some circular thing."

"I will. I helped him pack up the stuff from his clay table in the poolhouse before swim classes began last spring—it's still in his room."

"Well, I hope you're enjoying your teaching. How has it been, working with children again?"

"Easier than I'd expected. My breath catches, though, when I see eyes or hair or little noses that remind me of them. Little boys seem obliged to hug me, but tears are easily camouflaged out there; plus I can always duck underwater if it gets too bad. But I really am lucky to still be involved in these lives."

"Well, don't doubt for a minute that your boys are proud of you for going on with your life," she said. "How is Jim?"

"Fine. When's he's not at work he's busy with the yard and pool."

"He hasn't retired yet, then?"

"Oh, no; hasn't even talked about it."

"I have a feeling it'll happen quickly when the time comes," she said.

"We'll see. By the way, I've been meaning to tell you," I said, "Brax's leather jacket never turned up all winter. Friends were serious about searching for it; we sure thought it would've shown up by now."

"Well, he's still trying to get it home. 'Gettin' it home to Pop,' he says. He wants his dad to have it."

"Any vibes about where it could be?"

"It's definitely in a closet," she said. "He's showing me a box in a closet."

"Like a storage closet?"

"No," she said. "It's for clothes, though no clothes are there—just boxes. Have you unpacked all his things?"

"Everything. We looked through Tate's closet, too. It's not here."

"I think it's coming—don't give up yet. And let me know about that circular gift in the woods—it's coming, too."

I went up to Tate's room to poke through a laundry basket full of carefully towel-wrapped pieces of clay—some fired, some still green. He specialized in busts of lifelike characters, mostly comical. A bizarre one was a curly haired man, his face and head split open—crown to chin—allowing a hand, holding a big eye, to emerge from his brain. Another guy, with a crooked grin and a removable hat, might have been a self-portrait.

I did see a piece that could possibly be considered circular. Its thick saucer-sized base of rounded hexagonal angles was crammed with symbols, including an obelisk and eight domes of teeny to thumbprint size, one of them centered in a ropelike spiral. There was a bridge connecting two geographical shapes, a small triangle, and a quarter-sized delicately pin-lined concentric maze: an intriguing collage that I couldn't fathom, but a lovely thing, nonetheless. He'd talked of colorizing this piece—I wish he'd said more about it. Maybe he had planned to give it to me, but not likely for outdoors. I carried it downstairs to the den table to set beside his metronome. I would definitely see about having it fired—and think of it as my Mother's Day gift.

The end of May brought the graduation of his senior class at Mount de Sales Academy. When the principal called to ask if we would get any comfort from having his diploma, we declined; it would be just one more reminder of his unfinished life. But I did want to be with his friends for their baccalaureate service at church the night before graduation. Jim's bad hearing was his usual excuse for avoiding large settings with predictably heavy dialogue or emotion, as this turned out to be. The most moving moment—when Tate's classmates presented his diploma as an altar gift during Mass—was nearly unbearable. Several spoke of him, and I was glad I hadn't missed it. But neither of us attended the graduation.

I'd scheduled no swim classes around July 4th, expecting to be crippled by memories. Jim had the week off, too. But like most other frightening milestones, this first anniversary passed pleasantly with family and friends. Russell had called the day before to say he'd bring hotdogs if we felt like having company on the Fourth. That idea hatched plans for a cookout with a spontaneous guest list that grew to forty—which would be more than enough hands for the laying of a rock labyrinth. I invited Dan and Gail Johnston, our neighbors, and after the cookout, he led our group through the intricacies of laying a seven-circle ancient Cretan-style labyrinth.

Our location was perfect. Dogwoods, oaks, and mulberry trees shaded the level terrace, and walls of tall bamboo separated it from the woods below. Dan anchored a 20-foot center rope as a radius, and as he walked it around a huge outer circle, he showed us where to place our stones, some big enough to stand on end, others flat. As we moved with Dan toward the center, our rocks gradually revealed the classically simple Cretan design, with its seven concentric rings. Within an hour we were out of rocks, but the loose outline was laid and we were able to begin our slow, thoughtful walk on the maze-like path within the rows of rocks. In bed that night, I realized we had received our lovely circular gift under the trees. I'd have to tell Olivia.

On July 15, a group of the boys' friends, again led by Russell, organized the second Bragg Jam at Jim Kee's Rookery. Volunteer bands were recruited to play, and Russell created a promotion flyer to post around town. The outcome was a lighter, less sad version of their first one, with a two-fold outcome: in addition to celebrating our missing boys' lives, we congratulated ourselves on our first year of survival without them. A general comment was that a bigger, cooler venue might better serve the growing crowd, who obviously wanted this to become an annual event. Again, the cover charge went into a fund at the community trust for the Ocmulgee Heritage Greenway, where a gateway trailhead—with plans for a dancing water fountain and small amphitheater—was well under construction. The overall project would cost many millions, so Bragg Jam's kinship was more soulful than fiscal.

The hectic summer had been draining. I had taught swimming on autopilot to over 300 children, never able to unwind, stifling raw emotions in order to focus on the physical and emotional demands of young swimmers and their parents. All I wanted was to retreat to a quiet place and recharge, which was exactly what another immersion in learning more about the Enneagram could provide. Jim approved, though I don't think he really delved into its spiritual aspects—he likened the system to aptitude tests he administered to job applicants—but he encouraged the getaway for the therapeutic effect it seemed to produce. I expect a fishing trip was like that for him.

At the end of swim school I left for Vallombrosa Retreat Center in Menlo Park, California, to begin my first weeklong training with the Riso-Hudson Institute. Our tentative goodbye kiss at the Atlanta airport felt like ones we exchanged at doors of operating rooms, when breast cancer brought worries about the future. Even though he would be in good hands with Susie and her kids, I felt guiltily self-absorbed as I flew away from him, especially knowing I'd be gone for our birthdays. I loved him for being so supportive and hoped that whatever healing I was grasping for in this trip would include a way to relieve his pain, too.

After an idyllic week with the Riso-Hudson class, I took the Bay Area Rapid Transit to visit my cousin Bev's family in Oakland. We celebrated my birthday at their north-coast vacation house at Sea Ranch, and after a few days hiking on a bluff above the Pacific's crashing waves, I flew home, anxious to tell Jim and the others all I'd learned and seen.

When my instamatic camera was developed I saw a startling image in one of the photos, taken during an afternoon of biking at Sea Ranch. I had asked a honeymooning couple to snap my picture as I stood by a stained-glass window in a tiny stone chapel, carved into a hillside under redwoods. There in the picture, encircling my waist from behind, enfolded in my shirt, was an unmistakable pair of hands.

27.

≈

Time Travel

Matthew Davis made another visit in September. Again, since he was combining a visit to his mom's with a business trip from Seattle, his time was limited. On the morning he called I was about to go for a run and he decided to join me.

We had run less than a mile when Sculley, having tailed us through woods along the road, showed up, long tail wagging in proud circles. For him to have crossed the busy highway was dangerous and having him along would cause territorial battles with neighbor dogs, so we headed back. Matthew toured the labyrinth, which I'd been adding rocks to since we'd laid it in July, filling gaps in its outline. He placed a rock in honor of his and Betsy's new life—his company was transferring him to Boston, closer to her family. We spent our remaining time in the driveway by his car.

"We loved your letter," I told him. "Your descriptions and symbolism were amazing—the hike, that cabin, the eagle's flight, the necklace."

"I loved writing it," he said. "Most of what I do now is technical, so it felt great to get back to something creative. As far as symbolism, I see some, too, but I can't say I have any idea of being anywhere except where I was that afternoon." He had opened his car door and was leaning on folded arms on top of it.

"I've thought back to all those years when you and Brax were together nearly every day during grammar school and junior high; but I never really worried about what you might be getting into," I said, laughing. "I doubt if your mom did, either. I can't believe we let you 16-year-olds take your old

VW van to Fort Walton Beach. We may've trusted you guys a little too much."

"We were okay, we probably got into a lot less than kids can these days." He sat on the edge of the car seat, his legs straddling Sculley, who had pushed in for attention.

"I've wondered if you two ever thought about making a pact—you know, like Houdini made with his wife. Brax was fascinated by Houdini's promise to communicate with her after he died."

"Never a pact, but after I wrote the letter I remembered some tapes I'd ordered when we were about 13. I talked Brax into listening to them with me, but I didn't think he was really paying attention to them."

I tugged at Sculley's collar to pull him away from Matthew's car door, which he was trying to close. "What kind of tapes?"

"Instructional tapes about astral projection," he said, grinning up at me through his open window. "We'd lie on my bedroom floor and practice controlled breathing and visualizations to see if we could enter the time travel that was being taught. Brax had trouble concentrating—I thought he felt it was too contrived."

"Time travel—why am I not surprised! What about you? Could you do it?"

"I liked trying it. I listened to them by myself—it was restful. There were times I felt like I'd succeeded with the exercise, but mostly it didn't produce any special results."

"Not many people have even experimented with it," I guessed. "Maybe without knowing it, you learned something you might need later. Maybe it's possible."

He shrugged, smiling, as he cranked the motor. "I know I'll never forget that afternoon. Maybe one day we'll understand some of these things."

"Well, I'm sure expecting lots of answers whenever my day comes," I said.

"Me, too," he said. We hugged through his open window and I watched him drive past our pool and around the screened porch—back to his life.

There was still that authentic, calm sense about him—as if he were the same boy, unaffected by his success at Cornell, or Seattle, or by mysterious facets of his good friend's death. I wondered what he thought about past lives, which I had begun thinking more about. What if their friendship had started in another lifetime and had been sealed with a pact to race each other back here for another round? Maybe it was no accident that his birthday precedes Brax's by fewer than forty-eight hours. Or that Russell's was only a few days later. And what about Jim's and mine? Had we been so intent on jumping from some other lifetime into this one that we landed here within hours of each other, even at the same Macon hospital? Do spirits collaborate on scripts beforehand then let them be *forgotten*? Is that why we must endlessly ponder the purpose of each Life? I'm more convinced than ever that we are meant to take notice of so-called *coincidences*.

Later that fall I was among a group of volunteers to launch Middle Georgia's first Komen Race for the Cure, a fundraiser for breast cancer research. Its early morning premiere race was in late October at Wesleyan College, the world's first college for women—the day before Tate's nineteenth birthday. We had his favorite chili dinner in the poolhouse the next night, contented with memories of that adorable boy and his years of Halloween birthday parties.

The Enneagram Institute offers sequential layers of training, and I really wanted to continue with their next workshop—more experiential than the first one—to be held at Kirkridge, a rustic retreat center on a mountaintop in the Poconos, in Bangor, Pennsylvania. It would include a session of Breathwork Therapy, developed by psychiatrist Stanislav Grof, as a form of self-healing, and I was excited, if a little nervous, when I left for it the morning after Tate's birthday dinner.

Jane Hollister, a Grof-certified Breathwork therapist from Tampa, along with Riso and Hudson, led our class of thirty-six through a full day of preparation for the next day's amazing adventure. It was similar to Lamaze breathing, which I'd done when Tate was born. We formed partners, and mine was Agnes Lau, a therapist from Singapore who was experienced in this. The partner's role is to sit protectively on the floor in our large darkened room beside the breather, who is lying on a mat, following Grof's quick-breath technique into an altered state, aided by loud evocative music. Sitting with Agnes that morning, I watched as she and others entered various states of consciousness, some joyous, others in obvious distress, yet everyone reemerged in trancelike ecstasy.

Being a witness gave me courage to experience it, though honestly, I wasn't expecting any radical healing—nor was I aware of any blockages I needed to work through, although that was the most commonly expressed outcome. During the morning there had been some who appeared to relive birth experiences or forgive abusive loved ones, while others sang or enjoyed viewing peaceful memories; I expected to be in that group, grateful for wonderful memories and for all the positives in my life.

After our lunch break I stretched out on my mat with Agnes beside me. In no time, loud music and my controlled, rapid breathing transported me to a winding mountain road where, through closed eyes, I watched a squared-back car travel jauntily along the edge of a steep hill. I couldn't see its driver, but I waved, hoping to flag him down—there was something, I didn't realize what, that I wanted to tell him. As the car disappeared around the hill, leaving me standing by the road, a male voice from somewhere in our darkened room wailed for his mother. The sound gripped me, the trance intensified, and I was gone—flung like a ragdoll toward the car, which was now plainly a green SUV, carrying my sons. All I had wanted was a chance to say *goodbye*. But the process of releasing deep, pent-up regret for not having been with them as they took their last breaths seemed to take hours and rivers of tears. Sobbing uncontrollably, I could feel their arms as we clung to each other and their love while they helped me let them go. My session finally ended with a feeling of swimming to the surface of cool water, gasping for breath; but, like the others, I was dazed with relief. When the long wall of curtains opened we were stunned to see the season's first snowflakes floating like cotton balls through late afternoon sunlight.

After dinner we gathered to share our impressions, and it was then that I thought about where the boys had been the last time I ever spoke to them. They had been in a phone booth on Big Sur's coastal highway. They were traveling happily along a winding, mountainous road toward Los Angeles for a few days of fun with their friend James Morris. Our last casual goodbyes had been as full of cheer as ever, but inadequate—with little concern of all we had to lose. In looking back on that experience, I realize it was a milestone in a long journey of healing.

28.

$\mathcal{Q}$

Bobcat for a Birthday

Jim's early retirement was arranged that January, about a year and a half after the family reading in August of '99, when Olivia had viewed the boys waving flags for him at a finish line. Our life was moving into another new stage.

We talked often about his disappointment in not finding Brax's leather jacket. When I mentioned it to Olivia that February, she seemed to have more information. "Brax says it's on its way," she said.

"Really?" I said. "We're almost through the second winter now; what makes you so sure?"

"I can hear him...," she said. "'Still trying to get it home for Pop.' He says, 'K is going to know where it is.' I think you'll definitely find out from a big K."

"A person named K," I reported to Jim. "Maybe that's Kirby or maybe Colleen Kelsall—she gave it to him." Despite talk of the jacket's recall during a break-up, all feelings had healed, it was regifted, and they were friends ever since. "But you know she's living in London now."

"I can't think of any other K's," said Jim. "Surely he didn't leave it at Kmart!"

Our labyrinth continued to be a place of peaceful energy—it gave and required lots of it. I hauled rocks to fill gaps in its outline, transplanted moss and ferns from our creek down in the woods, placed a cement statue of two boy angels at the entrance, and always could see more that could be done. Ever since the Kirkridge retreat I had wished for an altar-type center rock, like the one in their labyrinth in Pennsylvania. I even located the perfect boulder in our woods but hadn't thought of a way to move it, short of hiring someone with heavy equipment.

On March 9, the morning before Brax's birthday, as Rob, Anna, and I were leaving for school, we nearly collided with a young man at the end of our driveway. He was standing next to a flatbed truck parked on the right-of-way, about to unload a small tractor that had a front-end bucket.

"Look, Mimi, that guy has a bobcat on his truck," Rob said.

"Can I help you?" I asked, leaning across to Rob's window to speak to the man.

"I'm supposed to meet my boss here," he said. "I'm not sure why, or why he's not still following me, but this is the address he gave me."

"I don't know why he sent you here, either, but I'll be back in about twenty minutes. I've been hoping for a way to move a rock—I wish we had time now to show you where it is—I'd pay you ten dollars to move it, if you have time when I get back."

He shrugged. "Sure—if I'm still here. My phone's in his truck so I can't call him."

"I'll hurry!" I said.

He was still there when I got home. I stuck ten dollars in my pocket and led him and his noisy little tractor down into the woods. In five minutes the large ice-chest size boulder was exactly where I'd pictured it, looking like it had been the centerpiece of our sacred space forever. We had just returned to the flatbed when a white pickup rushed to a stop beside us. Its driver, obviously the boss, called through his open window, "Pack it up, and let's go! I had to go back to the office for directions—we're at the wrong house!"

Of course, I knew they'd come to the right house—and I smiled, thinking what a perfect gift I'd gotten for Brax's birthday that year. He would've been thirty.

There was a third and final workshop in the Enneagram Institute's training series—this one on utilizing the tool in daily and professional life—at Simpsonwood Retreat Center near Atlanta, within easy driving distance. I left for it the next morning. It was probably no coincidence that these retreats seemed to be tied to birthdays, first mine, then Tate's, now Brax's, and, though I felt guilty as the sole recipient, I saw them as gifts, which I could share. The peaceful setting along the Chattahoochee was another ideal place for a retreat. Riso and Hudson led us into a deeper understanding of how to utilize this transformational tool in working with others. Many in our class were therapists who would blend the Enneagram into their work with clients. I planned to try using it during my upcoming swim classes as a way to intuit a child's specific fears and goals. Maybe a modified teaching approach for certain types could speed up the process of helping every child become a competent swimmer, but, regardless, it was an invaluable tool for better understanding of myself and others.

During swim season I made no allowance for time off during July 4th, which fell midweek. That Saturday we welcomed the birth of Carolyn's first grandchild, baby girl Payton, seen playing at Melinda's feet during Olivia's reading two years earlier.

It was Jim's first year to finally see what a busy operation had been going on in our yard every summer. Cars, filling the circular drive, moved in and out nearly all day as classes changed. He especially loved to sit on his screened porch to watch the parade of children, noting the daily progress of their body language—from resistant to jubilant—as they passed his viewing stand with their families. The hot summer flew by.

The friends who organized both Bragg Jam concerts were committed to keep the boys' memory alive with an annual gathering, but general consensus was that it would have better potential for growth if it were moved out of July's sweltering heat. Russell Walker had begun Mercer Law School, so Kirby Griffin agreed to pick up the torch. He organized volunteers who played at the earlier concerts and rescheduled the third one for late October. Ocmulgee Heritage Greenway, now called Ocmulgee Heritage Trail, with nearly a mile of paved walkways, had been rapidly expanding during the two years since its groundbreaking in September of '99, and fundraising would continue to provide Bragg Jam the bonus of a dual purpose.

Susie's house had been on the market all that time, but 2001 was their last summer with us. A sale was pending, so she wouldn't be moving back into the poolhouse when swim season was over. When they moved into their new condo a few miles away, Anna was 16 and Rob was 13. After two years of a full house, Jim and I had mixed feelings as we faced a new, quieter future. We were going to miss them.

They had been gone a couple weeks when the horrors from the attack on the World Trade Center's twin towers destroyed peace everywhere. To avoid being overwhelmed by gut-wrenching visuals on TV that Tuesday, I drove our pickup to Bolingbroke for a load of small stacking rocks and garden soil and followed the news, via my radio, from the labyrinth, which had been my refuge for the past year. By Saturday there was a little retaining wall and bed of colorful mums around the base of a young dogwood at the labyrinth entrance—as our 9/11 memorial.

29.

❧

Homecoming

The following Sunday morning at 7:30, I nearly choked on my coffee when I opened a short, surprising email from Kate Dodson. She and Criss had married and moved to New Orleans, where she was in law school at Tulane, during the year since we'd seen them, but her email said she'd recently transferred to the University of Georgia and that she had exciting news: she had located Brax's leather jacket! The email was time-stamped at 3:30 A.M. She enclosed her phone number, asking me to call so she could tell me all about it—*but please wait until after 9:30 to call.*

I hurried to our screened porch, where Jim was reading the Sunday paper, to show him her printed email. "Sounds like Olivia was right about a 'K' after all," he said with a big grin. We could hardly stand it, but I waited till 9:48 to dial Kate's number.

"Hello," mumbled a groggy voice.

"Kate? I know I'm waking you. This is Julie—we got your email! Should I call you back later?"

"No, hold on—I've hardly been able to sleep anyway." There was a muffled commotion, like she was moving covers, taking her phone away from the bed.

"Can you believe it?" she said, much more awake. "I actually ran into a woman last night who has Brax's jacket."

"In Athens, how in the world...?"

"I was tempted to call you at three—it's so unreal. Criss and I haven't been here two weeks yet—you knew I've transferred to Georgia, right?"

"Not till I read your email—I thought you were still in New Orleans."

"We were—for a year. Criss had trouble finding work in the wine business there, so that helped us decide to move here. New Orleans is a hard town to break into."

"I imagine."

"Joel Bordman, from Macon, came yesterday and we checked out the local bar scene last night, but we got a late start. After a couple places, we went to the Roadhouse, but since they had a cover charge and it was so late, we moved on to the Georgia Bar on Clayton Street."

"Cool name."

"Yeah. It was nearly empty and I was tired, so I sat in a booth while Joel carried on a long-winded conversation with the woman bartender. Criss came and sat with me; we were both about ready to head home."

"So how'd you find the jacket?"

"I'm getting to that part. Joel came over to say that the bartender knew a good friend of ours. He dragged us back to the bar to talk to this woman. She didn't look like somebody I was interested in meeting, but he told us she was from Macon."

"He said 'Guess who she was a friend of,' obviously expecting us to be impressed and more sociable. I tried to act interested, but when she said *Brax* I really did perk up. I couldn't believe she'd been his friend. I'd never seen her and she was kind of hard looking, you know. I said, 'You were a friend of Brax's?'"

"What'd she say?"

"She said, 'Yeah, he was my friend. He died. I still have his leather jacket.'"

"Just like that?!"

"Yeah. I nearly fainted. I said, 'Why do you have his jacket? His parents have been looking for it for two years!' She was so disinterested, I couldn't believe it."

"Did you tell her you would gladly take it off her hands?"

"Yeah, after I told her you'd been looking for it, she said, 'Well, I don't want it; I offered it to some guy before I moved from Macon, but he didn't take it.'"

"Thank goodness for that!" I said. "I wonder how she got it."

"She said she was bartending at the Music City Grill in Macon when Brax played there one night. I think she said she helped him take some of his stuff home when they closed. It was June, so he didn't need a jacket. It wound up being left on her back seat."

"He and Tate left on the twenty-third of June; I bet he hadn't realized it was gone. We'd about decided he lost it on the trip—it was his *look*, even if it wasn't cold."

"I know. I got her phone number. I'll call her this afternoon and go get it."

"What a story! Did you know our friend Olivia told us that a 'K' would be the one to find the jacket? She said Brax told her that."

"NO!"

"She said it was in a box somewhere but that he was trying to get it home for Jim. You sure must be special, Kate—like his personal envoy."

"I guess I am," she said with a lukewarm chuckle. "First he wants my vase, now I'm the one he sends to find his jacket. I really miss that guy."

"Well, Jim's sitting here, waiting to hear all this. So, when do you think you'll have it? We'll drive to Athens anytime and meet you."

"No, we're coming home next weekend; we'll bring it. I'll call her today and see where she lives."

"Just email me when you're ready. This is so shocking—in a good way. I can't wait to tell everybody." Jim and I ate breakfast on the screened porch basking in this amazing outcome of a two-year mystery. We looked forward to reuniting with this relic.

Their plan to come home didn't work out right away. Kate was in school and Criss was working. But I was also very involved as registrar for the second Komen Race for the Cure, set for October 6, so we were content to wait; within a few weeks, Kate finally sent an email that the jacket was hanging on a chair in their kitchen. It's just as well that we didn't know what a hard time she had trying to get the woman to commit to a meeting or to arrange some other way for its return, but we eventually heard that Kate had been half expecting a demand for its ransom.

Kate and Criss were coming home for the third Bragg Jam in late October, and there couldn't have been better timing for the jacket's homecoming—almost like an extra gift for us on Tate's twentieth birthday.

TV and newspaper promotion had helped pack the Rookery. It wasn't so easy to handle interviews about the boys and our memories of them, but we would do anything to express our gratitude for this happy event that kept their memory alive for others. Seven groups were scheduled to perform, including Mal Jones, a longtime songwriter friend, who now lived in Asheville. At the end of his set, he sang a beautiful, heartbreaking song, written as his message to Brax two weeks after the tragedy. It was our first time to hear it. His lyrics and the anguish in his voice touched us all so deeply. While the next group of players was wiring up, Jim and I left our long front table and squeezed our way up to the bar, further back in the restaurant. Unknown to Mal, and to most of us, his third-stanza lyrics of "For the Jester" would be the perfect segue for Kate's triumphant entrance.

♪ So if you can send us ♪ If you've got some strength to lend
We're holding on hard here ♪ To a fallen friend
But each day brings ♪ Something new
Each day brings ♪ A little piece of you ♪

The glass door had swung wide, and in Kate swaggered, like a prize-fighter, leather sleeves dangling from her shoulders, headed straight through the crowd for Jim, with Criss, her cornerman, following close behind. Cheers went up when they hugged and she lifted the jacket from her slim shoulders up to Jim's. She explained how moldy and wrinkled it had been from its long captivity, but it looked and smelled marvelous. It had been a loose fit on Brax, but his Pop plans to pare down so the beloved thing will fit. The jacket was passed around with lots of welcoming-home, and then Annie wore it the rest of the night. It seems content these days, with its pockets full of memories—as we all must be—while it lounges on Brax's wooden valet in his old room.

30.

∼

Writing Sanctuary

Two weeks after the 2001 concert, Jim and I joined our cousins Barbara and Rick Collins for a long weekend at Pensacola Beach. Barbara had just read *Pull of the Moon* by Elizabeth Berg and brought it for me. Berg's fiftyish character, Nan, uses a road trip as therapy for dealing with the poor direction her life has taken. By journaling and writing letters to her husband, she gradually realizes that her focus—limited only to what has gone—begins to pivot. By the trip's end she sees how much she still has left. Berg's simple, direct writing style inspired me—I could imagine myself writing that way—and I could relate to being pulled along my own disappointing path, far off the one I'd signed on for. But I also knew that lessons of letting go made better reading than living.

My therapy program for that winter began with a serious overhaul of Tate's bedroom. We sent his tall chest-on-chest bureau to Susie, and I sorted through savables, as per others' requests. Then I closed myself in his room and began plowing through his closet and dresser drawers. I left way too many things, including the boys' unpacked duffel bag, which may stay forever, along with his bookshelf and music stand. I saved Little League caps, pottery pieces, a fat stack of Mad Magazines, and souvenir t-shirts that would soon fit Rob. Truthfully, most of his dresser drawers are still full. Then, while I listened to audio books, I painted his room the deep burgundy he'd selected when we were painting downstairs the winter before he died.

I've always enjoyed wallpapering and painting. I spent most of Tate's last winter, in 1998, repainting downstairs rooms; but our kitchen color had been a tiresome ordeal. He and Jim redid cabinets and laid ceramic tile and I stripped wallpaper and prepped for paint. Then I double-coated walls, not once but twice, until the third color finally hit it right. But what stands out for me isn't the memory of the work but of a rare instance when Tate ever caused us any worries. He and several junior classmates had conspired to tell their parents a cover story for where they would spend a Friday night—some had even said they'd be at our house. As word spread among anxious parents, we realized that none of us really knew where our boys were until they showed up next morning. Tate was ashamed of the worry he'd caused (I'd hardly slept) and confessed that they'd been drinking beer in some older guy's apartment. He was ready for sentencing, especially after hearing that some of his friends were doubly punished for lying to their parents. I remember telling him I was too relieved to punish him, because if anything ever happened to him I would just paint the kitchen black! Tears sting to this day thinking of how sad he was as he hugged his dad and me that morning.

Eventually we liked the new color of his bedroom for its rich, vibrant burgundy tones, as he had seen it, instead of its being too dark, which had been our first reaction to it. The process was so satisfying that I moved on to include painting the other three bedrooms before Christmas while Jim took over our entire kitchen and grocery department. We faced 2002 as a team with three empty guest rooms.

In late January it was pure pleasure to produce a weekend workshop for my world-renowned Enneagram teachers, Don Riso and Russ Hudson. We had a fine turnout at the Crowne Plaza, Macon's only downtown hotel, for "The Enneagram and Relationships," and it gave my family, local friends, and institute students from elsewhere a chance to learn firsthand the basics of this intriguing life tool from the two pioneer writers on the subject. Russ did a second well-received workshop here two years later. My heart overflowed with gratitude for the help that had come to me though all their various workshops. The next step could be to become a certified teacher myself, but a career launch hadn't been my goal.

That March, on Brax's birthday, Jim and I were in Siena, Italy, attending Mass at the fabulous Duomo there. He would have been thirty-one. We spent a few days with Dot and Phil Brown's daughter, Katey, in the gorgeous hilltop town of Cortona, where she directed UGA's Studies Abroad Program. Then we ventured off with Rick Steve's guidebook to Assisi, Cinque Terra, Orvieto, Florence, and finally into Rome, where we visited with the true love of Brax's life, Christina Cellie, and her family.

Back home, I listened to Frances Mayes narrate her memoir, *Under the Tuscan Sun*, about her home in Cortona while we hefted large stones into Cortona-like steps to connect our labyrinth with the terraced lawn above it. Positive results from all this activity supplied ballast for melancholy that so often threatened a sinking spell when I risked slowing down.

The Enneagram had served me well as a personal tool for healing, and it also improved my technique for teaching swimming. By giving me a way to see beneath a child's fear, I could make a best guess as to his "type." That was a real help: I could tweak my approach in how to motivate a child and help him speed up his skill and love for swimming. We all benefit by being "seen" more and judged less.

When swim school was over, Jim and I took a five-hour cruise to Grand Bahama Island, different from Brax's and his friend Mick's voyage all those years ago. I came home from that week rested and eager to finally begin writing, and on Sunday, August 11, 2002, three years from my first conversation with Olivia, I began.

Seventy pages sped through our shared desktop computer, one thin wall away from our TV, before I bought my own laptop and created a serene writing studio in our poolhouse. There, I relived memories as they flowed with the tears. Jim was my cheerleader, delivering plates of food and calling goodnight over the intercom when it was obvious that writing would run into wee hours.

The place was a sanctuary where incense wafted around cups of delicious tea and spa music quietly blocked out the cares of an outside world. The labyrinth was thirty yards from my table at the picture window, where I watched birds defend feeders from acrobatic squirrels and listened for hawks circling on warm updrafts high above the trees. At night deer moved noisily in fall leaves, raccoons scrambled along tree bark, and owls haunted our woods with their spooky three-hoot calls. I practically lived in our poolhouse that fall and winter. When the heat pump wasn't enough to chase away winter's chill, I wrapped in a fleecy throw next to a portable heater and wished for nothing more than to be a happy hermit, obsessed with writing.

Bragg Jammers were determined to carry on in their friends' memory, and since it had definitely been more comfortable last year, to bypass July's raging heat, number four was also scheduled for late October, three days before Tate's twenty-first birthday. Frankly, we marveled that anyone had time to plan a concert at all. Kirby, the main organizer, had recently met his future wife and Russell was buried in law school, plus several volunteer performers were busy with day jobs, or living elsewhere. Schools were back in session and football may have caused a slimmer turnout, but Bragg Jam's five entertainers gave a wholehearted concert that night for a very appreciative crowd. The fact that our third Race for the Cure had been another huge success that morning, culminating weeks of volunteer work, made the night a two-fold celebration.

Modest concert proceeds went to the trail, which was making enormous progress. A bronze life-sized statue of Macon's Otis Redding had been unveiled at Gateway Park five weeks earlier, and over a mile of paved walkways were now in constant use. Donations, huge grants, and constant dedication by Trail organizers were creating beauty where centuries-old mud had been. Brax must have been daydreaming about visions like these ten years earlier—he was 20 and Tate was 10 when he wrote these lines, discovered by Russell and Kirby:

The old Ocmulgee's not the scene but a great view nonetheless
If we laid cafes around her banks and strolled in fancy dress
We could turn the sludge-mud into beauty on her breast

31.

ᴤ

Bullet Proof Bible

After my winter in the poolhouse I gathered enough nerve to mail pages to Sandhills Writing Conference in Augusta. Rosemary Daniell, the well-known author from Savannah, was the nonfiction/memoir critic, and her kind words were enough to encourage me to keep writing. That weekend of hanging out in the friendly atmosphere with real writers—some very accomplished—gave me the boost I'd hoped for. I suffered withdrawal pains when I had to convert my haven back into a swim school soon after I got home.

The real highlight that spring of 2003, in time for Brax's thirty-second birthday, was *Bullet Proof Bible*. Russell and Kirby had finished transcribing over 450 pieces of Brax's poetry, lyrics, and essays and published their extraordinary labor of love under his name, with one of his unique titles. They arranged the thick paperback alphabetically and included a chronological index, with earliest entries written when Brax was only 17. Russell wrote about his best friend in a foreword:

For those who knew him, the memory of this brilliant young man will not fade with time. It is hoped that, through these writings, others might share in his recollections, insights, and experiences. As you will see, the world is a better place for having experienced Brax Bragg.

As an afterword, they included Tate's precious letter to us. The book, which touches our hearts on so many levels, is available online.

All this time, behind the scenes, Bragg Jam 2003 was about to reveal its huge metamorphosis. Russell, despite facing a summer bar exam, and Kirby, busy with fall wedding plans, were still serious about keeping the event alive, so, when their energetic friend Johnny Harrison offered his vision for launching it as a regional festival, they gladly passed him the joystick. To improve turnout, as well as to preserve its origin, it was reset for late July. Mike Ford, president of NewTown Macon, a nonprofit partner with Community Foundation of Central Georgia, agreed to help with expenses. After years of working to revitalize downtown, which had been knocked to the ground when Macon Mall opened seven miles away in 1975, they had helped the faded beauty get back on her feet. Maybe New-Town figured Bragg Jam's youthful energy and music could get her dancing again!

Many sponsors, including the swim school, partnered with full-spirited media to enable booking of performers and to provide extensive publicity. Instead of one venue, there were at least six, and the roster of acts—thirty in all—included local volunteer bands as well as pricey imported ones. Jesco White, the inebriated "Dancing Outlaw" from West Virginia, added hilarity with his tap dancing, and three chauffeured belly dancers added drama by bursting into each venue heralded only by exotic music and tiny brass bells jingling around their gyrating torsos. Loud appreciation rocked every venue and, when space allowed, dancing went on all night.

Our generation coerced nearly 100 peers into being shift workers for selling armbands, beer, and t-shirts. Partiers rode NewTown's green trollies along the concert crawl, even way out to Jim Shaw's and beyond to a rocking little pub, the Shamrock, in Payne City, an unincorporated village off Vineville Avenue. Macon pulsed with cheerful, sweaty people following a trail of music up and down crowded sidewalks until 2 A.M. No one seriously complained about the heat. Volunteers assembled early Sunday morning with our brooms, blowers, and trash bags to remove all evidence. NewTown was quite impressed with the festival's success, despite a few budget challenges, and decided to continue sponsoring Bragg Jam, obviously a goodwill magnet for downtown.

The next week Susie, Annie, and I flew to Santa Monica. I attended a weekend international Enneagram conference there, but our real excitement was for our next stop. We took a Metro bus to Los Angeles to meet James Morris, with whom Brax and Tate had stayed four years earlier. Bart Stephens came from New Orleans, and we spent hours in James's tiny apartment hearing about the boys' last fun-filled days. The four of us—Susie,

Annie, Bart, and I—laughed and cried as we listened to James share his treasured memories of our boys. The Chinese pipe Tate held in that last photo was on a shelf beneath posters that had been the last-photo's back-drop. James took the Magritte poster right off his wall to send home to Jim, and we recorded our long conversations for him to hear when we got home. We girls enjoyed the touch of luxury in our vintage Best Western on Sunset Boulevard and relished being driven around to see all the sights. On our last night, James's fiancée met us for poolside drinks on a bronze-washed roof-top on Sunset Strip.

The trip had been wonderful but not without its poignant moments— it had brought us to another milestone. Even as these two thoughtful young friends, who had been classmates at UNO, whirled the girls and me through our nonstop, fun tour of Hollywood, there had been no escaping that final reality—we all felt it: we were treading through the closing chapter of Brax's and Tate's lives.

32.

❧

And That's That

Jim and I were on a day-tripper ferry to Nantucket a few weeks later, during a fall leaf-watching trip, when we got word that Richie, his mom, was gravely ill from a rare flesh-eating bacteria; she was being prepped for an amputation of her right leg. We jumped on the next high-speed ferry back to Hyannis Port and drove straight home. We hated what lay ahead for this gentle woman, who had braved so much already. The family rallied to sell her house and car and help her settle into assisted living, where, despite an annoying prosthesis, she would be wheelchair-bound. There was much rejoicing for her eighty-fourth birthday that November—it evolved into a family reunion at John Wesley Villas, her new residence. Within a couple of years, Richie's health declined and she transferred to a nursing home as a bed patient. Jim's sister, Carolyn, distressed by their mom's exhausted condition, took her home to Roswell, Georgia, in 2006, for their brief time left together. Sadly, Richie passed away a month before her eighty-seventh birthday.

Fall and winter months after 2003 were focused mostly on family life. I kept my connection to Komen's ever-growing Race for the Cure as registrar, and that year, its fourth, was the first run I ever competed in. I was surprised how hard it was to get that trophy, even if only in my age bracket. Running 5Ks around Middle Georgia became my new winter passion, but very little memoir-writing was getting on the page.

In mid-February of 2004, during a morning run with Sculley, neighbor dogs caused us to collide and I slammed the ground on my left shoulder. A neighbor drove me home, where I hoped an icepack and Advil would dull the pain, but nothing was going to interfere with plans for grandson Rob's sixteenth birthday party that evening. He may have forgotten his Uncle Tate's promise from seven years ago, but old Yoburt sure hadn't—he was spruced up for a big night out at Jim Shaw's Restaurant!

Midway through dinner a sudden burst of car horns on Vineville Avenue, right outside the restaurant door, grabbed everybody's attention. At the red light, drivers were saluting a giant waffle cone as he pranced across the street from Annie's salon into our crowded grill. Mylar balloons bounced along the ceiling while Yoburt searched for the birthday boy, his red face bent low over a plate of empty oyster shells. Cooks, waiters, and patrons joined in the singing, but Yoburt had to leave in a hurry because he, or rather the cute girl inside his musty old shell, began a fit of sneezing. As he waved goodbye and dashed back across the busy street, his big eyes still had that beguiling gleam. Yoburt had surely exceeded his life expectancy, but at the ripe old age of 19, he had fulfilled his final obligation—at the very place his first two birthday boys had worked their last night of working together.

My shoulder didn't improve after three weeks of painful rehab, so my doctor ruled out a rotator injury and prescribed an MRI, expecting an obscure fracture. The test, which I dreaded, was set for nine o'clock on a cold March night. I was at our door, keys in hand, when a ticking sound from the bathroom startled me. The only nearby clock was a little automaton Brax had bought me at a flea market in Morocco—it hadn't worked in years because one of us had overwound it. But now the clock's little orange hen was busily pecking corn from the faded red barn's yard, enunciating each nod of her head with *tick-tock, tick-tock*. Her timing had me laughing out loud when Susie called.

"I'm on my way out," I said. "But you've got to hear this—remember Brax's little chicken clock that wouldn't work?" I took the phone closer. "Hear it?"

"Oh, that's great!" she said, chuckling. "I figured they'd be surprising you somehow, with his birthday so close. I can't believe he'd be 33 tomorrow."

2004 was leap year, with dates falling on identical days of 1999. We had come full circle. July 3rd began as another lovely, innocent Saturday—and we had survived five years. Innocence was gone, if it meant we would ever take the future for granted, or that life would present only solvable problems, but acceptance allowed us to be grateful for all we'd learned, despite its high price.

We were excited about the upcoming Bragg Jam. Not that we hadn't relished the others, but it required less emotion now to brace up for them. I feel bad admitting it, considering all the work that went into them, but there was no escaping feelings of loss that arose from being with the group, grown now, with their careers and young families.

Bragg Jam 2004, again directed by Johnny Harrison and under the still-watchful eye of NewTown, now had dozens of sponsors, including, again, the swim school, and it was about to become a two-day extravaganza. On the last Friday in July, a horse-drawn carriage carried formally dressed patrons and sponsors down to the lantern-lit river trail for a Moon Dance, where a full moon was filtered through foliage of giant trees, which sheltered tables of food and drinks. The Five Tams sang seventies beach music from a stage near the bar, and further down the trail two girls danced gracefully on long white aerial silks, dangling from a tree limb high above our heads.

At daybreak, serious competitors tested themselves in a certified adventure race of boating, biking, and hiking along the muddy river bank. By noon, a delightful kid's festival drew families onto the trail for a myriad of booths, games, and music. Onstage a parade of little girls competed for hours in a Hannah Montana lookalike contest. The concert crawl began downtown at 5:00 P.M. with nine venues and forty-three performers, requiring 100 volunteers. Jim and I enjoyed helping—I even filled in at the last minute as chauffer for three belly dancers.

There was no putting this happy monster back in its box, nor was anyone so inclined, as long as its soulful origin would always be part of its story. NewTown had been patient and very generous in covering predictable overruns, but it was decided that Bragg Jam should become an independent nonprofit group, with a board of directors who could curb enthusiasm and project a budget in time for next year's event.

Writing, which had been my earlier obsession, definitely took a back burner that year. In September I joined a church group for a trip to Eastern Europe. Our crowd of thirty, led by two local Polish priests who were returning home for a brother's wedding, had a whirlwind tour of Prague, Budapest, Vienna, Krakow, and Zakopane, the resort town where the fun, vodka-fueled wedding festivities took place.

In late October of 2004, a few weeks after I got home, my 91-year-old Mother decided, after a couple minor fender-benders and a fall in her condo, that it was time to stop driving and stop living alone. My sister, Margaret, and I managed her moving sale, and she was soon settled in Pinegate, a hilltop high-rise for seniors, overlooking spectacular sunsets. It met her prerequisites: a big walk-in closet, decent food, and an active social life. Our Irish mother was practical, with a real talent for making the best of situations, of gracefully letting go of places, things, and even people, and putting the past behind her. She maintained her independence there for several years, until a few mini-strokes required a move to assisted living and then on to Bolingreen, a rehab/nursing facility north of town. She was a cut-throat bingo player there—playing three bingo cards per game—known for her colorful wardrobe and determination to live to be 100. And she almost made it. But when she could no longer manage Sunday outings—we had driven her here for lunch for over two years—in December of 2012, eight months shy of her goal of 100 years, she decided it was time to leave. It took about three weeks for her to wind down, and then she was gone. Her usual maxim for letting go was "...and that's that!" For Mom it was a punctuation mark—*period!* She was no mourner, at least not outwardly, but I'm sure she loves how her children hated letting her go and how much her family still misses her.

When Bragg Jam 2005 came around after swim school the next July, the group had become a certified nonprofit with a busy year-round volunteer board of directors, chaired by Heather Evans, who had been involved for years. Friday night's preview party was an outdoor concert in front of Macon Terminal Station featuring the well-known Drive-By Truckers from Athens. Cherry Street was closed throughout Saturday for the free kids' festival and also for the night's thirteen-venue concert crawl, which involved nearly fifty entertainers. Gail Mansfield from NewTown served as fiscal advisor and there was enough revenue to hire bicycle cops and street cleaners, make a sizable donation to the trail, and even to set aside a reserve for next year's start-up.

The festival had grown strong legs by its seventh year, with plenty of creative young people to dedicate energy and music savvy toward its unique brand of year-round community service. The best way for us to share in it was to continue being among the throngs of sponsors and happy jammers, and to simply show up!

The next year, Bragg Jam 2006 premiered a documentary produced by locally owned Bright Blue Sky in the newly reopened Cox Capitol, downtown's 90-year-old theater, where Jim and I had gone to see *Giant*, chauffeured in his mom's pale yellow 1951 Pontiac, on our first date sixty years earlier. We had shared a cherry coke at the soda fountain next door, at the Roy G. Williams Drugstore, while we waited for her to come drive us home. The new documentary presented a well-rounded history of the festival, along with photos, excerpts from past shows, interviews with founders and friends, and a conversation with Jim and me, staged in our labyrinth. Bart Stephens shared his 1995 film, *5700 Miles*, starring Brax, on the big screen that night, too. To see close-ups of his face and hear him speak was still a heartbreaker.

Our real miracle in 2006 was the birth of granddaughter Taylor Evans—Annie had finally gotten the child we all longed for her to have. Taylor is blue-eyed and talented like her daddy, Chad, whose local group, Hank Vegas, has been a popular performer at most Bragg Jams. Annie still runs one small salon, limited only to skin care. Taylor's arrival brought a new chapter of hope into our lives.

Susie reentered Mercer and completed her degree after kids, Anna and Rob, left home and married. She's a grandmother herself now: Rob and his wife Kaile have two little boys, our great-grandsons Logan and his baby brother Braxton.

Our labyrinth grows prettier each season as moss spreads over pathways and rocks, and I enjoy a sense of peace whenever I walk it. There's a little goldfish pond with a bubbling fountain at the entrance. An artist grandmother, Claudia Hartley from Phoenix, did a vibrant acrylic painting of the labyrinth for us after a 2008 visit with her Macon family.

Each fall, when I reopened the manuscript, it was necessary to read from its beginning in order to get in the writing groove again. It reminded me of paring an onion, both for its tonic effect and its tears. When folks surmised that I was writing as part of my healing process, I agreed—and then added that I hoped it could also be part of theirs. After seven years, I reached out to author Rosemary Daniell, the critic from Augusta's Sandhills event six years earlier, and joined Zona Rosa, her writer's workshop in Savannah, 150 miles from Macon. During winter months I made day trips to join her first-Saturday women's group for feedback and inspiration. Occasionally I cut the drive with a side trip to St. Simons Island, sixty miles south of there, to retreat in a friend's vacant beach condo, where I could binge write after long sunrise walks on the beach. March was always my last month for Zona Rosa, due to swim school, but I truly loved the bond that developed with these women, who shared so honestly with each other. Rosemary Daniell's mission is to teach that writing, especially memoir, is therapeutic—not only for the writer, but for readers who may be inspired by reading it.

We all have a mission—I trust that our boys accomplished theirs. I like to think that they remained as our sons and brothers in their afterlife and that their first mission there was to join a band of angels who could calm our horrified spirits.

Passing on, more than a graceful euphemism, is a lovely way to describe how our spirits travel. Our sons and loved ones have passed on. We were astounded that a window could be opened into their afterlife, allowing them to pass briefly through our lives again. That life has been described by prophets and seers throughout the ages as an intelligent world of memories, humor, and love. It confirmed that our spirits dwell in a universal pool with the Source of all Energy. Eternity is not to be feared, nor is there a chance we will miss it—we have always been part of that world, where there are no beginnings or endings.

I wish the slope into doubt and hopelessness wasn't so slippery—it blurs our vision of nature's bond with the divine and robs us of the peace that is promised if we trust the Creator with our life's purpose. Soul anatomy includes a resource for intuiting spiritual energy—some have far more of it than others—so, when our souls connect, our bodies receive a blast of chill bumps. I believe chill bumps are the soul's stamp of approval for having struck a chord with the supernatural.

Epilogue

❧

Olivia moved to the West Coast for several years, during which time we had little contact. But during the early months of that first year, when she bravely responded to requests from the spirit world, she helped restore our hope that a lively world filled with departed loved ones is waiting for us. Her arrangement—bartering with our boys—resulted in her providing readings for overlapping circles of our friends, lending truth to the boys' forecast that we would help each other. Her role in our recovery fit in with spiritual teachers, physicians, and comforting friends, whose various gifts help lift spirits of fellow travelers during life's inevitable dark times. Within the year after I shared my writing with Pam Morgan, "Olivia's" real name, she was diagnosed with cancer and to everyone's shock and dismay she passed away in October of 2017. To be sure, a huge welcome party greeted her. With love, we, along with her children Prissy, Marty and granddaughter Spencer, will remember her forever.

The boys still bring surprises. I tried all last winter, 2016, to convince Jim that we needed a cat. Gradually his resistance wore thin and he agreed, but only if we could find an orange tabby like Sarge, his dad's yard cat. On a cold, moonless March 10th morning, shortly after midnight, there was a persistent meowing at our back door. Our orange tabby had arrived just in time for Brax's forty-fifth birthday. Mango turned out to be the gift that kept giving—and we kept two of her four kittens, Sarge and Archie.

The following October, coincidently on Tate's thirty-fifth birthday, Bragg Jam sponsored an impressive concert at the City Auditorium, presenting two of Macon's world-famous musicians, Mike Mills, founder of R.E.M., and violinist Robert McDuffie. We thought of it as a great way for our family to celebrate Tate and his love for music. That morning I glanced out an upstairs window to see a sparkling red Mylar balloon, its ribbon snagged on a pine branch thirty feet above our side yard—it had made its way, like a falling star, through the tall, dense hardwoods to help us celebrate. I wondered whose hand had loosened its grip and let it slip away, but I like thinking that a Mylar balloon escapes heavenward because an angel needs it somewhere else.

Bragg Jam continues as one of the many partners that support the Ocmulgee River Trail, which is now fifteen miles long. A memorial patio of bricks, inscribed by school children, was installed as a riverbank overlook in 2008, complete with three iron benches and a raised plaque honoring the boys and their Bragg Jam legacy. The week before the festival, I joined hundreds of runners for Bragg Jam's Moonlight Miles 5K along the trail. Brad Evans, owner of *The 11th Hour*, Macon's weekly magazine, was in his second of four terms as chair of the festival board that year when Bragg Jam received NewTown's Partners in Progress Award for "Creating a Sense of Place."

By the end of the festival's seventeenth year, in 2016, nearly 800 performers had come across dozens of stages and more than $200,000 had been donated to the community. Media outlets understandably believed that by weaving our family's narrative into their publicity it might heighten interest in Bragg Jam's celebration, and in those early years, maybe it did. But eventually we all preferred to focus on the wonder and gratitude we felt for this exuberant regional festival, which, despite its sad origin, had become, in such an astonishing way, a legacy for our sons.

Tate would love his pretty namesake-niece, Annie's daughter, Taylor, who's 10 years old now. And Brax would be a proud chief of the growing tribe of little Braxtons—there are three now: the first grandson of Jack and Sue, my Atlanta cousins; Mick Allen's newest pride and first grandson; and Brax's own great-nephew, Rob's second son, Braxton Slocumb.

Afterwords

RUSSELL WALKER, Founder and title author of *Bragg Jam* and coeditor of *Bullet Proof Bible*...

When I'm asked about the first Bragg Jam, my mind's eye takes me back to the last time I saw Brax and Tate. For years, that image was crystal clear. I admit the picture is a bit faded now. But the memory is still alive.

Brax and I loaded some music equipment into the bed of my little blue truck. We drove down Vineville Avenue to Martha Roddenberry's art studio (Elements) in Payne City. Brax was excited to have put together the perfect group of accompanying musicians: my brother and now law partner, John Gray Walker, on drums, Frank Kern on lead guitar, and Tim Potts on bass guitar.

When Brax doubted whether these three—particularly Tim, lead singer and guitarist for Macon's Gypsy Train—would be interested in playing with him, I told him, "Just play them the songs. They will be interested." They were interested.

Brax spent a great deal of his free time lounging around, listening to all variety of recordings. He studied them. While he most enjoyed gifted singer-songwriters and great bands, he also appreciated the spoken word. He especially liked the antics of 1950s comedian and monologist Richard Myrle Buckley, a.k.a. Lord Buckley. Although Brax's new group was not familiar with its eponymous jester, they readily accepted the name Brax bestowed upon them. In short order, the quartet became Brax Bragg & the Buckleys.

The art studio rehearsal was only the third for the fledgling group. Fellow musician Rob Evans was enlisted to record the session in anticipation of Brax's and Tate's cross-country road trip so the three Buckleys could listen to and learn the songs in Brax's absence, in preparation for their upcoming gig at the Rookery.

When I listen, now, to that recording, I can still see them playing. I can still see Tate beside me, sunk down into that old sofa, grinning contently as he witnessed the realization of his big brother's dream. The songs were profound and powerful. And with the new compliment of musicians, Brax had done it! This *was* beautiful music!

My mental photograph, which has lost clarity in the more than 6,000 days since that third and final rehearsal, becomes vibrant and sharp again when I press play and listen. "Funny the pain the memory of happiness brings..." Goodbye, Brax. Goodbye, Tate. Have a great trip.

I was sleeping soundly on the morning of July 4, 1999, in the hot, still quiet of rural, dirt-road Warthen, Georgia. I had spent the night at the old Walker home place, where my father played, picked cotton, and spent summers with his grandparents in the 1940s. Those same grandparents lived off that land. It was in many ways unchanged.

The old house had no air conditioning—only a few box fans in the windows, without which sleep would have been difficult. There was no television. There were no phones. A wooden swing and a few rocking chairs provided the setting for gatherings on the dusty screened porch. I was far away, both geographically and mentally, from my friends back home in Macon. I was sleeping soundly.

A hand pushed against my shoulder. Someone gently shook me. As I struggled to gain consciousness, I heard, "Russell, wake up. Wake up, man. We have something to tell you."

"What are y'all doing here?" I responded, groggy and confused. I knew, even half asleep, that Tim Potts and Kirby Griffin did not belong there. I heard distress in their voices. When I managed to open my eyes, I saw anguish on both faces. "What's going on? What's wrong?"

I tried to hold back tears as I sat on the side of the bed. I hugged my mother and father goodbye. Tim said, "I'll ride back with you, Russell."

For a while, we rode in silence, numb. I could hardly process the news. "Brax and Tate are dead? Is this real? How?" Then it suddenly occurred to me—Brax had given me some board tapes from two of his recent solo performances.

Without saying a word, I lifted my arm, opened the center console, pulled out a cassette, and put it in the player. It felt like a dream. For the next hour, Tim and I listened to the voice and music of Brax Bragg, alive and in his prime.

As we approached Macon, I looked at Tim and said, "We have to play the show, the one that's already booked at the Rookery." Tim agreed. With that, the seed for what would become known as Bragg Jam was planted.

Every musician I contacted, all friends of Brax, said "Yes." Some canceled other shows to be there. Some traveled from as far as New Orleans. Nobody was paid. Nobody brought an ego. Everybody was cool.

We may have *called* that first night a celebration, but it wasn't. The first Bragg Jam was really an effort to hold on a little longer, to put off letting go. By keeping those songs alive, we might somehow keep Brax and Tate alive.

As the years go by, and as Bragg Jam continues to thrive and grow, I realize we succeeded in holding on. Brax and Tate are still with us. We don't have to let go.

* * * *

KIRBY GRIFFIN, Coeditor of *Bullet Proof Bible*...
I remember a Post-It note I saw next to the Braggs' wall phone at their house (when we still had house phones!) shortly after the accident. Three words were written: Responsibility Remorse Repair.

These words might always be a relevant process to guide the grief-stricken through a traumatic ordeal, but I'd like to reverse their order to better organize my thoughts and feelings around what Bragg Jam has meant to me.

It's likely that our repair from the loss of Brax and Tate will continue for the rest of our lives; yet, to echo Julie's sentiment, to think about their absence is like a pinprick in the eye, not the soul-slamming devastation that we felt in the past. Nonetheless, there are things we've done to get us through the darkness.

Brax's friends have performed in every Bragg Jam since the first in 1999. The first four Bragg Jams were comprised solely of performers who were friends of Brax and Tate. As one of them, I believe that playing was both an honor as well as therapeutic. Hearing Brax's friends sing his songs is both music to my ears as well as a comfort to the discomfort of their loss.

Another aspect is the volunteer work—any time you can put someone else's cause or need above your own, it becomes a medium for renewal and repair. In addition to coordinating the third and fourth years of Bragg Jam, I served on the board in 2005 and volunteered in other years. From the ticket takers to the catchers-in-the-rye of the Kid's Festival, hundreds have expressed their love through volunteering.

Finally, there is solace and rejuvenation in Brax's art, not only his songs but the writings that Russell Walker and I compiled to create *Bullet Proof Bible*. To call it a labor of love is an understatement; the labor became one component of the emotional therapy. To hear Brax sing is one thing; to hear his prose, poetry, and insight not only speaks to us, but guides us, makes us think, and brings his friendship back to us in the present, wherever we are.

Remorse comes and goes, influenced by friends, time of year, a book, or a song. In 2006, when the Bragg Jam board filmed a documentary on the festival and its roots, many of Brax and Tate's friends were asked to speak in it. When my stint was over, I walked out of the Hummingbird with my wife, Beth. When she said how good it sounded (whether it did or didn't, she is very sweet), I wasn't listening. Instead, I began to cry. When she asked why I was crying, all I could say was, "It hurt." In that moment, I understood what Brax meant when he sang, "Funny the pain the memory of happiness brings."

I was also reminded of this when I read the first chapters of Julie's memoir. To live through it again, through hers and Jim's eyes, is both heartfelt and heart-wrenching—it gives new meaning to Stephen King's observation that writing is "telepathy." It took me back to driving with Tim Potts to Warthen to get Russell, sitting behind Father Cuddy with my head in my hands when we played "Just a Minute of Your Time" at the wake, greeting the boys when they arrived at Hart's, looking for clues from the Man in White by the Braggs' mailbox. I feel it as I type this—I have just learned to accept it without understanding why it had to happen.

Finally, there is the responsibility that Bragg Jam has brought to us. Economically, it is a huge windfall for the city of Macon and a bright spot in the otherwise dastardly days of summer in Middle Georgia. The money that has been raised and donated has served its purpose in supporting the Ocmulgee Greenway Trail—the river played an important mythological part in Brax's writing.

Perhaps the biggest responsibility that Bragg Jam holds is the continuation of Macon's musical heritage. From Lena Horne, Little Richard, Otis Redding, and James Brown to the Allman Brothers, Capricorn, R.E.M., Jason Aldean, and Zac Brown, we can add Bragg Jam to the great musical history of Macon, and one that points to the future of adding other talent to that list.

Through my lens, Bragg Jam is these emotions and memories and even more that I can't find the words to describe. What gets me through it all is two things: there will always be a Bragg Jam, even if it means Brax's friends busking on a street corner. Most of all, it means that Brax and Tate will live on. Someday, we'll be together; until then, we'll sing praises of their lives and patiently wait until the day we see them again.

* * * *

EVERETT VERNER, *Bragg Jam board president, 2015–2017. Board member since 2011.*

Since becoming involved in Bragg Jam in 2010, it has grown tremendously. Our single weekend concert-crawl music festival has more than doubled in scale and attendance and feels more like a staple event for the whole region rather than an event for friends, family, and locals.

Beyond that, from April to October, Bragg Jam runs the Second Sunday concert series, a free outdoor monthly concert series on Coleman Hill Park. All told, Bragg Jam has positioned itself as a premiere events-organizer for the community, creating and promoting events throughout most of the year.

The board is still comprised of amazing volunteers who pour a great deal of time and energy into each and every event. Unlike early formations of the board, no one on our current board knew either of the brothers whose tragic passing inspired the inception of Bragg Jam—many of us did not even live in Macon at the time. I personally believe in the incredible value that these events bring to our community and am honored to be able to be a part of its history in any capacity. Bragg Jam gives us—myself, others on the board, and countless volunteers—a vehicle for contributing to our community. The payoff is the joy we experience with each successful event; we expect to cheer it on from the sidelines long after we have all moved on to other endeavors.

* * * *

MIKE FORD, *former President of NewTown Macon...*

Bragg Jam, which began as a heartfelt tribute at the Rookery by fellow musicians and friends of the Bragg brothers, had been gaining momentum each of its first four years. Seeds for a citywide festival had been planted when the friends came to us at NewTown Macon for help with expanding it to meet its potential.

"A citywide concert in *July* in Macon? You want NewTown to sponsor on behalf of the Ocmulgee Heritage Trail? You want NewTown to provide the cash to grow it?"

These were questions that jumped in my mind when NewTown was asked to sponsor a citywide Bragg Jam. No sensible person would think it could work. While NewTown was having some success bringing life to downtown Macon, this might just help. The festival's objective of honoring the Bragg brothers and raising money for the trail was sufficient reason to give it a try.

It was tough going financially for a few years, but we continued because downtown Macon needed a push and music has been a big part of the city's history. The good news was that the young people behind Bragg Jam loved music and were very smart. There were also college kids from all over who were looking for something to do in July.

The outcome has been huge for all of Macon. Today, there are over eighty bands performing on twenty stages, and people come from all over for this wonderful weekend of music. It has raised awareness of downtown Macon and raised money for the trail.

New events, activities, and businesses have started because of Bragg Jam and its people. We have more restaurants (Dovetail), more concerts (Cox Capitol Theatre), and more tours (Rock Candy Tour) springing directly from Bragg Jam. We even have the Creek, a downtown radio station focused on local interests and playing Macon music.

In a word, Bragg Jam is great!

Acknowledgments

My heartfelt appreciation and love for all who will be forever in my memories, especially to you who understood my need to share our times together in this memoir. Hopefully, I've made it clear how essential you are to my life and to my story, especially since I've talked of little else since beginning this writing project all those years ago:

Jim, Susie, and Annie; grandchildren Anna, A-Jay, Rob, and Kaile Slocumb and Taylor Evans; great-grandsons Logan and Braxton Slocumb; Margaret Wallace; Bobby and Harriet Wallace; Carolyn and Marshall Mattingly; Shelley and Danny Cummings; Hazle and Larry Hamilton; Christine and Joe Wilson; Melinda West; Jalaine Ward; Jim Morris; Bucky Buxton; Herm Slocumb; Jack, Jake, and Andy Burch; Beverly Burch; John Lert; Dot and Phil Brown; Katey Brown; Cile and Jim Messer; Trisha and George Barfield; Gina and Dave Hersh; Beth McKinnon; Earlene Tuft; Barbara and Rick Collins; Tommy Patterson; Milton Heard; Russell Walker; Kirby Griffin; Bart Stephens; Matthew Davis; Kate and Criss Strain; Mick Allen; Johnny Harrison; Mal Jones; John Wood; Chris Sheridan; Christina Cellie; Colleen Kelsall; Tim Potts; Happi Potts Burnett; Judy and Steve Bowden; Terry Cantwell; Laura Endres; Nelda Chapman; Father Tim McKeown; Richard Keil; Gail and Dan Johnston; Belinda and Skipper Zimmerman; Ed Grisamore; Russ Hudson; Jane Hollister; and especially Pam Morgan.

An extra nod of appreciation to Ben Sandifer for suggesting I contact his friend Marsha Luttrell at Mercer University Press—something I'd never have dared to do otherwise. And to Marc Jolley, who saw something in my story that he could take a chance on: I can only say Thank You for making a dream come true!

* * * *

Special thanks to my many "readers," especially to Jim, and those of you who took time to share your fine editing skills: Katey Brown, Rosemary Daniell and members of your Zona Rosa Writers' group, Joy Raynor, Niki Collins-Queen, Linda Conger, Susan Mucha, and Eric Jones.

* * * *

Special gratitude for the kind souls who allowed me to shift my writing sanctuary into their St. Simons condos: Linda Philips, Connie Altobelli, and Fay Knight

* * * *

In memory of departed family and friends who wondered why a memoir should take so long... Peggie Wallace, Richie Bragg, Sue Burch, Marie Sears, Regina Casson, Ellen Harvey, Sherry Murray, Ellen Flannigan, Shelley Lert, Sister Felicitas Powers, Monsignor John Cuddy, Don Riso, and especially Pam Morgan ("Olivia").

To thousands of young swimmers, whose courage has always touched my heart and inspired hope for our future—keep your kicks up!

In honor of all parents who have suffered the loss of a child. Though no list could exist to include everyone, I am compelled, risking unintended oversight, to mention some mothers, mostly local, whose resilient spirits inspire us.

Patty Able, Marilyn Adams, Annette Arnold, Valli Berg, Lillian Binner, Judy Bowden, Brenda Bridges, Gerri Brooking, Coy Bullock, Laura Campbell, Janet Carter, Nell Chapman, Ashley Childers, Betty Cork, Midge Cutright, Rosemary Daniell, Margaret Finn, Cindy Gaskins, Kay Gerhardt, Betty Glover, Pat Godsey, Laurie Hardin, Charlotte Harrell, Kathy Hawkins, Sharon Hayes, Julie Hodges, Melanie Hoffman, Dixie Holton, Christine Jones, Lynn Kernaghan, Betty Sweet Ladson, Betty Lewis, Barbara Majors, Carolyn Mattingly, Anne Meroney, Carol Olsen, Jodi Palmer, Janet Pharo, Misty Portillo, Paula Raffield, Joy Raynor, Kim Rheeling, Betsy Robinson, Lauren Rutherford, Nancy Sasser, Claudia Schlottman, Marie Sears, Hope Shields, Annette Stilwell, Marcia Stramiello, Linda

Stuart, Judy Trout, Earlene Tuft, Joyce Wade, Katherine Walden, Krissy Walker, Shirley Walsh, Erin Weaver, Becky Williams, Kathy Wills, Betty Young.

Last but not Least!

There are not enough words to express our appreciation for the magical legacy of Bragg Jam! Nor could there exist a list of all who have worked tirelessly to make it a thriving regional festival that far outshines any sadness of its birth. Bragg Jam magnifies the beacon that continues to draw people to "Macon, Where Soul Lives!"